Waking Up In
LONDON

Printed and bound in Great Britain by Antony Rowe Limited,
Chippenham, Wiltshire

Distributed in the US by Publishers Group West

Published by Sanctuary Publishing Limited, Sanctuary House,
45–53 Sinclair Road, London W14 0NS, United Kingdom

www.sanctuarypublishing.com

Copyright: Robert Ashton, 2003

Photographs: Courtesy of Corbis, Redferns Music Picture Library and
Chris Harvey

Cover photograph: © Redferns Music Picture Library

ISBN: 1-86074-491-5

Waking Up In
LONDON

Robert Ashton

Sanctuary

Contents

1 Electric Leg

This is the pub. The Percy, The Earl Percy to give the Ladbroke Grove boozer its full name. It is one of the last dog days of December. A wet, unfriendly grey affair in west London. Rain is slashing at the pavement. A wicked winter wind whips around the sides of the corner pub, dragging an empty crisp packet – zigzag, zigzag along the gutter – in its wake. The trees lining the Grove are bare and, behind curtains, the dregs of Christmas decorations are twinkling in darkened rooms. On a wall, someone has scrawled 'Hate and War'.

A few hundred metres south, past the grime-crusted stucco, I can make out the drone of the cars and trucks speeding in and out of London on the Westway. 'I'm up and down the Westway, in an' out the lights,' The Clash sang on 'London's Burning'.

I am visiting The Percy to toast the group's singer. Joe Strummer is being buried in a few hours.

Beneath this flyover, outside the underground, two teenage mums, underdressed in denim and Nike, push by a scrum of parka-clad tourists spilling across the pavement. They want directions.

'To the Portobello Road market... Please?' They get no change from the dealers sharking for business.

A Rasta waves the tourists in the right direction. On up the Grove, there's a strange sight. A small knot of sodden zoot-suited greasers milling outside a funeral parlour, John Nodes. It's straight out of central casting – black windows, gold signage, heavy curtains and a clock to remind us that it's not for ever. The cortege is getting ready to roll. The Rasta watches, then slips into Dub Vendor opposite to flee the rain and check the sounds.

The street outside The Percy is quiet. A lady with a taste for pre-lunch liveners and a scruffy-looking mutt huddled inside a scruffier fur coat shuffle from the Chesterton Road side of the pub. She snatches a look into the saloon and struggles with the door. 'Do you mind, young man?' I see a face tinged blue by the cold. The stench of the Guinness- and whisky-soaked carpet is immediate. It rises up and hits my nostrils and, although it is minutes past opening time, there is already a thick fug of smoke.

Two solitary drinkers sit on a long tatty couch against the wall nursing half-pints of lager and lime. Put a top in that. To my right, at the bar, a few groups of middle-aged men, some balding, some with greying quiffs, most long past their best game, are supping their first round of the day. Judging by their garb – black suits, black Crombie coats, black jeans, black ties, black crepe-soled shoes – they are at the pub to raise a glass to John Mellor. Conversations are low monotone.

The old lady with the mutt takes a table beneath the heavily draped window. Next to her, a ducking door through to the snug. I take up a bar stool near her and the barman glances up from the sports pages. He folds the *Sun* away. 'Yes, mate?' I nod at the old lady. There is no rush. 'Yes, love. What can I get you?' He's off the bar and polishing a glass. She orders a port and lemon.

Before I get my order in, the door is yanked open and the cold kicks us in the kidneys. A man – sharp, but louche, in a dark-blue corduroy suit, black shirt and black Chelsea boots – dashes in. He joins me at the bar. He could be an estate agent. There's thousands around here trying to punt two-bedroom apartments to City bankers for 400, 500 grand ($650,000 or $800,000). Then I clock his shirt, which is faded, but still easily readable with a slogan stencilled in white lettering across the front: 'Be Reasonable, Demand The Impossible'. An old Vivienne Westwood design when she was knocking out gear from Sex on the King's Road in the punk days. 'You here for Joe?' he asks.

I am. But, I'm also here to start a journey. To travel around London, to walk its streets, drink in its bars, dance in its clubs. But, I need an angle – something to hook it on and which binds the city.

Then I get it.

Someone feeds pound coins into the jukebox and it kicks out 'Armagideon Time' by The Clash.

Music.

Things are falling into place. A travelogue of the city with a musical twist. London has a rich and varied musical heritage; it is a major force in shaping contemporary music around the world. I can work the pubs, clubs and venues, knock on the doors of glitzy music companies, skulk backstage in sticky-floored sweat pits, run-down recording studios and beer-soaked rooms above pubs.

I'm going to meet some people, those who like music and those who work in the business. They will be able to put me in touch with some other people and then they will put me in touch with still more. I'm going to soak up their stories and the sounds. It is all clicking into place. London, England – capital of the UK music industry.

After the US and Japan, the UK is the third largest music producer in the world, with sales of $2.8 billion (£1.7 billion) or an 8.3 per cent share of the global market (Germany and France, the next biggest markets, have just 6.3 per cent and 5.4 per cent shares respectively).

The five major labels (EMI, Sony, BMG, Warner and Universal) and countless independent labels have their headquarters in London – producing something like 90 per cent of the country's new music. With the London labels and recording studios employing around 10,000 people with another 40,000 musicians, managers, venue staff and promoters, the economic impact of the music business on London is substantial. Big.

A 2002 report estimated the contribution of the music business to the UK economy was around £3.6 billion ($6 billion) – a massive figure considering the relatively small numbers of people employed by it.

London music fans are also some of the most passionate consumers of their favourite bands' records. UK record buyers buy more CDs per year than any other country in the world – on average 4.1 units per capita, compared to just 3.3 units in the US. Over one third of all records bought are pop, about 28 per cent are rock, 11 per cent dance, 10 per cent R&B, 4.2 per cent hip-hop, 4.2 per cent classical, with the remainder made up of jazz, country and New Age fans.

It is 30- to 39-year-olds who spend the most cash on music, and pop and rock are the best-loved genres amongst London record buyers, with Robbie Williams easily the most popular artist of 2002 in terms of sales.

There should be no problem finding music being played live, either. There are an estimated 600 music venues in the city offering a wide range of different ways to experience music. It's possible to watch U2 at massive rock stadiums such as Wembley Arena and Earl's Court or to chill out to a solo singer-songwriter at a more intimate venue such as the Union Chapel in Islington.

There are another 1,000 venues also licensed for public entertainment, making music easily accessible to the city's eight million inhabitants. Researchers have also identified that in a typical week in the capital there are over 700 different musical events being staged. While most of these are in clubs in the heart of the capital, trips into the suburbs can also be rewarding. Thus Blackheath, located on the city's southeast periphery, boasts its Concert Halls, which have witnessed performances by Jimmy Webb, Roger McGuinn, Randy Newman and The Brodsky Quartet.

The city's parks are also regularly used as venues. The summer brings with it a host of outdoor concerts, including classical recitals at Kenwood House in north London, the regular pop bonanza Party In The Park in Hyde Park, or one-off events such as the Three Tenors or The Sex Pistols playing Finsbury Park in 1996. Each year the South Bank also hosts the Meltdown Arts Festival, usually curated by a well-known musician.

The West End of London is awash with theatres, and musicals also provide some of London's major musical draws, with hits such as *Fosse, Chicago* and the Queen and Madness musicals, *We Will Rock You* and *Our House* respectively. Boy George's *Taboo*, based on the '80s music and nightclubbing scene, is also a major attraction, and transferring shortly to Broadway.

I only have to look at the number of songs with London in the title or taking the city as its inspiration or subject, to also realise how the rich melting pot of the city has come to influence musicians and the music they create: 'Waterloo Sunset', 'Plaistow Patricia', 'A Bomb In Wardour Street', 'Guns of Brixton', 'Portobello Road', 'I Don't Want To Go To Chelsea', 'London Boys', 'London's Burning' and 'London Calling'.

A tour through London's music scene is like a world music tour, and the capital contains something that will strike a chord with every musical taste. Nowhere is the city's multiculturalism more apparent than in the vast array of musical styles hosted every day and night. The rhythms of rock, pop, R&B, jazz, reggae, folk, dance, Latino, Asian and rap emanate from clubs, pubs, concert halls, the radio (there are scores of radio stations alone in London) – even the capital's underground tube network. Whether it is Debussy or disco, it is possible to find a venue, a festival, a hole-in-the-wall club or a busker playing it.

In some neighbourhoods it is possible to hear different styles all within the space of one or two streets. And on any given night, one can find each one of them performed live somewhere in the city. There is reggae here, in west London's Ladbroke Grove, bhangra in the East End, hip-hop and garage south of the River Thames in Brixton, while the alternative and indie scene are based in NW1's Camden Town and DJ culture is blossoming in the clubs of Hoxton. Woven between all this is pop, which rears its head anywhere a teenager with a hairbrush has found a mirror to sing in front of.

London is also the stop-off point for visiting rock and pop bands. No world tour is complete without London on the schedule. And artists gravitate to the capital from all over Europe and America, ensuring a continual regeneration of the city's musical scenes. The influx of styles and cultures adds to London's influences and also retains its freshness.

London also reigns among the best dance-club cities in the world. Club culture, which found a natural home in the city with the emergence of dance music in the early '80s, has made many London DJs into global superstars. Recently, the taste makers and more stylish promoters have moved away from the superclubs, attracting the bridge and tunnel crowd, to host smaller clubs. Each has their own genre of music and fashion style.

Beyond the actual music, London also holds many historic musical landmarks. Rock fans can check out Jimi Hendrix's former house at 23 Brook Street in Mayfair, the EMI's Abbey Road studios where The Beatles recorded many songs in Studio 2, or World's End (formerly Sex) at 430 King's Road, Chelsea, where Johnny Rotten auditioned for The Sex

Pistols. There's also an incredible number of London streets used as backdrops for album covers, including David Bowie's *Ziggy Stardust* and Oasis's *(What's The Story) Morning Glory.*

The death of Strummer is a good place to make a start on this journey. Punk was about a new start. A new musical order. For a few short years in the '70s, Strummer and The Clash were the sound of west London. The Westway was their turf. Strummer had squatted in a place about 1km (½ mile) away from The Percy, across the Harrow Road, taking the name of his first pub rock outfit from the address 101 Walterton Road. The 101ers were regulars at their local, the Chippenham on the nearby Shirland Road, and for months had a residency at The Elgin, a pub a few blocks south of The Percy.

Strummer traded playing The 101ers' 'Keys To Your Heart' for punk and The Clash. He penned 'White Riot' after he and bassist Paul Simonon were caught up in the Notting Hill riots that raged along Ladbroke Grove – and outside The Percy – in 1976.

Mick Jones lived on and off with his nan in a 18th-floor flat in a council block, Wilmcote House, Royal Oak. You can see it from the Westway. And after watching the cars zip up and down the Westway from the flat's balcony, Strummer returned to a squat in nearby Orsett Terrace to knock out 'London's Burning': 'I'm up and down the Westway, in an' out the lights'.

I knew Strummer had also sunk many pints at The Percy. It was the right place to be right now.

By chance, I had bumped into Strummer just days before his death. He was drinking in a Bohemian drinking den, The Colony Room, which is up a narrow staircase on Soho's Dean Street. I was with a friend, Jimmy. Strummer was standing at the tiny bar, dressed head to toe in black, looking like a rock star, not a punk rocker. He was 50.

Blue clouds of cigarette smoke hung heavy that night. It had already passed turning-out time in the pubs and I knew the barman was about to ask his regulars to ship out. Jimmy leaned over. He was a little drunk by then. 'Hey, Joe.'

Strummer looked up from his drink. 'Yeah?' Strummer's eyes narrowed. He was probably thinking, 'What now?'

Jimmy had a little speech prepared. He was slurring, 'I jus' wanna say my favourite Clash record of all time, my favourite, it's "Hitsville UK". That's it, "Hitsville UK".'

Strummer laughed. He'd heard them all: 'White Riot', 'Complete Control', '(White Man) In Hammersmith Palais', even 'Tommy Gun' sometimes makes the Top 10 fave. But, not 'Hitsville UK'. 'Oh yeah?' says Strummer. 'Well, I've never heard that one before.' We shook hands. A few days later, he took his dog for a walk near his Somerset home and died.

So I say to the guy in The Percy:

'Yeah, I'm here for Joe. What are you drinking?'

'Jack and coke, mate. My name's Paul. And I should probably chase that with a beer. Get us a Guinness.'

We shake hands. The Jack Daniel's comes quickly. It rests on the wood bar for less than a second. In what looks like a choreographed move, we raise our glasses together, quickly. In a toast. 'This one's for Joe.' The bar looks over. Nods and then everyone in the pub raises their glasses. 'To' – louder – 'JOE.' Someone puts 'Tommy Gun' on the jukebox and there isn't a dry eye in the house.

I hear someone ask, 'Were you at The Rainbow?'

Paul saw Strummer and The Clash play The Rainbow in Finsbury Park, long shut and now a religious drop-in centre. He was 17. A Hendon boy, he's seen Bowie at Earl's Court, he's drunk with Sid Vicious in the Roebuck pub on the King's Road, he's seen Strummer's 101ers at an art college in Elephant & Castle. But The Clash – that was something else. 'It was like getting a blood transfusion, a fix of adrenaline, doing a gram of speed and then being hooked up to 1,000 watts,' he recalls. Clash gigs made an impression: Paul wasn't going to be a nine-to-fiver after hearing 'Career Opportunities'. He's made his living since, variously, as a stallholder (selling punk records), a shop boy (selling clothes) and writing (about fashion, music and culture). This is like hitting the mother lode. I order up another round to squeeze some more juice out of Paul.

'So what's happening with music in London?'

'Got a couple of hours?'

'Sure.'

'I'll tell you, then,' says Paul.

It seems I've pitched up in London as the music business in the capital faces something of a crossroads. Some might say a crisis. Figures suggest the London labels are having pretty rough time. They are losing the battle against a 9 per cent turn-down in the global music market, which is expected to decline further over the next couple of years. Latest figures from the trade body the BPI (British Phonographic Industry) show the value of the UK market fell by 3.7 per cent in 2002 – the first value decline since 1997. Sales of albums were down for the first time since 1999. And sales of singles fell for the third successive year, by almost 12 per cent. With just 52 million singles delivered in 2002, the market is 40 per cent down on 1997, when 87 million singles were bought by the public, making this the worst year for the format since figures were first collected in the early '70s.

In the face of this some companies, like EMI and BMG, have restructured. Many have shed acts. Most have shed jobs. Some, like Zomba, Mushroom and Mute, have been bought, while others have simply gone to the wall.

Music shops are also having a tough time. Fewer and fewer big album releases are keeping the sector buoyant and, again, chains and shops have been sold or shut down. Among those was Virgin's V Shop brand, whose 40-plus stores were sold to an Australian group.

Games, clothes, digital TV, drinking, drugs – they're all competing for the same pound in kids' pockets and have all been blamed on falling revenues in shops and on the live circuit. The latter has taken a pounding recently because of the ascendancy of pop and dance culture: squeaky-clean pop doesn't play well in spit-and-sawdust pubs and many venues have taken to installing DJs rather than booking bands. MTV and other TV music stations have been blamed for the demise of pub rock. Bands can record videos rather than string a few dates together for a tour. Now venues also face the prospect of tough new licensing laws, which the Musicians' Union believes could fundamentally destroy small music venues and put many jobbing musicians on the dole.

On top of this, the business is having its profit margins cut, dramatically. Albums once commonly sold for £13 ($22) or more; now they are being knocked out for a tenner ($17). In 2002, nearly 40 per cent of new releases were bought for £10 ($17) or less. That means less money to reinvest in the talent – the bands and acts that the A&R men sign. But with the massive amounts now needed to make a splash in the crowded marketplace – typically it costs upwards of half a million pounds to launch a new signing – getting an act to earn money for the record label is tougher than ever. In fact, fewer and fewer new acts ever earn a buck. Some estimate a hit rate of less than 10 per cent.

London's music business is also facing massive levels of piracy. A major chunk of the estimated $4.5 billion (£2.7 million) of worldwide revenue lost to pirates has not been seen by the capital's labels because of downloading of music from the Internet and unauthorised copying onto recordable CDs – CD-Rs.

The problem isn't going away. It is estimated that around half a billion tracks are available on the Internet despite the closure of the illegal file-sharing service Napster. The industry is belatedly launching its own subscription services and has recently had some successes, but many worry that kids have now got into the habit of not paying for music. It will be hard to persuade them to pay a few quid for a legitimate single download when they can get it for free.

Then there is the music. Oh dear. For the first time since 1963, no British act was represented in the *Billboard* Top 100 singles chart during a couple of weeks in 2002. The acts that are selling are dinosaurs: Pink Floyd, The Beatles, Led Zeppelin – all back in the charts despite disbanding decades ago.

London is kicking up its fair share of new talent such as the garage stars Ms Dynamite and So Solid Crew, but it is the TV pop show-derived acts that get access to the primetime mass media and set the cultural agenda. Manufactured pop, served up by good-looking young boys like Will Young and Gareth Gates, may have had its time in London. But, it has already tied up valuable label resources, which could have been helping to nurture a new Bob Dylan.

And, even if a new Bob Dylan is discovered, he needs to sell from day one. Anything less than a major hit with the first single is deemed a failure in many boardrooms now. U2 would probably have been dropped after their second album in this climate.

Four or five rounds down, and a little bit wiser about the workings of the business, Paul, me and the rest of The Percy empty onto the street to watch Strummer's hearse race up Ladbroke Grove. No slow burial for Joe. Electric Leg. The car screams by fast, like one of his songs, with a Stetson resting on top of the coffin plastered in stickers like his guitar – 'Question Everything', 'Vinyl Rules', 'Disobey All Authority'.

We follow on up to the crematorium, over the Grand Union Canal and left at the Harrow Road. The place is teeming, a TV crew is trying to get a story. There's a fire truck, and firefighters with emergency equipment form a guard of honour. The coffin is unloaded and carried into the chapel, where a wall of remembrance has been created from wreaths shaped like guitars and beatboxes. Strummer played a benefit gig for the striking firemen just weeks earlier, and now here they are turning out for him, as are his old bandmates.

Huddled inside out of the drizzle, Simonon, Mick Jones and Topper Headon shift awkwardly, preparing to deliver their tributes. There's also a brace of Sex Pistols – Paul Cook and Glen Matlock – who played with Strummer on the Anarchy Tour. Rat Scabies from The Damned, Chrissie Hynde, Kurt Cobain's widow Courtney Love, documentary maker Don Letts and film-maker Jim Jarmusch. A crop of grey-haired former punks in black suits and Crombies.

The church is way past bursting and a heap of mourners are stuck outside. It doesn't seem to matter when '(White Man) In Hammersmith Palais', inspired by Strummer's night at a reggae show in late '70s London, is played.

'All over people changing their votes/Along with their overcoats.'

It is played at ear-splitting level, louder than I've ever heard it. But, the sound is rubbish. Just like a Clash gig. More tears are being spilled and I see one tough nut reaching for a pair of shades to hide his welling eyes.

'If Adolf Hitler flew in today/They'd send a limousine anyway.'

An informal queue forms for mourners to file past the coffin and offer their last respects.

'I'm the white man in the Palais/Just looking for fun.'

The place is quiet, apart from the stifled coughs and crepe-soled shoes shuffling over worn slabs. I watch one old rocker bend over and barely breathe the words, 'Goodbye, Joe.' I couldn't find any words at all.

There's a wake down the road at another bar, The Paradise. Free bar. The place is rammed. The flags from the funeral have been hoisted in front of the bar and an impromptu sound system is blasting reggae, just like they did before Strummer and co launched into one of their shows. It's a very cool scene for a very packed room. Spliff is being traded and everyone is getting drunk. I see the guy who had choked up by Strummer's coffin earlier – his name is Nick. 'It's like looking down the bar at the [old punk haunt] Roxy and seeing all the faces from '77, but now so much older,' he cracks. 'You can feel him with us now,' Nick tells me.

'Who?'

'Joe.' Nick looks surprised. 'He was a real man. He had huge integrity and remained true to the ethos, the essence of what he started with his music. We're all poorer without him. I'll miss him.'

2 Carnival W11

The fierce bass rumble is making the ground shake, duh-duh-duh. And the glass in the large double doors behind me is rattling in its pane. The bass vibrates upwards, through my legs and up my spine. The noise is deafening, like ten jumbo jets landing in my head. Below me, the street is moving. Or at least it seems to be, slowly, like a lava flow. But, with more colour – red, green and gold.

I'm standing on a first-floor balcony of one of the stucco-fronted houses lining Ladbroke Grove, several blocks south of The Earl Percy. Drinking ice-cold Red Stripe beer. Someone has a spliff on. Someone is mixing a Muddy Waters. There are around a dozen of us dancing out here and watching one of the 60-odd floats taking part in Notting Hill Carnival pass by.

That's where that bass is coming from. From the enormous speakers double-stacked, high on the back of an articulated lorry, which is moving less than 3kph (2mph) through the throng in the street, while a dozen half-naked dancers stomp and skip atop it. It's in a convoy of floats carrying steel-pan players bashing out calypso or sound systems blasting everything from hip-hop to house, salsa to soul, and soca, calypso's modern, energetic alternative.

This is a carnival party, one of hundreds taking place in this corner of the capital. Across the street, flags and banners hang from balconies packed with people, swaying to the reggae rhythm exploding out of the truck between us. And on the flat roofs above them, another dozen drunken revellers are silhouetted against the dying sun, dipping low in the late summer sky.

With around a million people roaming these narrow streets of W11 today, it seems like the whole of London has been invited to the party. Carnival, the biggest street festival in Europe, takes place over the last – Bank Holiday – weekend in August. Some 65 masquerade bands, ten steel bands, a dozen calypso singers and over 50 sound systems are creating the most incredible cacophony, and probably the loudest party I've been to.

As one speaker-laden lorry passes, another drives by our balcony, adorned with gigantic inflatable bananas and palm trees. The music on the two floats' sound systems clashes for a moment before the only thing in the world I can hear is the music pumping out of the truck in front of me. This time it's a calypso tune. Trailing behind the lorry – 'maddening up de place' and doing a typical masquerade slow shuffle – around 50 masked and painted women and children are dressed like giant silver butterflies in sequins with huge peacock-feather plumes.

These are Mas (short for masquerade), the costumed processions that are the backbone of carnival and also give it its colour. It's probably taken a team of seamstresses, fuelled on a diet of rum punch and curried goat, weeks to stitch those costumes together. The competition for best Mas on the road is fiercely contested, and judged today, the final day of the carnival.

Someone taps me on the shoulder. It's Paula. She's lived on the Grove for nearly two decades and holds a carnival party every year. She's speaking. Shouting, actually. I can't hear a word she's saying. I wave my half-empty can. 'NO, I'M OK,' I shout back. Now she's pointing again. 'WHAT?'

And then the bass cuts out for a split second. '...ON THE STREET...'

Got it. She's going down. 'OK,' I grin, nodding. We're going to get amongst it.

About half a dozen of us snatch up our Marlboros and head down the stairs and out the front door. I hadn't seen them from the balcony above, but every inch of the steps and walls of the house are being fought over for dancing space. There's half a dozen or more people sitting on the window ledge, legs dangling over the drop to the basement, a stash of bottled beers and discarded food piled amongst them. At the entrance, two Rastas have set up a makeshift stall selling jerk chicken. Next to them a man is selling cans of Red Stripe out of an ice-filled dustbin. Two quid ($3) a pop.

There's only one way to go – right. The direction of the floats and the mass of bodies. It takes ten minutes to get 10m (10 yards) in the crush. This isn't walking. I give in, and let myself be pushed by the weight of the thousands of people snaking slowly up the kilometre (half-mile) up the Grove behind me.

I spot a gap where the crowd thins out at the corner of Cambridge Gardens. I duck in and land in front of a booming sound system struggling to get its sounds heard above the garage being blasted from another passing truck. This is the Lord Gelly sound system.

A regular at the carnival, ragga, reggae, soca and soul are his speciality. There's no escaping the din, not even on a side street. Paula pushes a rum punch into my hand and Dr Alimentado's 'Born For A Purpose' is cued up for action.

'If you think you have no reason for living ...'

I am swaying to the beat.

The Notting Hill Carnival has been taking place in London since 1959. Initially it was a response to racist attacks taking place in Notting Hill in the late '50s, when white youths regularly went 'nigger hunting'.

Someone on Brixton's *West Indian Gazette* had an idea to brighten the mood – a carnival.

On 30 January 1959, London's first Caribbean carnival was held in St Pancras town hall. Televised by the BBC, it was timed to coincide with the Caribbean's largest and most famous carnival in Trinidad, which was first held when slaves were set free in 1833.

Any doubts that a sun-drenched Port of Spain carnival would not translate well to a civic building in north London on one of the coldest days of the year were soon dispensed with. The following year it moved to Seymour Hall, alternating between there and the Lyceum until 1963, and growing larger each time.

And then, in 1965, a local Notting Hill woman, Rhaune Laslett, decided to organise a fête in what was then a poor working-class ghetto. At this time Laslett knew nothing of the indoor carnivals already taking place, but she invited Caribbeans alongside all the other ethnic groups then living in Notting Hill – Spanish, Portuguese, Irish and Africans – to take part in a week-long festival, culminating with a parade on August Bank Holiday.

Sue McAlpine of the Kensington and Chelsea Community History Group says, 'the histories of these carnivals are both independent and interlinked. They were linked by their motivation and the constituencies they were seeking to motivate'.

Laslett borrowed costumes from Madame Tussaud's, Portobello stallholders donated horses and carts, and the fire brigade had a float. And about 1,000 people showed up – 999,000 fewer than today – and, in a bid to assert their presence in the neighbourhood and recreate their own unique and vibrant carnival tradition, a small band of Trinidadian locals donned traditional masquerade costumes and picked up their steel pans.

The first carnival was both a social protest and a cultural celebration, with the pulsing sounds of calypso and soca the lifeblood. And when steel-band player Russ Henderson, who had played at the first St Pancras event in 1959, started to march his steel band up and down the street, making a route up as he went along, the seeds of today's modern procession were sown. People out shopping would join in, walk a few streets, then peel off and someone else would join in. Carnival – Trinidad-style, with no entry fee blurring the lines between participant and spectator – was up and running.

With its emphasis on masquerading and calypso, carnival takes popular subjects of concern as raw material for lyrics and costumes. It is owned by the people and for the people. Massive, spontaneous, sometimes subversive and often political, the ingredients for carnival can be explosive. They sometimes are – literally.

By 1975 the carnival was attracting 150,000 people. The police presence also started to increase. And then, less than a century after disturbances at the original carnival in Port of Spain, there were riots at the Notting Hill Carnival in 1976. Strummer was there, and Simonon.

The 1976 riot took most people by surprise. Bottles started flying and the police were largely ill-equipped and ill-prepared, defending themselves with dustbin lids. I see a copper on duty today, one of around10,000 police lining the 5.5km (3½ mile) route. He's too young to have been at the 1976 carnival, but he knows the story. 'Yeah, some guys from our station were there,' he tells me. 'I know it got quite heavy and they lost control of the streets. But that just doesn't happen any more. There's some trouble, but it is isolated incidents. I've been doing this for four or five years solid now and everyone is really friendly dancing with us.'

Unfortunately skirmishes the following year, in 1977, contributed to media stories about crime rather than culture. From then on, thanks largely to the press, carnival moved from being a story about culture to one about crime and race. By the '80s, growing tensions between the police, carnival organisers and carnival goers led to a 7pm curfew for bands and sound systems and there were calls for banning the event.

Tory shadow Home Secretary Willie Whitelaw said, 'The risk in holding it now seems to outweigh the enjoyment it gives.' Kensington and Chelsea Council suggested holding 'the noisy events' in White City Stadium, 1km (½ mile) or more away. As recently as 1991, following a stabbing, *Daily Mail* columnist Lynda Lee-Potter described the carnival as 'a sordid, sleazy nightmare that has become synonymous with death'.

By this time, however, its detractors were in the minority. Like the black British community from which it had sprung, there was a common understanding that it was here to stay. Latest police figures suggest attendance of one million; organisers say it is almost double that.

Fortunately, these calls have been resisted and the carnival has become a celebration and reflection of London's unique musical and multicultural make-up. It's big now, but also safe. After 2002's carnival, 241 tonnes (237 tons) of rubbish were cleared from the streets of Notting Hill. And there were only 74 complaints about noise.

I leave Lord Gelly and make slow progress south towards Kensington Park Road. I pass a dozen food stalls, producing a dozen different smells and serving up Jamaican patties, mangoes, coconuts, sweetcorn and rice and peas. I grab another beer and fill up on a slightly burned chicken wing toasting on a barbecue set up on a wall outside a house on Westbourne Park Road.

The music is deafening. As I walk up the street – swaying, twisting and pushing through the crush – the sound systems clash. One minute I hear reggae, the next it melds into R&B. The wind might change and it's a steel band. But all the time I can hear whistles. Everyone seems to have one. And they are blowing on them – hard. People are singing, hollering, crying, laughing, shouting. What a fantastic racket.

In a nearby tent I duck in to see a bunch of veteran calypso singers in pork-pie hats and tight, black suits, shiny through age. Amongst the audience of women in colourful, sequinned dresses, Tony is waiting his turn, clutching his lyrics scrawled on a few scraps of notepaper. On stage a black man in a white shirt and braces is leading us through a topical ballad. His voice is deep, but couldn't carry a tune.

'Oh man,' says Tony conspiratorially, leaning in close. 'This guy, he sings like he's just died.'

His act is dying, dying on its feet, but when he finishes the applause and cheering are as loud as if Nat King Cole had just dropped by.

Outside the tent, on Kensington Park Road, I fetch up outside one of the chic restaurants that have moved into the area, O&E. Run by Australian Will Ricker, it's on the same street as the fashionable bar 192, which is a favourite with media luvvies. Then there's a Café Med and Mediterraneo. Roger Moore and *bon viveur* Michael Winner eat there. Private members' club Soho House has a sister joint, Electric House, nearby on Portobello, which services the locals working in the music business, advertising and PR. Nearby there's a fancy deli and, around the corner, on Colville Terrace, Mr Christian's, serving prosciutto, *pâté de foie gras*, Roquefort cheese and Cava for the Notting Hill set.

Now Notting Hill is probably one of the hippest areas in the whole of London. The designer Paul Smith has a large shop in a converted house further up the street, on the corner of Westbourne Grove. Agnès B is also here. A fashionable lingerie and sex shop, Myla, near the Edwardian butcher's on Portobello, sells designer vibrators. Joseph on the site of an old gas station on the corner of Colville Road, Earl Jean on Ledbury Road. And then there's a clutch of rinky-dink boutiques run by girls called Amanda or Amelia. The Cross, Willma – they get written up regularly by *Vogue*.

In this part of London, the girls wear local girl Stella McCartney, Bella Freud, Alexander McQueen, Julien Macdonald, Chloë. Maybe teamed with something they picked up from the Portobello Market or the boutiques on Westbourne Grove. An old Hermès scarf, perhaps, or a Smashing Grandpa tee. The men are in Paul Smith, Dunhill and Savile Row, with shirts by Duchamp on Ledbury Road and leather bags from Bill Amberg. The boys dress in Diesel and skate/surf wear.

They like to eat and drink well. Boozers like The Percy are on the wane. No spit and sawdust now. They've become gastropubised. O&E was once an old-man-and-his-dog pub. The Warwick on the Portobello was a solid market traders' bar, but now it's a Chardonnay and gastro grub – leek mash with pork and apple bangers. Tom Conran, son of Sir Terence, turned a rusty old pub, The Cow on Westbourne Park Road, into a destination joint when he served up oysters with the Guinness. He also runs a deli on Westbourne Grove.

But, just a few decades ago this ritzy piece of Kensington and Chelsea was a slum, a no-go area. Two centuries ago, the area was little more than wasteland. A few cornfields, a meadow, an occasional lane. It changed when the Great Western Railway opened up North Kensington to development in 1838. The Ladbroke family commissioned architects to develop the area and the Ladbroke and Norland estates were built in 1840. Spacious, neoclassical mansions with balconies and loads of stucco, they're referred to as birthday-cake houses because of their bright colours today. Upper middle-class families moved in.

At the time, Notting Hill was known as the Potteries because of pottery works around Princedale Road, towards Holland Park, or Notting Dale. And it was this poorer area that Irish and Jewish immigrants occupied in the late 19th century. The 1930s saw the arrival of Fascist demonstrations against Jews and local immigrant groups. The houses, mostly large, three- and four-storey jobs, were carved up. They became multiple dwellings, let out by the room for a few shillings a month rent. The mass murderer Christie lived in Rillington Place, off St Mark's Road near Ladbroke Grove tube. He drank in the Kensington Hotel on the corner of Lancaster Road. His house and the street were pulled down and renamed Ruston Mews.

After World War II, the area worsened. It became a slum. It also became home to a large Afro-Caribbean community. The notorious slum landlord Peter Rackman preyed on them in the '50s and '60s and the area was rife with racial tension. Inter-ethnic tension culminated in the 1950,s when teddy-boy gangs engaged in open warfare against Afro-Caribbean immigrants. Britain's first race riots occurred in August 1958. These devastating riots formed the backdrop to *Absolute Beginners*, a cult novel by Colin MacInnes, later filmed as a musical starring David Bowie.

The area started to become upmarket in the mid-1990s, when house price inflation saw many new arrivals from Chelsea and Fulham funded by their families' trust fund, the Trustafarians. And the film *Notting Hill*, starring Hugh Grant, sealed its reputation. When the festival isn't raging, Notting Hill is fairly quiet. However, the Portobello Market on a Saturday, the biggest street market in Europe, is always rammed. For sale – everything: from 10p (17c) secondhand and thirdhand castoffs to Victorian antiques.

Steve Lewis knows about Notting Hill. 'Talk about how Notting Hill has changed,' Lewis tells me. 'When I first worked around here I could only get a Jamaican patty for lunch. Then, I suppose, along came Kensington Place.' Now the area is top to tail with fancy nosheries, and Lewis got fed up with eating patties.

Steve Lewis met Richard Branson when he was a teenager. He was still at school at the time, 16 years old. He saw an advert in a newspaper, which was placed by the Virgin entrepreneur. Branson wasn't much older than Lewis. He was running *Student* – a magazine for college kids – and a mail-order company for discount records.

Lewis went to the offices in Albion Street, Bayswater, across from Hyde Park. He was offered a job handing out the paper, selling it to longhairs. He didn't want it, he wanted something better and he got it. He started working with Branson, stayed with him while at college and helped grow Virgin during the '70s and '80s. It grew into Virgin Records, with offices in Vernon Yard, off Portobello Road, and artists such as Mike Oldfield and The Sex Pistols. Then the company moved to Ladbroke Grove, and finally up to Virgin's current offices on the Harrow Road.

Then Chrysalis' Chris Wright appeared on the scene. Another entrepreneur, he tapped Lewis from Virgin. Wright had joined forces with Terry Ellis in 1967 to set up Chrysalis. In 1985, Wright took Chrysalis public, then sold a half-share to Thorn EMI in 1989 for $96.6 million (£57.8 million). In 1991, he sold the rest of the record division.

In 1993, Chrysalis set up Echo, and Lewis was put in charge. In the same year, Pony Canyon, a subsidiary of Fujisankei of Japan, agreed to pay £11.5 million ($19.2 million) for a 25.1 per cent stake in Echo. Lewis was getting rich. Three years later, Babybird's 'You're Gorgeous' gave Echo its first big chart hit. Then Julian Cope and Moloko also joined Lewis's outfit.

With Wright, Lewis also set up the first TV and film department in a publishing company. He was head of the group's music division, calling the shots. With all those tunes, the company was earning money while its employees slept. Lewis built the top independent music publisher – twice. At Virgin and Chrysalis. Then, just when things seemed hunkydory, Lewis quit. Big surprise. That was a couple of years ago.

There's a fish restaurant on Uxbridge Street, W8. Geales is just behind Notting Hill Gate and along from the Notting Hill Arts Club. Fish and chips, cod, haddock, plaice – all the favourites and mushy peas, too, for a couple of quid ($3) extra. There are disposable paper tablecloths, wood panelling, sailing paraphernalia, portholes. This could be Cape Cod. They sell beer out of bottles – I have a Budvar.

Lewis is small with short cropped hair, and he looks younger than his 49 years. Neat and tidy, he's a little bundle of energy. He's in a blue T-shirt today, jeans. Casual, but everyone working for him knows who's boss. He has the big office on the first floor of his publishing headquarters in a nice-looking terraced house around the corner from Geales. There's a stereo, a desk. Nothing else. It all looks new. And it is. Lewis is just setting up a new publishing company called Stage Three Music. Why? Because he's at the third stage of his career. After Branson, after Wright, now he's on his own – his own group.

Lewis has had a couple of years to mull over his next move. To plan things. He did a bit of writing and a lot of thinking. He says now that he wasn't enjoying life a few years ago. Not corporate life anyway, at the top of a music company. 'I left Chrysalis because I felt the industry was going into a brick wall. It wasn't as much fun as it was 30 years ago. It was the general direction the industry was going. The marketing and promotional costs were going through the ceiling,' he elaborates.

Lewis believes the relationships in the London music industry are changing. The power is moving away from the record companies towards other areas. It is becoming increasingly difficult to get shelf space in retailers because of the competition. Not just with other music releases, but computer games, DVDs, T-shirts and other merchandise. 'Basically the business model we had is no longer relevant. The balance of power is now more towards publishers and managers,' he says.

Why? Because of economics and technology.

'In the old days,' continues Lewis, 'you only needed record companies. But, now you only need an Apple and Pro-Tools. You needed a record company for distribution, but technology has changed all that.'

Lewis uses the analogy of when formats changed from vinyl to CDs. Bands were asked to provide the same amount of material that they would have used to fill a vinyl album. But, the way people think about music and use music has changed. 'Consumers think more in terms of individual songs, compilations,' he adds. 'If consumers are interested in compilations, then we have to sell it to them.' The music industry needs to think greater volume, at lower unit price.

Also, it is difficult for record companies to resist technology. They may have tried or been slow by not establishing their own subscription online services before Napster and KaZaA got into the mix. 'You can't resist technological change. You can't sue your own customers. But, you need to find out how you can give people what they want at a price they want. So the very business model has changed.'

Fortunately, Lewis believes he is in the right business – publishing. 'I can see a clear way forward for music publishing. People always want the songs. Artists are selling all kinds of product now. Music is only one thing they sell. Recorded music will be bundled with other product and in different ways. But, it is the publishers that can drive those alternative revenue streams. You always have to pay for copyright.'

Stage Three Music is, therefore, going to be positioned to exploit this. There will be the traditional functions of a good music publishing outfit, giving service to songwriters – the men and women who sit at home or studios with their guitars and pianos bashing out tunes.

Register copyrights, get royalties. That's the basic business. But Lewis believes the publishing business can be a little bit more creative. Part of that means developing relationships with the advertising and film community, putting resources into creative exploitation, getting films to use music by bands whose work Lewis owns or getting an unknown act in an advert. Levis use The Clash. The band has its first No.1 ever. Levi's use Babylon Zoo. The band has its first and only No.1. TV has a lot of power. So does film. Eminem and *8 Mile*. Lot of synergy there.

Lewis only has to watch TV to see that. Especially, the reality TV shows where unknowns fight it out over a number of weeks to become a *Pop Idol*, like Will Young and Gareth Gates. 'Reality TV programmes, that is what is creating success. But, these are cabaret singers propped up by great songs and propelled into the charts by TV exposure,' he says. The winners, when the careers of Young and Gates are long forgotten, are the songwriters and the publishers. Guys like Lewis. 'The whole reality TV thing is really TV production, not music. Just putting on a bloke on singing a great song.'

There are also increasing avenues for Lewis and other publishers to place their songs. Digital TV, websites, games – they all use music. And there are increasing numbers of them. 'With broadband connections, all these things are going to use music and they have to pay for the music they use,' Lewis argues. That's why developing real talent, people who can write songs, will also be important to publishing executives like Lewis. 'That's what's interesting to me. Working with great talent,' he adds.

Back at the carnival, I turn onto the Portobello and try to head northwards towards the Golborne Road. I'm trying to get back to the Ladbroke Grove apartment. The narrow little thoroughfare is hardly moving. On a corner someone had a beatbox pumping out drum 'n' bass, but his sound is being swallowed up by the incessant shrill of the whistles and a powerful sound system a block away.

A little salsa band comes out of a side street and the trumpet players, like pied pipers, lead half-naked Brazilian and Portuguese girls down the hill. I stop for a moment and survey the scene – an endless sea of people. And they always seem to be walking in the opposite direction.

As the sun begins to set, the crowds begin to thin. I fetch up at another sound system for some serious dub. The air is thick with weed and the black booze dustbins are empty except for melting ice. Paula hands me a plastic glass of warm rum and Coke. And a version of 'Everything I Own' kicks off a spate of dancing. A couple of cops stroll by, jackets off, one with a Hawaiian lei around his neck. They turn a blind eye to the smoking.

Finally we make it to Paula's place and, after the systems have been wound down, we watch the refuge crew sweep into action. Huge dustcarts, their lights flashing, rumble behind an army of brush-wielding workers. On her doorstep three Rastas are sleeping off the day. Every step is sticky with beer and the windowsills are littered with empty beer cans. It looks like a makeshift bar which has been drunk dry. As Paula and I rejoin the party upstairs on the balcony, I ask her if it ever gets dangerous. 'You're more likely to get into a ruck at a football match than with a million stoned people. I don't think I could ever move.'

I hope she doesn't. The ice has melted in Paula's buckets, but the bottle of rum is still cold. We crack it open.

3 Busking It

I don't want to hear 'Baker Street' or 'Mr Tambourine Man', not again. They are the touchstones for buskers. The fall-back option. When all else fails, hit them with Gerry Rafferty's big hit or Dylan. Everyone can handle Dylan in rush hour.

I spend a day under ground on London's tube network – from Aldgate to Acton – and I hear both songs being played: on bata drum at Bank, on rinky-dink electronic organ at Old Street and classical guitar at Chalk Farm.

Thankfully Steve isn't playing either tune right now. Steve's a busker; he plays his guitar for a living. His audience can run to hundreds of thousands of people. His stage – the streets, railway stations, the bottom of escalators on the tube, Underground platforms and tube tunnels. A lot of work is underground. Now he's tapping out Oasis's 'Wonderwall' on his ratty Fender guitar. The axe is plugged into a practice speaker powered by a pack of batteries.

'"Wonderwall",' I say.

Steve, teeth like broken skittles, matted long hair, looks happy that I stop to chat. No one else is stopping. Not at this hour – 5:57pm. It's rush hour and the suits are rushing home. I stand and watch Steve for ten minutes. He dispenses with Oasis, bashes through a Beatles song, I think, and then turns in a pretty good version of Mike D'Abo's 'Handbags And Gladrags'. That gets the punters turning out their pockets. The Stereophonics recently recorded Rod Stewart's old standard and it's the theme of the critically acclaimed *The Office*. People recognise it. A couple of 50p pieces (85 cents) clatter into Steve's battered guitar case by his feet. He thinks he's on a winner with the Rodney. Next comes 'Maggie May'. It's now 6:16pm and 'Maggie May' isn't attracting any cash. Steve calls it a day. He picks up the loose change from the case, unplugs his guitar and straps it and the speaker onto the frame of an old shopping trolley. Then he joins me for a coffee.

Buskers live life on a bum note. Their trade is low earning. And they're always on the receiving end of comments. Few of them good. Steve leans his guitar case against the window of the burger bar and eases himself into one of the red vinyl chairs. We both look out onto Pentonville Road. Watch the world go by for a moment.

'Jesus, what a day,' offers Steve finally. He digs deep into the trouser pockets of his Oxfam suit. It's a Burton's job. He spreads out a handful of the coinage on the Formica table in front of him.

'How long did you need to work for that?' I ask.

'Two hours, maybe two and a half.' Steve looks tired.

He spends three or four minutes counting through the loose change. No notes. Two well-worn guitar picks, a few Euros and what looks like a dime coin are carefully picked out. It looks like six or seven quid ($10 or $12), tops. I place another coffee in front of him.

'It's not a bad spot there, you know.' Steve reckons he can make fifty ($80) on a good day. Sometimes more. Sometimes less. That's it for the day. He slides the coins across the tabletop, into his left hand and into his jacket pocket. Then he reaches for a pack of Regals.

'How does the day pan out?' I ask.

The schedule is rigorous. Monday through Saturday, Steve plays from 10 or 11 in the morning until 6pm, sometimes longer if he's hitting pay dirt. He's been playing the Underground for four years now. But is only just accepted.

'No one likes new faces around here. Someone new comes along, they're taking our patch or it's another mouth to feed. Know what I mean?' He tosses a Regal into his mouth, snatches a Zippo from his pocket, turns it in one hand, flips the lid open with one jerk of his wrist and, with one finger, pops it alight. Steve takes a long drag from the cigarette. Snaps the Zippo shut. His first fag for hours – no smoking on the Underground. Not since the King's Cross fire.

'How did you get into the busking business?' I ask, as Steve exhales his cigarette across the café. He keeps the tab fixed tightly between his lips when he speaks.

'I came down from Sheffield. Used to work in a dye factory up there, but was always playing music. Played in a band – we did the clubs and pubs around Yorkshire.'

When Steve lost his job, he thought he would give London a try. He was only 24 then. He still lives in the same Bayswater bedsit he found four years ago. '£60 [$100] a week, but it's an absolute shithole.'

Steve didn't have any friends. Busking was work and his social world. At first, he went about it like a science.

'I travelled all around the Circle Line getting off at each station to see which was busiest or had a good spot. Sometimes I'd get chased off by one of the old guys, who had been around years. King's Cross is OK because there is a mix of tourists and there's loads of different lines and subways here. I don't like pushing a guy off my patch, so I'll find another place. There's always a spot around here if you get here early enough.'

Early on, Steve's repertoire was rubbish. He's improved it.

'I used to sing and play stuff I like, you know? Quite a lot of obscure stuff. Talking Heads, er, "Changes" by David Bowie, actually people like that. But, I was also playing "China Girl". You know, the song Iggy Pop did? It's a good tune, but I found out after experimenting with different songs that people like to hear what they know. Not necessarily what they like, but just something recognisable. You know?'

Steve got wise. He bought himself some Beatles, Bob Dylan and Oasis songbooks. Bob Marley's stuff is also popular.

'Now I like it. I don't think I could get another factory job. You know, I work for myself. I can get by most weeks, always pay my rent. I can't say I'll be doing this for the rest of my life – I still think maybe I could get a band up and running again, give it a shot. My playing is like 500 per cent better now. I've got to say that. This is good practice for a musician. You can learn a lot of craft down there by the tracks.'

Then there's running from the law. Buskers can spend a good chunk of time dodging the British Transport Police. Busking is illegal. The charge is trespassing – up to £200 ($340).

Steve owes something like a grand ($1,700) in cumulative fines. That's just in four years. He's got a deal with the courts to pay at a rate of £20 ($33) each month. He doesn't ever expect to square it.

'How can I? Every time I play, I risk another £50 [$85], £100 [$170] fine. They can sing for it.'

But that may change. A new scheme aims to license the guerrilla musicians in London. Buskers hopping from station to station, one step ahead of the police, may be a thing of the past. As I sit with Steve, a pilot scheme to license busking on London tube stations is being greenlighted. I head down the Northern Line towards Canary Wharf station. The busker licence is being rolled out at 25 officially branded pitches at 11 key stations. Canary Wharf is one of them. The others are Charing Cross, Oxford Circus, Tottenham Court Road, Bank, Chancery Lane, Green Park, Leicester Square, London Bridge, Piccadilly Circus, South Kensington and Westminster.

The move follows bylaw changes won by London Underground. After surveys showed that eight out of ten tube customers backed the busking initiative and wanted to hear music performed – legally – on the network. Good-quality busking is appreciated, it seems.

Tony Maguire, London Underground's Director of Communications, says, 'We listened to what our customers want. Now we'll be listening to some great music from some of Britain's best buskers – coming soon at a station near you.'

Auditions start today and I'm checking them out: 20 buskers will audition in front of a panel of musicians and tube employees. Eventually a pool of several hundred musicians will be created.

New schemes have new rules. The London Underground busking licence is no exception. The rules are as follows. Licensed buskers will still rely on tube travellers for their earnings; only passive collections will be allowed; actively soliciting money can lead to licences being revoked. Busking on trains will be prohibited, as will unlicensed busking at stations not included in the trail. A busking licence does not give the holder the right to free travel on the Underground. Steve thinks it should.

No mime artists or comedians will be licensed under the scheme because they could attract audiences, which cause congestion and safety problems. Pitch licences are for solo artists only – however, some may eventually be categorised as suitable for two or more performers.

Buskers must report to the station supervisor and sign in before playing. They will receive a visitor's pass allowing access to the station only; any busker who misuses the licence or pass will have these revoked.

Before being licensed, buskers must agree to abide by London Underground's terms and conditions; failure to comply with these also risks loss of licence. Buskers will only be allowed to play at officially recognised pitches; the revoking of a busking licence or visitor's pass will automatically follow misuse; there will be no right of appeal. Photographic ID cards will be issued and must be displayed while busking – these cards must also be presented for identification, on demand.

Buskers will not be allowed to use staff toilets or canteens. These will remain for staff use only; staff will have the right to suspend performances if these are causing problems or disrupting services.

That's a lot of rules. Impact tests have already taken place at pitches to check the effects performances have on customers and whether they drown out the PA system. 'Mind the gap... The train approaching is a Northern Line via Bank...' The success of the licensing scheme will be reviewed at the end of the trial. Customer surveys will play a role. If positive, it may be extended across the whole network. Martin Penney, Customer Programme Implementation Manager at London Underground says, 'Musicians will be chosen based on musical competence and good character.' He adds, '[The] majority of the buskers are excited about the scheme. They will have to sign the terms and conditions but will not have to pay for their licence.' Once chosen, buskers will have to adhere to a schedule, which will be drawn up a week in advance.

The auditions, dubbed Tube Idols, have attracted a rum bunch of about two dozen hopeful buskers. At Canary Wharf I spot a violinist, blues guitarist and an accordion player with a beret and candy-stripe trousers. A trumpeter called Alf is not happy. He tells me the licensing scheme could cause friction. At present, buskers operate an informal system of occupying a pitch for an hour. This could change under licensing.

'I know some guys think it is more Big Brother. We have quite a good system going, what's the point of having a licence? Will it make us better musicians? I doubt it. And what happens if I get a licence and then some guy without one wants my patch? How will it work? I think there could be a few fisticuffs.' The official guidance from London Underground is that if licensed buskers are harassed by unlicensed buskers, they should inform station staff. They will call the cops. Alf shrugs when I tell him that.

'Sure, that's going to work. In the meantime, I got a black eye, lost my takings or worse.'

Alf doesn't seem long for the busking game.

Another busker (he won't give his name) is more positive than Alf. 'Been one for nearly a decade and told no one. Yeah, I had doubts. But, the tube people have included me in the scheme, how it will be set up and the like.'

When the licences are issued, he expects to be one of the first to pick one up. 'On account of the fact that I have been busking for a while. I should get first choice in the pitches I want.'

Another busker, Charlie, is nervous because he has a conviction for busking. The organisers tell him that won't count against him. Not unless it is for assault on tube staff or police officers. Charlie shakes his head.

'It were only trespass.'

They think he'll be OK, but police checks may be made. A woman asks for Charlie's full name. He looks apprehensive. I pull a judge aside.

'What sort of music will you license?'

He is a jazz drummer, but they'll be looking for everything from pop to classical. 'The judges' decision is final. Buskers will have to pass a test of professional opinion, but we want tube travellers to have the widest selection of musical styles and, therefore, buskers may be drawn from many different musical backgrounds such as rock, folk, world and classical. But I'm afraid there is no appeals procedure if they fail the audition.'

Alf is back. 'I want to know. Will you lot keep records on what we earn and so forth?'

A London Underground official looks perplexed.

'Count my takings at the end of the day?'

'No,' Charlie is assured. And the tube won't inform the tax man, either. He looks happy at that.

I watch for an hour or so. The standard of the audition is pretty high. Alf looks good for a licence. I head back to central London, to King's Cross. I pass a sax player at Embankment. At the exit leading up to Charing Cross station, there's a bongo player. I've seen and heard enough buskers to draw up a few recognisable schools. Here are some.

Instrumentalist: Real pro busker. Probably with a miniature amp and well turned out. His repertoire was popular in the '70s.
Heavy-metal dude: Black leathers, tatty jeans, these metal kings pile on the distortion and heavy riffs. 'Smoke On The Water' is the only song they have learned.
Jazzman: This saxophonist will always have a purple-lined instrument case brimming with coins.
Acoustic guitarist: Will know The Beatles' catalogue from front to back, but very often can't play it.
Accordionist: Will often make the move from the platform to the train with a baseball cap for a collecting plate.
Bongo or percussionist: Usually the biggest noise pollutants. Moroccan drummers are the most popular, Keith Moon impressionists the least.
Tuneless: No tune, no song, usually no money.

On the ride up to King's Cross, I consider Steve's school. I guess he is a cross between instrumentalist and acoustic guitarist. I find Steve back at his usual pitch. He doesn't look happy to see me. But then he doesn't look unhappy. Steve is not a well of emotions.

A poster behind him advertises toothpaste. The girl with the perfect white teeth and big smile has been defaced. Now she has a black molar. Up the side of the ad I can see Steve has printed his name above someone called Bongo Brian. After his, Dave, Machine Mike, Mick, Eve – the other buskers Steve shares his pitch with.

Steve is knocking out 'Wonderwall' again. It's not a bad version of the song. Of the top tunes on the street, 'Wonderwall' is a favourite in the busking jukebox. Other favourites include 'Mr Tambourine Man' by Bob Dylan, 'Let It Be' by The Beatles and 'No Woman No

Cry' by Bob Marley. Within minutes Steve is relieved by Bongo Brian. I know this because Brian is second on the list on the toothpaste ad. He also ambles along the subway with a pair of bongos under his arm. Brian – black, 5ft3in (158cm), Kangol hat, check pants – eyes me cautiously. But he is genuinely pleased to see Steve. Brian has a thick Glaswegian accent.

'Hey, how you doing?' asks Brian.

'Yeah, OK,' replies Steve.

'Good man. Fucking good man. How much have you made?'

They both look over at me.

Steve tells him, 'Ten [$15], maybe twelve quid [$20].'

Brian laughs. 'I could make that in ten minutes.'

'See you, Bongo.'

Brian is still laughing. He reminds me of Sammy Davis Jr.

There is some competitiveness between buskers. Professional rivalry. Steve has told me that most jealously guard their exact earnings from others. They often exaggerate. And a tenner ($15) is often turned into a £20 ($30) spot.

Busking is their living, so keeping the pitch is everything. Keeping on good terms with their colleagues too. No one wants to upset the apple cart. Buskers have enough trouble from drunks, football supporters, City boys and every other tube rider with a grudge.

Brian says, 'OK, man. Now take care. See you tomorrow?'

Steve gathers his gear and Brian unpacks his. He hasn't much. Bongos. A Thermos flask. And a mouth organ. He places the mouth organ on top of the Thermos. He sees me watching.

'Chicken soup, brother. I make it up myself. Way too much salt, though.'

He laughs at that and then gets a rhythm going. Just getting his wrists warmed up. Bongo Brian is good. Just then a Northern Line train deposits hundreds of commuters on a nearby platform and they swarm out of the tunnel exits, past Bongo. He hits those skins hard.

A little groove gets going. Everyone is in too much of a hurry to take much notice of Bongo. Some probably don't even hear him in the racket. Steve has his amp loaded. He nods at me. I follow him upstairs. We hit the same café. Steve isn't going for a licence.

'No way. You can't call us beggars one minute, get the feds on our backs dawn 'til dusk and then bring in a licence for just a few. They'll be outlaw buskers and then this group who are licensed. I can't see it working.'

I ask about Bongo, Machine Mike, Mick.

'I dunno.' Steve sips his coffee and takes a drag off his cigarette. I can sense he's uneasy. 'Well, yeah, Bongo thinks it is a good idea. Eve too. I don't see her much now anyway. So I don't know how it'll work out, because they'll move on. I don't think this patch is going to be under the licence.'

He's right. King's Cross isn't part of the trial scheme.

'But, I don't know. Buskers are full of bullshit. They are always trying to tell you they've earned a fucking fortune and maybe they've made a fiver [$8] out of the whole day. Could be they'll sign up; more than likely not.'

Same place tomorrow?

'Same time, same place. You know, I'm working on putting a new song into my repertoire.'

'Yeah?'

'Yeah, that Stones song "Fool To Cry". Might go down with the ladies. Wanna hear?'

Steve reaches for his guitar.

'You know, maybe tomorrow, Steve.'

4 Camden Town

Camden, a north London borough, northwest one, NW1 – that's the postcode. It's lively, this junction at Camden High Street and Parkway. Crawling with belching diesel trucks and screaming scooters.

This is the main artery for London's music. And all music tribes have a constituency in Camden. Just outside the tube station are jazzers, blues boys, rappers, hip-hoppers, R&Bers, rock 'n' rollers, house addicts, beat boys, fly girls. Cartoon punks, tartan bondage trousers, bum flaps and green Mohawks. 'Anarchy' painted in white paint on their newish-looking black leather motorcycle jackets, a can of Special Brew – the street lager – in their paws.

A little further down Kentish Town Road, black velvet-caped goths, reeking of patchouli oil, scurry into the Devonshire Arms. Black-painted timbers on white, it's mock-Tudor, built by the Victorians. It's also London's premier goth venue. I know that because a neatly painted banner, hoisted above the pub's door, tells me.

A Sikh is parked on his ass outside, catching rays: a goth Sikh or Sikh goth. He's wearing a black turban. I can hear a track being played, 'Dark Entries' by Bauhaus. I nose inside and spot the DJ. He's a strange-looking boy with lopsided hair, mascara and black nail varnish. I start to count the number of piercings on his face, but give up at a dozen – and that's just his right ear.

He is drinking a can of booster booze Red Bull through a straw. On a tiny dance floor in the middle, four women goths are dancing, kicking their legs, waving their hands above their heads like they want to dry their nails. The song is 'Terror Couple Kill Colonel' by Bauhaus.

The DJ likes Bauhaus. An old man, barely started on a pint of Guinness, is the only other paying customer. I nod over, but he ignores me. No – he's asleep.

On Camden High Street, there's a greaser in a black leather jacket with 'ROCKERS' spelled out in studs, oil-stained 501s, engineer boots and a red-and-white rag tied around his neck. He has wispy, thin, nicotine-coloured hair, all that remains of what was once a proud DA cut. He must be pushing 50.

Nearby, an enormous roly-poly woman with dyed red hair down to her waist, Oxfam threads, laddered black tights and enormous platform shoes waddles out of the Elephant pub on Jamestown Road. You don't see people like this anywhere else in London.

There are also tourists, hundreds of them. In a 100m (100yd) stretch from Camden Underground to the Buck's Head pub, I hear conversations conducted in French, Italian, German and an east European accent, maybe Russian. The whole world is in Camden. Japanese girls want to buy saucy knickers in Pink Piranha on Chalk Farm Road. Japanese boys want to buy magazines in Mega City Comics on Inverness Street. 2000 AD is popular.

More clothes stores along the High Street. Punkyfish by the canal bridge. A giant cat carved out of fibreglass is scaling the walls above the racks and racks of Metallica T-shirts and camouflage army pants. Across the street a fibreglass tank crashes through the brickwork of a store selling the same Metallica T-shirts. In the middle of all this, the market. And more T-shirts – this time, Paul Frank, Gucci, Calvin Klein and Adidas rip-offs.

There are records, too – CD, vinyl, tape. Stalls and shops and lots of them. There are few other places in the city where I could get hold of sounds by Nigerian, Jamaican, Cuban and Japanese acts at one stall. I try Record and Tape Exchange and pick up some dance on vinyl. In the vicinity, you'll also find Bar Vinyl, Rhythm Records, Resurrection Records, the Music and Video Exchange and Out On The Floor.

Camden Town first came into existence in the late 18th century. In around 1791, developers – including Charles Pratt, Earl of Camden, who gave his name to today's Pratt Street – began to build on open land and fields north of Tottenham Court Road. Initially they developed the east side of the southern part of what is now Camden High Street. Then, this road was an old coaching route to Hampstead, often used by highwaymen and boasting just a couple of inns including the Mother Red Cap, now the site of World's End. Some highwaymen were hung from the gibbet nearby, close to Camden Town tube station.

The Grand Union Canal, which cuts Camden High Street in half, arrived in 1820, and by 1850 Camden had its own railway station. Railway and canal construction brought the first Irish settlers to Camden, accelerated by the famine in Ireland in the mid-1800s.

Warehouses and other businesses soon flourished along the canal banks, and by the end of the 19th century Camden High Street was a popular shopping centre, patrolled by trams and horse-drawn buses. The Underground station was opened in 1907, linking the area with the rest of London.

However, the destruction wrought by World War II and the development of roads and railways, which largely killed off waterways transport, meant many warehouses fell into disrepair. In 1971 some of these disused, old industrial buildings, including TE Dingwall's timber yard, were leased from British Waterways Board for use as craft workshops. In 1972, a weekend market, selling the products made in the workshops, was started on the cobbled yards outside. The market gradually broadened its range to include antiques, clothing and food.

Because the site was allowed to open on Sundays, before laws eventually relaxed the Sunday trading restrictions on other shops in the capital, the market became a popular weekend destination. By 1985, three other markets had opened on or near Chalk Farm Road. In 1990, many of the old buildings at the Lock were renovated and a new indoor market built near Middle Yard.

Being music central, live music and clubs are Camden's thing. The area is steeped in the live experience and has the biggest concentration of music bars, clubs and venues of any area in London. Count them.

The first rock gig in the area probably took place at the Roundhouse, the big brick dome on Chalk Farm Road. Built in 1847, it was originally a turning shed for railway engines. Then, in

1966, it became a concert venue. It hosted the launch party for the underground rag *International Times* – Marianne Faithfull and Paul McCartney were among the guests, offered a cube of sugar spiked with LSD when they tipped up. Soft Machine and Pink Floyd provided the tunes.

The list of other bands that have played the Roundhouse is endless. Here's a few: Led Zeppelin, David Bowie, T Rex, The Who, The Ramones. The Stranglers liked it so much they recorded two live albums there – *Live (X-Cert)* and November 1977's *London Ladies,* featuring 'Something Better Change'.

Dingwalls, named after the timber yard, opened in 1973, followed by the Music Machine four years later (in 1982, this was renamed the Camden Palace). The Camden Palace is at the southern end of the High Street, by Mornington Crescent tube. It opened its doors as a venue after nearly a century hosting variety acts and, later in the 1960s, BBC studios. *The Goons* was recorded here. The Heartbreakers, with former New York Dolls Johnny Thunders and Jerry Nolan, The Police and Siouxsie And The Banshees were early attractions.

The Electric Ballroom opened in 1978 next to the tube station and, when it is not being pressed into service for bands or club nights, holds a rarities record fair at least once a month.

These and other venues in Camden feature live music every night of the week, mostly young bands looking for their first record deal. In 1990, the state-of-the-art Jazz Café was opened on Parkway, giving the area another musical shade next to the predominant alternative-rock scene. Pubs have also had a strong tradition of hosting live music, especially The Monarch, the Devonshire Arms and Dublin Castle.

Camden has been – and is – a significant player in British music because it is where every new band in Europe pays its dues. It has been – or is – the backdrop to most new scenes. The Good Mixer on Inverness Street and Arlington Road was the official birthplace of Britpop in the mid-1990s when Blur, Pulp, Oasis, Elastica, Supergrass and Suede played in the borough. Some band members lived in the area; all of them drank at the Good Mixer.

This musical reputation has also done much to attract media and production companies such as MTV, which has studios on the canal, and record labels, like Creation. In the early 1990s, Prince opened a purple-painted store on Chalk Farm Road.

Then there's neighbouring Kentish Town. It has mopped up some of Camden's musical overspill. The Verge just by the abandoned tube station on Kentish Town Road. TV Smith, from The Adverts whose big hit was 'Gary Gilmore's Eyes', is playing tonight. Ubiquitous live catch John Otway is a forthcoming attraction. One tube-stop ride north of Camden, there's the Forum and Bull & Gate.

One cold Friday night, I'm outside The Electric Ballroom. This has a long history, too. Once an old dancehall for the local Irish community, now it's a venue and night club. Local boys Madness played here. So did The Sex Pistols, Adam And The Ants, Moby, Talking Heads, Elastica. Tonight it's Full Tilt. That's a club, not a band. The queue is nonexistent when I arrive at 11pm.

Downstairs for goth, synth-pop, industrial, techno and hard-house. Upstairs they play nu-metal and rock classics.

I get frisked by the bouncers. No knives, no guns – OK, I'm in.

I go down some stairs – there's a round bar in front of me and the Ballroom opens out. It's a cavernous space. On the floor, it's packed. There are black leather trench coats and someone is wearing a rubber mac and a jockstrap. There's pink hair, blue hair, jet-black hair. Jet black clothes. Big boots like Tank Girl. I climb the stairs, AC/DC's 'Highway To Hell' is playing. A man in his 30s is playing along on his air guitar. A girl in her early 20s pretends to fellate him.

Julie Weir knows all about Full Tilt. She runs Visible Noise, a metal label, and one of the best in London. This is where I come to get the lowdown on goth, metal, whatever. Julie is an authority on the scene. She did a thesis at university about subcultures like this.

'The Birmingham and Chicago schools of sociology in the 1970s stated that subcultures can be pigeonholed; everyone looks like this and that,' declares Weir. 'In my thesis I said they were becoming more amorphous. It has, because if you look at kids now, they're not mods, rockers, punks, goths. If you see people coming down to the club everyone looks like a mishmash so you get a kid who could be a goth wearing bright pink, which they'd never had done. I think it's bringing things together. Not mods fighting rockers, it's all the kids who look a bit weird together. Styling has got a lot less interesting. People have grown lazy. Hardcore kids are just jeans, trainers and sweatshirts. Dressing down – they could fit in anywhere.'

I agree to meet Weir in her office on the Portobello Road at number 231, above Intoxica Records. It's a rabbit warren up there. A hobble of tiny rooms stashed full of CDs.

Julie. Big shoes. BIG shoes. Black tracksuit top. She's been in London for ten years. Born in a big steel town in Cumbria. The Lake District. She likes metal. In her nose, too. That is pierced, so are her ears, lots of times, and her chin and her tongue. But Julie isn't as intimidating as she appears.

Her first single was 'Ghost Town' by The Specials. She likes Queen. Not that intimidating. 'Everyone likes Queen, don't they?'

I say nothing.

'They're a great band. It's all to do with the theatrics, I think.'

Weir used to listen to Iron Maiden, still does. Then she left Workington at 18 to go to Salford University in Manchester. At college she studied Sociology and Popular Culture. 'I was interested in why people dressed like this – the whole tribal identification in cities and stuff,' she explains. She also discovered the indie rock scene in Manchester and became secretary of the college rock society. 'I ended up spending a lot of time in Manchester writing and doing photography. I got involved with a lot of bands and was into the goth, punk, heavy-metal scenes,' she says.

In 1992, Weir left Manchester to go work in a record store in Leeds and later she ran a club called Asylum, whose speciality was industrial hardcore, hip-hop and metal. Then she came to London study for a MA in Film and Media at the University of London. She recalls, 'I did it the right way. Record shop, clubs. I moved to London because...Leeds is a small town and if you want to get on in music you need to be in London.'

Weir specialised in modern culture. But the course didn't last. About halfway through, she started applying for jobs and got an interview to do merchandising. She was interested in design. It worked. This was at the group Vinyl Solution. She soon moved on from merchandising to do label management at a new imprint, the metal setup called Cacophonous. It was the first label Cradle Of Filth signed to in 1994.

I'm losing track of the genres and subgenres. Julie helps me out. 'Yeah, metal is still about teenage rebellion, but it is a finicky scene. Cacophonous is traditionally known as a black metal label, which is extreme Scandinavian, metallic metal.'

OK.

'We started doing different stuff – death metal, which is more thrashy extreme stuff, then there's grindcore, then doom, which is slower math metal.'

OK?

'Nu-metal is commercial. More than that. There are very, very tiny differences. Math metal is very technical. Death metal and thrash metal are very similar, but death metal is slower. Black metal and satanic metal can be different because black metal can be orchestral or can be doom-laden, angst-ridden. Satanic is all about death, destruction, suicide and pestilence. But, it can all flood into one genre. Nu-metal is the other end of the spectrum. Nu-metal is really chart metal – an all-encompassing term for bands like Limp Bizkit, which doesn't apply to the metal we have over here. Nu-metal got kids into rock music. Once they were into rock music, kids wouldn't know about the history of older bands and would start finding out more. Your tastes get honed as you grow up.'

Right, I'm hearing it, but I'm not sure I'm getting it.

Julie gets going.

'A lot of extreme metal is fantasy, storytelling. Doom is different. The politics is mainly in grindcore – it's fast and chaotic. Grinding guitars and drums doing blast beats. Black metal bands can be racist. Black metal is black magic and Satan. We've all done it, wearing black, but you grew out of it. Metallica and Megadeth are old-school metal.

I don't think there's a term for them now. Everyone is compartmentalised. There are thousands and thousands of different categories. A lot of kids run around in the clubs, who have Slipknot T-shirts. Slipknot were classed as nu-metal, but they sound like an old-school thrash band. Now with nu-metal and post hardcore comes the emo kids. This is like slowed-down punk after they've split up with girlfriends. Emo is emotional. This brings more girls on board. The scene is around 50:50 girls and boys because the bands are better-looking and they're more conscious about what they wear.'

Many of the majors, such as EMI, don't have a recognisable label identity. Once it was the home of The Beatles, but so many groups and different musical styles have come and gone through its doors that it cannot claim ownership of a particular genre. However, many small labels purposely generate a culture and an image to package their music. It may be a reggae label like Greensleeves, dance with Ministry of Sound, or metal like Julie's Visible Noise.

But, that can be a drawback. Visible Noise has a label identity as a young metal label. It appeals to 10- to 25-year-olds. It has found its audience. They know what they want, they don't want anything else. It can be difficult then to expand from that base.

Julie needs to start a new label to attract new and slightly different bands to the group. Her answer is to launch a new imprint called Surrender. 'You can get compartmentalised. We got sick of being compartmentalised in the nu-metal vein. There's only one band on Visible Noise that is nu-metal and that's Lost Prophets, but you get branded as a nu-metal label and you get five million demos that sound the same.'

A few years back Julie says every demo she got was from bands that wanted to sound like REM. She wants Surrender to attract more varied groups and ideas. She is aiming at people who 'have been to university and are looking for the next band they can paint their room black to'. She adds, 'Surrender is being set up because I'm 31 and I'm listening to different types of music these days. I'm branching out. Everyone in the office doesn't listen to metal 24/7. There was one band I really wanted to sign and there was no way they would fit on Visible

Noise. They are more grown-up. They sound like a mixture of Death In Vegas meets Sonic Youth meets some bizarre '80s electronica.'

Julie is trying her best to find a handle on this whole thing, to provide me with the road map to metal and an understanding of Full Tilt.

'Kids are starting to look at what's available in the metal scene. Like my first single was The Specials, then I would have bought an Abba single when I was 11. Kids today won't do that because it's not cool enough. Kids are so tuned in at 10 or 11 years old, whereas I was wearing skinny-rib polo necks and Crimplene when I was 10. We didn't have much choice at the time. Kids are a lot more sussed now. They're loyal to what they like – they won't just jump ship.'

OK? Again, I think I am beginning to understand the subtle metal differences. I put this to Julie: is it like a kid walking down the road? He is not just metal if he is wearing a Slipknot T-shirt. He is Slipknot metal. Another kid might be walking down the same street with a Limp Bizkit T-shirt on. He won't be Slipknot metal. They won't necessarily connect.

Julie nods her head. Then she adds, 'As more bands come along, the whole thing is separated down into different genres. The attention span of kids is limited. They're looking for something different all the time.'

Julie believes metal is so fragmented that trying to construct a continuum from hardcore to ska punk is impossible. But, what really riles her is when metallers, Full Tilters, can't be bothered. And they're not bothering. They dress in any old gear nowadays. They're even less interested in politics.

'I don't think kids are that politically aware. Most don't care. They're more interested in the best trainers. Music has always gone hand in hand with fashion. Everything is a step on. It's going full circle. When nu-metal came around it was more fashion-conscious and more fashionable. But now the new street uniform is baggy jeans, trainers and a hooded top. That could be anyone. You can buy that anywhere. People are losing interest in image. When I was about 14, I used to go to London and the Intrepid Fox pub on Wardour Street. It was like walking into a zoo. You'd see all these fantastic-looking individuals, which is why I think Marilyn Manson and Cradle Of Filth are so popular because they've been given shitloads of money to spend on new clothes'.

I look at Julie's black top. It's slightly faded.

'They spend a ridiculous amount on a new video. Kids need something interesting. Any kid can pick up a skateboard and say they're into Limp Bizkit.' Julie believes a change is in the air. 'I think kids will start digging a bit more to find something a bit more interesting, instead of just following charts. They're going to do something more interesting instead of S Club 7 and Steps. Kids evolve and everyone's life will take different turns.'

I look at the guy with pink dreadlocks waiting at the bar, downstairs in Full Tilt. Despite Julie's briefing I still have no idea if he is nu-metal, old metal, death metal, satanic metal, goth, emo, grindcore, math metal, doom, metallic metal or black metal. When he turns around, I see he is wearing an old Hawkwind T-shirt. Old school? Or is this an ironic twist from a doom merchant? The DJ plays The Cult and he wades into the sea of black on the dance floor. I guess I'll never find out his tribe.

A few weeks later I'm sifting through boxes and boxes of records in The Stables, a tumble of cobbles and rickety, old abandoned Victorian sheds and railway arches given a lick of paint and a new life. Another market, this time mostly antiques, furniture, secondhand clothes and, oh, records.

I pass the ramp where The Clash stood for snapper Kate Simon. The result was the cover shot of their debut, eponymous album. The band squatted in the '70s in a nearby disused building (known as Rehearsal Rehearsals) to practise.

I rummage for some rare grooves at a stall run by Jon.

'I only do secondhand,' says Jon.

'Good. I'm looking for *Metallic KO* by The Stooges'.

'Vinyl, yeah? Might have it. That is on Skydog, I think.'

Jon pulls out a couple of large cardboard boxes filled with hundreds of albums.

He pulls out *Fun House*. 'No, hang on.'

He pulls out Iggy Pop's *The Idiot*.

'No. mate. Don't think I've got it.'

He grabs another box and flicks through the dog-eared sleeves. 'No, that's *Raw Power*. No. Sorry, mate. But, I know the guy that runs the label.'

That's how I came to be sitting in a café on Camden's Delancey Street with Frenchy, Skydog boss. He hands me a CD, *Metallic KO*. 'With some tracks not on the vinyl release,' he says. His accent is thick French.

'Thanks, Frenchy.'

Frenchy was born in Grenoble, France. He played the 100 Club Punk Festival on the same bill as Glen Matlock and The Sex Pistols. Frenchy was one of the Stinky Toys.

'I came over with the Stinky Toys. On the first single I was credited with being the guitarist, although I didn't actually play on it. I did one gig with the Stinky Toys at the 100 Club. The Clash were on the bill and Siouxsie And The Banshees with Sid Vicious on drums. I could play a few chords. Nobody cared at the 100 Club. There was so much noise. It helped me get to know a lot of people very quickly. It was fantastic. Coming from France, I'd never heard anything like it. I couldn't believe it. We'd heard of punk through magazines, but didn't know much else. When I first arrived we went to the Roxy and the Vortex and I said, "Fuck, I want to stay here, this is far too good." You could sense that anything you wanted to do there was a chance. Doors were being held open. It was a once-in-a-lifetime opportunity.'

One door that opened was the opportunity to set up his own independent record label in London, but Frenchy believes that scene is now dying. Partly because of finance or, rather, lack of it. Partly because bands aren't interested in becoming part of an alternative culture. That's his story.

Frenchy's real name is Marco Gloder. He came to London in 1976 after running a record store in Grenoble. 'I was always into music, mainly English and USA music because there's no scene in France. In

France, if you listen to English and American music you've usually got long hair and you belong to this group called zone – freaks, basically, who smoke dope. That was late '60s. I left my shop with my partner and he sent me my share over to London.'

Once in London Frenchy quickly fell into the punk scene. He shared a flat in Chelsea with Adam Ant and Julien Temple. 'It was quite arty, a lot of people in bands were living there at the time,' he recalls. '[The actress] Amanda Donahue used to come round after school.' He used to do a bit of dealing too, did Frenchy. 'They used to call me three for-a-quid Frenchy. The Old Bill knew – in late '78, early '79 we used to squat in Terror City in King's Cross. There were lots of council houses, which had become squats. A couple of guys from Madness and their manager lived there.'

Frenchy began as a roadie for bands in the UK – Sparks and The Dickies – before founding his own record label, Flicknife in the late '70s. 'I wrote this song, but I had no one to record it with. My best friend then was this guy called Henri Padovani, who was guitarist with The Police at the time. He left The Police to join Wayne County And The Electric Chairs. They'd fallen out with their record company and were doing nothing, so I said, "Why not record these songs with me under a different name?" – sort of like a mystery band. That's how Flicknife started.'

Frenchy recorded called the band the Mystère V – after a French plane. The first single, 'No Message', charted. His label was up and running. Then he met Michael Moorcock, science fiction writer and Hawkwind lyricist, at the Marquee. 'He was one of my favourite writers and he had two tracks from an album that he did in the early '70s and asked me if I'd put them out.'

Various Hawkwind-related projects followed, with Frenchy contributing all the artwork and indie label Cherry Red helping. At one point the label had Nico, Alien Sex Fiend, The Specimen and The London Cowboys, featuring Glen Matlock. Frenchy would license records to friends in the business and they would return the favour. This was the indie spirit of the London music scene in the '70s, '80s and '90s.

However, Frenchy believes that that spirit has died. Nowadays, very few indie labels are actually independent. They are owned by bigger companies eager to cream off the top bands. When Creation discovered Oasis, it was not long before Sony pounced. Mute is now part of the Virgin empire. 'There weren't many labels apart from Mute and Cherry Red, Rough Trade, Beggars Banquet and 4AD. We all got on great. There was a real indie community. We all helped each other,' explains Frenchy. 'If I did a compilation album and needed tracks from other labels, there would never be any problem and I'd do the same if they wanted a Flicknife track. That's all dead now because in the late '80s majors would sign indie bands even if they did nothing with them, they just didn't want the indie labels to have them.'

We decide to repair to the Dublin Castle, around the corner, halfway up Parkway. It's a beautiful, sunny evening. But we make slow progress along Arlington Road. Frenchy had a bad motorbike accident in 1991 – 'It was about 4am, 4 January.' A drunk driver sailed through a red light and Frenchy didn't stand a chance. Now, he is limping. He shows me the scars. 'It was a really, really bad bike crash. I had a Norton Commando. My leg completely exploded and they gave me the last rites twice in one week. They told my girlfriend I'd be dead in half an hour. I was in Hammersmith Hospital for nine months, then had 18 months of physiotherapy to walk again.'

The Dublin Castle is the breeding ground for bands – it has already seen Madness, Travis, Blur, Stereophonics and 3 Colours Red pass through its doors. There is an old Madness poster on the wall behind the bar. We order a couple of pints of Guinness. There's a cramped, smoky backroom where bands play every night of the week. It's a good atmosphere. I check out when the first band is on – not for another half hour at least.

Frenchy is working with Marc Zermati. Zermati is a legendary figure in the European record business. A friend of Lou Reed and Iggy Pop, he ran the Open Market record store in Paris in the early '70s and supplied Frenchy's Grenoble shop a few years later. Zermati also started the influential Skydog Records label in 1973, releasing ground-breaking records by Velvet Underground, Gang War, New York Dolls and Iggy Pop

And The Stooges. Zermati and Frenchy also organised the legendary punk-rock festivals in France, in 1976 and 1977, with bills featuring The Damned, The Heartbreakers and The Clash.

In 2003, they decided to relocate Skydog from Paris to London, and relaunch the label with Frenchy as A&R. 'Marc was getting pissed off in France. He fell out with his distributor and he rang me and said, "We should establish ourselves in England."' Before they find new rock bands, Frenchy and Skydog plan to mine the extensive catalogue. It's the right time. Skydog has the albums bands like The Strokes and The Black Rebel Motorcycle Club are always namechecking. The first releases are going to be classic Iggy Pop, The Stooges and Johnny Thunders. 'Marc was friends with Iggy and Johnny Thunders and they gave him tapes. That wouldn't happen now. *Metallic KO* was the last gig by The Stooges, so Iggy didn't care. He ended up doing three albums with Marc. The back catalogue is very strong and always sells. DVDs will have classic gigs.'

Then Frenchy will go into A&R overdrive. That's what we are doing in the Dublin Castle. He's signed four already, including a band of four Japanese girls. But, there is a problem with London A&R, according to Frenchy. Every A&R man follows another. They turn up at the same gigs mob-handed. It's down to money, he says. 'Going to see bands isn't as exciting. The scene has changed. You see 19-year-old kids, the way they dress is different, big baggy trousers. They have no rebellion in the way they dress. The young have had it too good – there is nothing for them to rebel against,' he claims.

'The point is I'm all for kids having a laugh, but they don't seem to be having a laugh. They should make their own fun. Kids these days spend their money on computer games. In the old days you'd go out with £3 [$5], £1 [$1.70] to get in and a few drinks, and walk home with about 30 others. I would walk home with Billy Idol and we'd all talk about forming bands and getting famous. We had all those ideas and it happened for some and it didn't for others. There was possibility and some of us grabbed that.'

Now Frenchy believes the music business is too corporate and, therefore, it's much harder for people to open a business from scratch.

'With Skydog we're not opening a business from scratch. We've got a strong back catalogue. We've got licences from all over the world. 4AD went bankrupt, as did Factory Records. Creation found Oasis, you can't deny that. They had a back catalogue so weren't starting from scratch, but if you're starting from scratch you're going to find it very difficult.'

He also believes many companies are just to plain lazy to develop talent and give a band the A&R support they need in the early days. 'A lot of companies are doing compilations, but in ten years' time they won't be able to because all the compilations will have been done. Where is the new talent going to come from? Now if a band hasn't got a hit within two singles, they're out on their ear. In the old days even the majors would allow two or three years to nurture a band. But now it has to be instant, radio-friendly. It's sad to say. Bands used to tour and tour and tour until they were picked up by a record company. Now the bands are manufactured. It's back to the '60s – writers and marketing people would pick up four or five boys and girls in the street and get them to front the band; the five prettiest people to front it. They let the public do the judging and if they say Gareth Gates is what we want, Gareth Gates is what we get. Before Gates made his first single, he'd never been in a studio.'

We turn to see the first band limp into the Dublin. Shaggy hair, sweatshirts, baggy jeans, no style. Frenchy shakes his head. We'll give this band a miss. 'We desperately want to sign an English band, but we can't find one.' It doesn't look like he's going to do any A&R business tonight. 'We've signed a Japanese band, French band and American band, but we just can't find an English band at the moment.

'I'm the A&R guy. So first and foremost I have to like the music. But the music scene in London is dead at the moment. Most of the good bands are coming from the US, bands like The Black Rebel Motorcycle Club, The White Stripes. Too many bands sound the same, like Coldplay or Travis. They all sound a bit wet, a bit MOR [middle of the road].'

Frenchy also believes the venues are a problem because they have become part of major chains. 'A lot of big promoters were nice when they started – they'd help you with new bands, find a gig – but now they won't give you the time of day,' he claims.

It's the same with DJs. They stick to their playlists too rigidly, he believes. He targets around a dozen DJs who are sympathetic to the Skydog sound. 'We have particular DJs, it's not worth having a plugger. I've sent stuff to Virgin because they may play it – they play stuff that isn't just in charts. Between all of that we may get about 30 plays, which may not seem a lot but it gets things played and started.'

Just then the band that limped in an hour before limp back out again. I don't look at Frenchy, but I know he is shaking his head again.

Dingwalls is right in the heart of Camden Market in a mess of tight little cobbled alleys behind the Chalk Farm Road known as Middle Yard and overlooking the canal. I passed through during the day. A hot day, the sun was baking the dozens of stalls set up in the middle of a large yard, hemmed in on three sides by cafés and cluttered shops. The aroma of chicory wafted up from a coffee stall – someone was frying veggie sausages.

I stuck close to the shops, missing the hustle and bustle at the centre. I went from one tiny shop to another, idly window-shopping. I could have bought a secondhand domino set, an Edwardian globe, and after climbing the wrought-iron staircase to a second level of stores I came across silk from India and silver from Africa made into jewellery in Battersea then sold in Camden. I poked my head through the door. It was shady and cool in there. The owner was asleep in a deckchair, a book by the philosopher Noam Chomsky open on her lap.

Back out on the walkway, I looked out across the yard, towards Hampstead Road Lock and a roof terrace built on the back of Dingwalls. Scores of drinkers were lapping up the sun on the decking. Maybe some would be going to the Suicide gig tonight, at the venue below them.

The sun set hours ago, though it's still light when I return to Dingwalls. At night, the atmosphere in the yard changes. It's calmer, quiet even, with just a few tourists passing through. Dingwalls is a decent-sized room. There's a lot of history in there, too: The Stone Roses, The Fall, James, David Gray, U2 have all played at Dingwalls. It also hosts the biggest comedy club in Camden, Jongleurs. Midweek bands make tunes, weekend comedians deliver the laughs.

The intimate venue is perfect for up-and-coming bands. After three decades of playing the 'Be Bop Kid', New York electronic punks Suicide are long past 'up and coming'. Perfect for bands on a second coming. Marty Rev and Alan Vega have been rediscovered.

The room is occupied, but not packed. There is a stage at one end with an open floor space in front and a raised area at the back with bar and tables. I'm in early and stake a claim on one of the tables. Dingwalls serves up food, and I order up a burger and fries.

Pockets of space open up in front of me as people drift back to the bar to recharge. There are a few hundred of us, I'd guess. There's a nice feel about the place and there seems to be a good view of the stage from every angle of the room.

A synthesiser on stage is set on drone. It drones. And then Rev and Vega appear. Vega leans on his mike and wails – it sounds like 'Rocket USA'. I leave the table in order to get a better view. At the front, I can see the sweat on Vega's face and the stitching on his thrift-store jacket.

During 'Ghost Rider' I move back to the bar to catch a beer. Susanna is standing on her own. She's 19 and looks like Patti Smith in 1975. I tell her this, but she's never heard of Patti Smith. Susanna is a Photography student at the Royal College of Art in Kensington. She also models part-time to help fund the course, and just got back from a job in Cuba.

'*Horses*,' I say.

Susanna shakes her head. No, never heard of her.

'What brought you here tonight?'

Susanna fetches a flyer from her jeans. In Biro scribbled on the back is a list of bands and some albums – Suicide is fifth on the list.

'A guy, I guess he's a friend, gave me this at Nag Nag Nag. Do you know that?'

I nod.

'He's putting together an electronic album,' she continues, 'and wanted me to do vocals. But he told me to listen to a few bands first that he was influenced by. I'm not sure I like Suicide, though. They sound really, really bleak.'

Behind us Alan and Marty are drifting into 'Fast Money Music'. I take her point. I ask Susanna who else she has seen.

'Not seen because a lot of it is old' – her musician friend has also listed on the flyer The Velvet Underground, MC5 and Stooges – 'but I've bought a couple of their albums and I saw Death In Vegas, which was cool. I live up the road, and whenever I've come here there's always a great atmosphere, it's quite chilled. I come on my own. Sometimes bands will just walk off the stage and have a drink here. Do you think these two will?'

She gestures over to Vega, and Rev, who is motionless behind his synthesiser. It doesn't look as though Suicide would be happy with a post-gig beer.

'I like Dingwalls because it doesn't seem like one of those air-conditioned places, you know? It's not too...corporate.'

Frenchy would like Susanna.

'It's the best place to see fairly big bands and there is a good sound.'

She glances over at Suicide.

'In Cuba, a lot of the bars where they played music were small and family-run. This has the same feel because I think London is in danger of becoming soulless like every other high street with a Starbucks and Gap.'

I take her point. In 1970s London, there used to be hundreds of pubs and small venues, like Dingwalls, that provided an alternative to larger concert venues. However, stringent licensing laws, health and safety issues, concerns about noise pollution, the demise of freehold pubs and the rise of dance culture and clubs, has helped shut many of them. Bands and music are the victims. There is a danger that the future stars will never make it onto a stage because getting gigs is becoming more difficult.

Dave is a promoter and I met him at the Good Mixer pub. We arranged to meet at this Suicide gig. Dave doesn't want me to use his full name in case it lands him in trouble with the council. Dave isn't a fan of the council. It recently cut the capacity – or number of paying customers – allowed into the venue he works at, a nearby pub. He arrives just as Susanna decides she can take no more of Suicide. He is late. He is promoting tonight.

'It was OK, we were about half-full, which is good for nowadays. And the band weren't much cop, to be honest.'

I tell him Susanna's theory about sameness and her concerns about live music.

'She's right. A lot of places have closed or new, brighter pubs have replaced them. London and this area, Camden Town, has been putting on live music for decades. I think it's important that we encourage live bands because it is in places like this that they learn about stagecraft and hone their songs. See which tunes go over best with an audience. This is where talent is made and found, not on television programmes. So it's a real shame if young talent is being excluded. Where would Madness have been without Camden's pubs or Blur? There used to be a decent pub called the Camden Falcon around the corner, which had some great nights, but it has closed now. I think they are turning it into a restaurant. A lot more pubs in the old days would have live music in Camden, but the council has been tough on landlords. They have withdrawn licences or cut down on the numbers of people allowed into gigs. It's a big problem.'

Dave adds that many bands simply find it impossible to gig.

'First off, you've got to convince someone like me that you can pull in a decent-sized crowd. Where I promote, the space can hold 150 people. That's quite a lot of people for a band that probably hasn't got a record deal, may not have released a record and has only been together a few months. I don't need to fill it to turn a profit, but I'll need more than one old geezer and his dog. Sometimes we'll put a few bands on, so if they all bring 20 or so mates that's 60 in the audience to start off with.'

That might be enough to break even, but often the band can go unpaid. 'I know bands who play for nothing or pay to play – they'll make up on any shortfall or place a large deposit because the promoter doesn't want to take the risk. It's the way of the market right now.'

But Dave is also happy for colleagues in the promoting game to take some of the blame for the state of the pub rock scene. Often he believes many are simply in it for the money. 'It's all to do with numbers, isn't it? Footfall. Clicks through turnstiles. There was a time when the promoters were interested in the bands. They'd want to put certain bands on and they'd get a following. So often now promoters wouldn't know hardcore from hard-house. You could go to a gig tonight and they would have mixed up a card with wildly different bands that only some of the audience like. In venues, small ones especially, you need to match up bands and acts so they complement each other and bring in a similar audience.'

But, maybe the time for pub rock has come and gone.

'Yeah, fashions change and people demand more from a venue now. Having a bunch of scruffy Herberts singing out of tune in a small pub with a pint of warm beer in your hand is no longer seen as fun. People today demand a lot more, and there are a lot more activities all demanding the same pound in your pocket.'

Suicide wrap it up. Rev leaves his synthesiser on drone and they leave the stage. The synth drones.

It's Easter Sunday and DJ John Peel's producer Louise Kattehorn told me about Track & Field. It sounds like an athletic event, but actually it's a record label. Steven Drew is behind it. With glasses and a fringe, he is clutching a 24-track double CD, *Pow! To The People*.

He buys a round of drinks at the bar inside The Monarch on Chalk Farm Road. The Monarch is relatively new on the Camden circuit, but has established itself as a cutting-edge venue. It's tasted the success of bands such as Death In Vegas, The Doves, Feeder, The Strokes, Coldplay and Muse. It has good talent-spotting ability, The Monarch. This afternoon, Drew is promoting an all-day event, as well as *Pow! To The People*. There are around half a dozen bands playing on the bill, including headline act Freeheat, featuring former Jesus And Mary Chain's Jim Reid.

Track & Field started as a night out for dancing in the Betsey Trotwood in Farringdon in the late '90s. Early shows included

Tompaulin, Birdie and Comet Gain, and attracted many from London's pop community, including Sarah Cracknell from Saint Etienne.

Drew's sister, Jill, is also playing with her band this afternoon, the six-piece London-based Kicker. Jill, who has a day job working for a performers' collecting society, PPL, takes me through the history of the band. Formed in 1998, the line-up is Jill on vocals and violin, Laura Bridge on bass, Cat Cormack on trumpet, Andy Jones on guitar, and Ben Phillipson and Phil Sutton on drums.

In the summer of 1999, Kicker recorded a two-song demo, which caught the attention of Rough Trade. They put it out on their own label. This was their first single, 'Get Rid of Him'. A compilation CD of the band's first five 7-inch singles entitled *fivefortyfives* was released in September 2002.

Kicker made their live London debut at the Betsey Trotwood, supporting Comet Gain, and have been regulars on the London circuit since, playing the Notting Hill Arts Club, the Scala, the Water Rats. 'We started out in 1999 with me Phil, Laura and Andy. The others came later,' explains Jill. 'We were the first band to have a record out of Track & Field, and since then we have played gigs across the UK, from Brighton to Glasgow, supporting various bands such as Birdie, Beachwood Sparks, The Ladybug Transistor, Saloon, Tompaulin and The Tyde.'

Jill says it is tough to get noticed above all the other bands gigging, but has managed to secure airplay for all of Kicker's single releases. 'Mainly through John Peel and Steve Lamacq on Radio One, John Kennedy on Xfm, and a bunch of other stations, but it is very hit and miss,' she adds.

I drift upstairs to prepare myself for Kicker. It's a good little space up here. A tiny bar at the back and at the other end of the room, the stage. No frills. Kicker play a blend of laid-back guitar pop, mixed with a splash of mellow old soul and bedsit indie.

After the set I buy Jill a drink and find out how hard it is to get a band going in London, keep it together and then find a foothold on the live ladder. She bums a cigarette off me, too. 'I was asked to join by our drummer Phil – he was putting a band together and he knew I played the violin so he asked me to come and play that,' she explains. 'I did for a couple of months and then one night after one too many cans of beer I decided I wanted a go on the mike. I'd always quite fancied being the singer in a band, but I'd never had the guts to tell anyone in case they thought I was being big-headed thinking I could sing.'

They've played The Monarch before, and like the place. 'The sound is really good here. It just feels homely unless you have the unfortunate experience of seeing it in the daytime. I like the fact you can nip down stairs to have a chat like this, have a little sit down and then nip back up again to catch the bands. In London, the Betsey Trotwood has fond memories as it was our first ever gig, and the Water Rats is a really good venue too.'

The audiences at these places are generally a bit more clued up than some venues, which helps Jill and her band. 'Yeah, the London audiences aren't especially tough unless you go on stage early and they haven't had much beer. Then they can be.'

Kicker rehearse at least once a week. They hire a rehearsal studio up the road on Camden Road. 'How much time we put into it depends, really. It goes in peaks and troughs. I mean, we always rehearse at Zed One in Camden and then of course we have to have a few beers until kicking-out time. Other than that, it depends if we have gigs coming up – you might go through a couple of months where we're having a few more get-togethers in the week to brush up on stuff.

'Sometimes, it's tricky juggling the band with a full-time job. When we have a gig, I usually have to take the afternoon off work to make sure that I can make sound check and stuff, and that's not always practical because I might have loads of stuff on at work. Then often it's weird being on stage and then having to return to the office the next day.'

Jill is fortunate her brother runs Track & Field because getting seen and heard doesn't always follow from putting a band together. 'It can be tough; I suppose it depends what sort of stuff you do. We've always been really lucky with regard to getting gigs in London and I think we've always had a pretty good crowd and always got paid. People like Track & Field and Fortuna Pop are great promoters for small bands because they put stuff on and they're doing it because they really love the music – there's no hidden agendas there. We've probably had a harder time when we've done gigs out of London. It's pretty annoying when you pitch up at venues and the promoter's pretty clueless. We did a gig in Sheffield last month and they didn't have a fucking clue.'

I take Jill's advice and nip back upstairs. To catch Freeheat.

Jim Reid's band is headlining. Sister Vanilla, fronted by his sister Linda Reid, played earlier. The room fills up.

Freeheat, with Ben Lurie on guitar, Nick Sanderson on drums and former The Gun Club member Romi Mori on bass, was formed after The Jesus And Mary Chain fell to pieces in 1998. They have stripped the music down to the bare essentials. Reid and co blast their way through the set with no feedback, just straight-ahead rock 'n' roll.

I give them four numbers before slipping out the side door and back onto Chalk Farm Road. A block south, there is a queue for The Lock Tavern, a joint run by DJ Jon Carter, husband to Radio One's DJ Sara Cox. I join it.

5 Pirates

Camden, again. I stop by a market stall selling bootlegs. Bootlegs of Lou Reed, Joy Division, Iggy Pop. And – under the wood table propped by four beer crates – pirated albums. I have a squint under the stall. Boxes of pirated big-name releases. Some very recent ones, some crudely produced. Some with almost perfect colour artwork. Photocopies of the album sleeve. But all recorded on CD-Rs. One or two MP3s. Probably in a front room somewhere in London. Maybe eastern Europe.

'Where did you get this?' I pick up a copy of *The White Stripes* by The White Stripes.

The guy selling it is reluctant to say.

'Why?'

'I tell you, you could be filth.'

'The police? No, I'm not.'

'Yeah. Well, I'm selling illegal gear, so get used to it.'

'Where do you get this from?'

No reply.

I check out the stuff. Some nice albums by Bruce Springsteen, Madonna, Rolling Stones and David Bowie. The White Stripes' *Elephant*.

'That's a good copy,' I say.

'Yeah, pleased with that,' says the market seller, before checking himself.

'I'll take it. How much?'

'Umm, six quid [$10], mate.'

'I'll give you four [$7].'

'Five [$8].'

'OK.'

I hand over a fiver ($8). 'What's your name, in case I come back?'

'Steve.'

'Thanks, Steve.'

Less than half the cost of the bona fide album being flogged in the Virgin store across the road. No wonder Steve is popular today. Only a few months ago, the US record chain Tower boasted a store in Camden. It closed – it's now another clothes shop. Steve and people like him can't have helped business.

A week later, I call in to see David Martin. Martin knows all about Camden. And the rest of London's many street markets, computer fairs, swaps and car-boot sales. He is Steve's nemesis. David Martin. Dave is how he introduces himself. He's the man when it comes to enforcement. In the music business, anyway. The man that Steve from Camden avoids, or at least tries to. Dave – the thin blue line between Steve and U2, The Rolling Stones and Madonna. His job is to ensure the bands don't get ripped off. But the line is being stretched. The job is getting tougher.

Martin works for the music business's trade organisation, the British Phonographic Industry. The BPI is near the sharks. Damien Hirst's *The Physical Impossibility Of Death In The Mind Of Someone Living*, his tiger shark in a glass tank of formaldehyde. It's displayed at the Saatchi Gallery, right next door to the record industry's trade body. I'm standing on the embankment, on the north side outside the Underground station. The sun's out.

Turn right, it's a 1km (½ mile) trot to Westminster. I opt for one of the new Hungerford footbridges running either side of the train tracks shipping commuters from Charing Cross to Waterloo and beyond. The pedestrian traffic on the bridge is light, a few late office workers stride towards me. Cell phones pressed to their ears. A clutch of tourists lean on the metal railings, watching a barge ship head seawards.

Halfway across, looking downstream, I can see St Paul's, the new mayor's offices. Then the other way, west, I see the wheel, the London Eye, the world's largest Ferris wheel. It's like a giant bicycle wheel, with massive spokes, left leaning against the old Greater London Council building. But this wheel is a couple of hundred times bigger than a bike's.

As I draw closer to the South Bank, the wheel gets bigger. Huge struts shooting up over 120m (400ft), triple the height of Tower Bridge, further east down the Thames. Designed by architects David Marks and Julia Barfield, it casts a long shadow over the block of a building where the BPI has its offices. I walk past the queue of customers waiting to take the half-hour ride in one of the 32 capsules and duck into an entrance to the former County Hall on Westminster Bridge.

Opened by King George V in 1922, this was once the seat of London's government. It is now home to the London Marriott County Hall, the London Aquarium, sharks at the Saatchi Gallery and the BPI.

The BPI used to be run from Savile Row, but a rent hike moved it south of the river. Up to the second floor and the lift door opens onto a glass-fronted reception. Grey sofas, four suites artfully lined up in a long pewter vase, ducts, big windows. It's styled like an advertising agency. No adverts, though. On the walls, photos of Rod the mod, Cher, Sting and a bunch of other big-name pop stars.

Martin is a bluff, no-nonsense Yorkshire man. He strides into reception and grips me with a vicelike handshake. Martin lives and works in London during the week and goes home to his family in Derbyshire for the weekend. He's been in the office since 8am. Likes an early start, does Dave. I spot his training shoes under a radiator. He's had a quick workout in the gym already, next door at the Marriott Hotel.

'Keeps this' – he rubs his stomach – 'trim,' he jokes.

In 1989, a man called Tim Smith was arrested at a manufacturing plant. He was holding *The Black Album* by Prince or the Artist Formerly blah, blah, blah. This was the first ever pirated CD seized in the UK. Since then, Dave and his pirate-busters have been busy. Martin makes two cups of tea in the BPI kitchen and tells me piracy is one of the biggest problems facing the music industry today. I believe him.

His unit attended, or gave evidence in, almost 700 criminal cases in 2002. Dave's been on hundreds of raids of premises from Brighton on the south coast to the Barras Market in Glasgow, Scotland, a notorious hot spot for pirates. In fact, he has just hired a local investigator to keep an eye on things there. He's busted record fairs in Brixton and banged up Beatles bootleggers trading in rare, unreleased demos and studio outtakes. His team, working with trading standards officers and the police, regularly busts people like Steve and the gangs of criminals supplying him. The Russian mafia are now big in record piracy.

Dave's been to Camden. But Steve's business is not the priority it once was. 'Camden is still a niche for bootleggers, but Hackney is where a lot of pirates operate,' explains Dave. The thing is bootleggers don't like their bootlegs on CD-R and the success of the BPI at closing down illegal plants supplying Camden, London and the rest of the UK has meant a downturn in bootlegging. 'There's still a small amount of stuff coming in from Malaysia, Singapore, probably the Czech Republic.'

Then Dave gets serious. He's not joking now. Wearing a crisp mauve shirt and silver cufflinks, he takes a pew behind his large desk and sips his tea. I can see the Houses of Parliament across the Thames behind him. Fresh from the BPI's research department, he has the latest piracy figures on his desk. They are grim.

'It's depressing reading,' Dave says.

The figures go something like this: levels of commercial piracy, illegal recordings, which are manufactured and sold for profit, rose by a staggering 81 per cent from 2001 to 2002. Martin says music piracy cost the UK recording industry £49.8 million ($83.2 million) in 2002. That compares with just £27.8 million ($46.4 million) the year before and £20.5 million ($34.2 million) in 2000.

The number of music CDs consumed in the UK between 2000 and 2002 rose by one third – from 314 million units to 406 million. That's equivalent to nearly seven CDs for every man, woman and child in the country. The problem is that 80 per cent of that growth was at the expense of musicians and songwriters.

The government is interested in the activities of music pirates. Piracy of music, film, games and computer software costs £9 billion ($15 billion) in lost sales. That works out to about £1.5 billion ($2.5 billion) that is lost to the Treasury.

'We need to impress upon the government that it is not just the creative business that is losing out, but the economy as a whole,' says Martin.

Martin has a map of London pinned to his office wall, and a map of the UK. Helps him keep track of the pirates. In the old days he and his team of ten pirate-busters used to put pins in the maps, tracking where illegal product turned up and where it was produced. He doesn't do that anymore. There are no pins because the problem got too big. Steve arrived and thousands of people like him.

Piracy affects every part of the music world – the bands, the singers, the record companies, the publishing companies, the distributors, the retailers. They all lose out when Steve knocks out a pirate copy to a punter – 'A fiver [$8], mate. Can't say fairer than that' – rather than a legit, proper, real-deal recording.

There are three main unauthorised recordings: counterfeit, pirate and bootleg. Martin is going to explain the difference. He's also going to tell me what he's doing about it. Dave sips his tea. Dave, the thin blue line between Steve and The White Stripes, Nick Cave and The Fall.

Pirate recordings are duplicates of the original. However, they are then sold with different packaging and artwork and often on different labels. Compilations are common: Greatest Hits, a collection of Love Songs, Hits From The '70s, '80s Chart-toppers, that sort of thing. Steve has a few of those, but they're not so common, since many of the factories producing them were busted, fined or closed.

Then there are the bootlegs. A lot of record collections have a few bootlegs. I've got some – a Sex Pistols album, The Buzzcocks' *Time's Up* on vinyl, and The Clash at London's old Lyceum. These are usually recorded by some enterprising chancer smuggling a tape machine into a gig or recording a concert from the radio.

But the big problem Dave is now facing is counterfeit recordings. Replicas of the real deal, some with perfect packaging. The artwork and disc can sometimes look identical to the product churned out by Sony or BMG.

'Six years ago I was chasing a dozen audio-cassette counterfeiters. It was quick and easy. There was only a finite number of factories. Now I estimate there are probably around 50,000 people in Britain who have set themselves up with CD writers and computers. They've made the quantum leap burning CDs. And if they work in a factory, they have a captive customer base to sell to. Maybe they sell in their local pub or over mail order.'

Martin taps the modish flat-screen computer that is on his desk in front of him.

'It's this. Technology. Now it is very difficult to trace where the product has been produced unless we have got good intelligence. It's very difficult to distinguish between whether the product is professionally produced by a pirating organisation or just comes from one guy knocking out one or two as a cottage industry. Is the guy down the road making 25 copies or 25,000?'

He believes the number of CDs recorded or burned at home will soon overtake those bought in stores. In fact, the availability of CD-burning technology is the biggest single immediate threat to the music industry. In the past there was a qualitative distinction between home taping and commercially pressed CDs. Home-copying technologies enable the creation of perfect copies in high volumes.

The scale of the CD-R piracy problem can be illustrated by the number of homes with CD-R and RW (rewritable) hardware and the number of blank CD-Rs sold. Technology consultancy Understanding & Solutions estimates nearly 350 million blank CD-Rs were sold in the UK in 2002. The consultancy also calculates that more than 50 per cent – equivalent to 176 million units – were used for the purpose of burning.

In 2003, Understanding & Solutions estimates 457 million CD-Rs will be bought, 204 million of which will be used for burning music.

The proportion of UK households with CD-R hardware was 24 per cent in 2001 and is expected to reach 40 per cent in 2003. This means that approximately 8 million households have the ability to create perfect digital copies of music CDs. Stand-alone CD copiers are now available off the shelf. Two grand ($3,400) gets a copier with seven CD writers each capable of producing high-speed copies at up to four times normal playing time. No host PC is required and the burners can be networked together to increase production.

DVD-R is also being used by pirates. They have over seven times the data storage capacity of a CD and can be used to create single-volume compilations of a band's entire catalogue.

Martin and his team are now having to tackle a qualitative and quantitative leap in piracy.

Spotting the pirate is also getting harder. Dave has already seen an ex-copper prosecuted for CD fraud, and not a plod, either – he was a former detective superintendent.

'There is no archetypal music pirate nowadays. They are from a cross-section of society. It's not your typical Jack the Lad. You get blue-colour, professional white-collar people,' he adds. 'These guys have factories. Multi-drive towers capable of making 200 CDs every hour set up in the bedroom or the garage.' The policeman, caught by Martin, had produced thousands of counterfeit music CDs from home and sold them at local markets.

How do they meet? Pirate chatrooms.

'These spread by word of mouth,' explains Martin. 'You need a password to enter but, once in, you can swap illegal stuff. There are a lot of guys doing that now. And computer fairs.'

Martin reaches behind him. It looks like a closet, but this is where Martin keeps the seized goods. One box is marked 'COUNTERFEIT'; another, 'MP3'. He picks out a few CDs, pushes them across his desk and sips his tea. I can see CD-Rs similar to those that Steve had, which are very crude. There has been no attempt to disguise their illegality, with just the album title and track-listing scrawled in biro – Ministry of Sound's *Ibiza Annual*, Sash's *It's My Life*. Someone has drawn a childlike figure on a piece of paper jammed into the plastic CD case. Inside is the *Now 51* compilation, illegally downloaded, which was seized by Martin and his team.

'They're not very sophisticated,' I say.

'Don't have to be,' says Martin.

I open the case. Just a common CD-R with 'Now 51' written in a thick black marker pen. Whoever buys it would know it isn't legal.

Martin is on a roll. 'These people, the pirates, they aren't music lovers. That's more reason why the creative industries are working together, pan-industry, to pool resources because we have a common enemy.'

Martin believes some of the titles are being knocked out for 'three or four quid' ($5–7). This is the economics of music piracy.

Martin believes a pirate can produce an unsophisticated copy – like the Ministry of Sound compilation I am holding – for around 80p ($1.40).

No overheads. Low anyway. A few quid for lighting, power, maybe a few employees on a ton ($170) a day in a larger-scale operation. That's it.

'It's just a CD-R disc, the case and a sheet of notepaper. You know, I've met a lot of criminals. Some who've got convictions for armed robbery...tell me they've learned the skills to pirate music in prison. They say, "Why should I go and rob a bank? This is a victimless crime".'

He gathers the counterfeits up and passes me David Bowie's *Heathen*. I inspect it, hand it back and take a sip of my tea. Then I get passed Oasis's *Heathen Chemistry*. Martin doesn't say anything, but sits watching me. These are more sophisticated counterfeits. The pirates have gone to the trouble of scanning a single sheet of photocopy paper to use as the inlay. However, it is still clearly a copy. There is no label information and the inside of the insert is blank.

'Mmmmnnnnnnnnnn,' I say.

'Yeah. It's not illegal to buy one of these. So the problem we've got as an industry is to convince people that they are hurting the record industry and shops,' Martin tells me.

In his office along the hall, Martin's boss, BPI Executive Chairman Peter Jamieson is sitting behind his desk. But he isn't being quiet. Not on piracy. No way. He's as vocal as Dave on this one. The night before Jamieson had been on the news, telling the viewers that piracy is crippling. Now he repeats his message for me. 'Whether it is home CD burning, which has seriously damaged the record business in some countries or, worst of all, full-scale commercial piracy linked to organised crime, every CD sold which does not benefit the creators of that music undermines the ability of the record business to create the music of the future,' he says. He is as passionate about stamping out piracy with only an audience of one. He means it.

So does Dave. He thinks there is a music pirate on every street in London, and on every street in every major city in Britain.

Steve, who sold me *Elephant* by The White Stripes for a fiver ($8), lives on a street in Kilburn. He is a pirate, a counterfeiter and a bootlegger. A few weeks later, I'm standing by his stall again. Steve is at his usual pitch. I follow up The White Stripes purchase. This time

I buy *Evil Heat* by Primal Scream from him. It costs me just £3 ($5), less than *Elephant* by The White Stripes.

'It's older, isn't it?' Steve says, by way of explanation.

Evil Heat pirate-style is also not the most faithful reproduction. Home-made probably, downloaded onto a CD-R with the title written in red ink across it. The inlay card looks like it is a photocopy of the original. But it is black and white. The tracks are spelled out on a piece of paper glued to the underside of the case. There's a coffee stain on the card, too. Looks like someone placed their mug of Nescafé on it.

Steve seems less suspicious. He even gives me a smile. Gold tooth, but he's no Goldie. At least three teeth, including one at the front, is missing. That's messy. I think I prefer the old, moody Steve.

'Awright?'

'Yeah.'

He hands over the counterfeit CD wrapped in a Tesco supermarket bag. I can see the receipt for his groceries is still inside. Steve likes baked beans, own brand. Not Heinz.

'Yeah, this looks pretty good,' I lie, examining my purchase.

I think Steve is falling for my charm. Really, he just wants to take more cash off me. He pulls out another cardboard box, which was underneath the stall.

'Have a butcher's at this, then.' He seems quite proud of this little lot. I can see why. Whereas *Evil Heat* in my Tesco bag is obviously home-made, this box of goodies – *Hunky Dory* by David Bowie is amongst the haul – look like they rolled off a kosher manufacturing plant.

'Do you fancy a pint after this?'

Steve doesn't look keen, but says yes.

I look around. The Buck's Head is metres away.

'Buck's Head? About six.'

'OK.'

'Six, then. See you.'

It's 6:20pm and I'm not sure Steve is going to show. I check outside. His stall is gone. The patch is now occupied by two goths who aren't selling anything, but are just staring into space. Back inside, I order another pint of Guinness.

It's 6:37pm and Steve is sitting next to me.

'Sorry I'm late, mate.'

He fetches out another carrier bag from inside his army surplus camouflage jacket, this time Safeway. There's a big superstore just up the road by the canal. 'Get us a pint, mate. Lager…with a top.'

Inside the bag, there are no receipts this time, but *No More Shall We Part* by Nick Cave And The Bad Seeds, *Forty Licks* by The Rolling Stones and *Forever Delayed* by Manic Street Preachers.

'So what is it you want to know?' Steve takes a big gulp of his pint. He's ready to spill the beans.

The CDs all look legit. Not so. 'This is from a factory in Poland, I think,' Steve says showing me the Bowie album. I've got the real thing at home and this looks identical. All the tracks neatly listed, some codes, maybe the right ones, I don't know. EMI logo. The artwork looks slightly bleached out and I know my copy has the lyrics and pics of the Thin White Duke, the one with a fag in a cigarette holder. Classy. Steve's copy doesn't have the photos or the lyrics, just the handwritten track-listing and credits. But, it's a good job.

'Poland?'

'Yeah, I think so. Maybe Russia. Good, isn't it? And look at this' – handing me the copy of *Elephant* – 'only just out. Good as gold, that.'

'Yeah, I bought one from you the other week.'

'Oh, sure. Yeah, I remember.'

'Was this made in Poland, too?'

'Nah, some fella up in Newcastle. He's got a factory up there.'

When Steve says factory, he actually means a house. A two-up, two-down turn-of-the-19th-century working cottage in a pit town. That's where Jerry lives. Steve tells me Jerry won't meet me because he doesn't trust his own mother. When Jerry lost his job in steel, he went into the CD counterfeiting business. Now he has a whole replication line plotted up in the lounge. CD-R burners, multiple high-speed CD recording equipment. Blank CD-Rs, inlay cards, stampers, optical discs churning out thousands of copied CDs each week. Every week.

Steve met Jerry at a computer fair. 'I saw Jerry. He was lugging around a fucking great big box of CDs and DVDs and it was all really high-quality stuff,' Steve continues. 'Well, see for yourself. He needs people to distribute it. That's me. I've also got a brother, who helps out.'

'What were you doing at a computer fair?'

Computer fairs are Dave Martin's new passion. He knows all about these geek conferences. Growing numbers of illegal MP3s and CD-Rs have been surfacing at computer fairs. The week before I meet him, Dave had busted a guy for running a mail-order Internet business from home.

'It's pirated product. And there's a lot of swapping that goes on now. You know one guy might say, "I've got 50 DVDs. Can I swap you for 100 MP3s?" So they can both copy each other's stuff and eventually build up a massive library of CDs, films, you name it.'

Dave is unhappy about that because it makes his job tougher. He knows one counterfeiter who employed a retired husband-and-wife team to put his CD-Rs in cases and insert the inlay card.

Martin digs deep into another of his brown cardboard boxes. The one marked 'MP3'. They look similar to the CD-Rs, but because of the capacity of the discs it's possible to get ten or more albums on a single one. I could pick one of these up at a car boot, market, computer fair or on mail order. A recently seized MP3 had the entire Beatles catalogue on two discs, from *A Hard Day's Night* to *Yellow Submarine*. It cost £5 ($8).

Martin hands over another MP3. The label, again no professional job, says U2. It lists 15 albums by the Irish group – *War, Boy, October* are among them, and every other album that was recorded by the group. As a bonus, two albums by REM are also included. A bargain. That little package, bought legit in HMV Oxford Street, would cost nearly £200 ($340).

Martin hands over another CD, *The Beatles 1*. The greatest hits album looks identical to the copy I have in my record collection at home. Robbie Williams's *Sing When You're Winning*, Whitney Houston's *The Greatest Hits. Barry White, The Collection*. This is the pro stuff. Manufactured in CD plants in Russia and the Ukraine mostly. Martin has evidence that the Russian mafia is moving into CD pricing, and flooding London with their illegal stock.

The CDs are exact replicas, with the title, act and record label printed. The artwork is indistinguishable from the real McCoy, right down to the barcode. Some have stickers on the front. The Whitney Houston CD includes an identical copy of a form offering membership of the singer's fan club. These are passed off as genuine and put into the retail chain. They are sold as new, as legitimate.

'The way this works is that some guy will turn up with a white van and load them into a record shop,' explains Martin. 'It's mostly small retailers, not your big high-street chains.' The CD, which cost very little to produce, will be marked up at full price, at £13.99 ($23.50). Just like the real thing sourced from BMG, Sony or EMI. Huge profits for the retailer and pirate.

Martin and his team can forensically match the product, if seized, to the manufacturing plants in Russia or the Ukraine. However, the criminals move their orders to other plants. Many are not running to capacity and need the work. A quick batch. Who will know? The illegal order could keep jobs.

Martin has a son at university. He's practical. He knows students have no money. They live on baked beans, like Steve. With only a grant to keep them in books and booze, they are not going to pay nearly six quid ($10) each month for the benefit of a legal music service. They can go to a website and get the same music for nothing. And that's a packet of fags and a pint they can buy with the £6 ($10) saved.

'It's a question of, do I press this button on my computer and pay? Or this one over here' – Martin's fingers are poised over the keyboard to his flat-screen computer – 'and get my music for nothing?' he explains.

Dave dangles his fingers over his keyboard again. 'And you know what it is? It's technology. That's to blame for all this.'

He has a point. Because, now Dave doesn't just have to contend with some chancer at a U2 gig with a Sony tape recorder hidden down his trousers. The Internet poses one of his biggest threats. Illegal use of music in the online environment is huge. And two-pronged. There's trade in physical CD-Rs and MP3s run from websites, chatrooms and online auctions. Highest bidder gets the U2 bootleg or MP3 compilation of gangster film soundtracks. In 2002, Martin's mob closed down 3,500 online auction sites dealing in pirate material and more than 500 sites offering illegal MP3 files for download. Martin says a lot of work is now being put into building a rapport with Internet Service Providers (ISPs); make sure they don't host illegal downloading companies.

As well as closing the website, Dave's job is also to trace the source of the leaked track. Someone at a recording studio might have posted the song on the Internet. Maybe someone has a mate in the press department. It could be anyone. Dave has to find out.

Then, there is file sharing and downloading of music. This is done without the consent of the artist or any of the other rights owners.

Napster almost single-handedly created this industry. Now closed, Napster enabled people to swap music files. And it was free. At its height it had some 60 million users. Abusers, Dave would call them. However, with Napster gone, the pirate-busters have a host of other networks, some of which don't use ISPs. These are called file-sharing peer-to-peer (P2P) networks. KaZaA is top of the pops with the kids right now.

Research done in March 2003 by Sound Trak found that 670,000 people were using KaZaA at the weekend. Together they had an incredible 135 million files available for download.

'Broadband makes it so easy and quick to download material now,' says Dave.

A dozen more Napster clone services were forced to stop trading in 2002. Some MP3 sites offer pre-released tracks. Get your favourite band's new single before the shops even stock it. One of Dave's team found a pirated copy of Robbie Williams's *Escapology* on sale at the Barras Market before it was officially released by EMI.

Illegal downloading in the UK is running at a rate of around one billion tracks each year. The effect of this is devastating – for bands and the London record companies. Jamieson explained: 'It is an abuse of the huge emotional investment artists put into their work. It is an abuse of the huge financial investment that record companies put into artists. When investors see an uncertain return for their investment, they inevitably reconsider whether it is worth investing at all.'

BPI research shows 40 per cent of the UK population use the Internet on a weekly basis. Of these, 26 per cent download music and almost 60 per cent use file-sharing services. More than half the downloaders are burning CDs and burn on average 4.2 CDs per month.

Even big, legit, companies have posed a threat. Dave and his colleagues recently saw off EasyInternet Café, part of the Easy Group of companies run by flamboyant entrepreneur Stelios Haji-Ioannou. The cafés had been running an illegal service, downloading music onto recordable CDs for customers. One of the songs downloaded – and used in evidence in the High Court case brought by the BPI – was by Blue. They say, 'We're passionate about our music, but it's also the way we make our living. Everyone who works with us from the writer, engineers, producers and crew really appreciates it when you buy our music rather than just taking it off the Internet, because that shows you respect the time and work they've put into getting it out there in the first place.'

Jamieson agrees. 'Illegal copying jeopardises the livelihoods of artists and songwriters as well as putting at risk the thousands of jobs directly and indirectly created by the recording and publishing of music.' He believes the ruling against EasyInternet Café sets a precedent in support of authorised licensing services.

Haji-Ioannou doesn't agree. He believes the music industry is charging 'rip-off prices'. He adds that, now the technology is available, 'consumers will continue to share music files online. The music industry has long been charging consumers rip-off prices for music and it is now paying the price for its own greed. If it really wanted to help its customers, it would promote and commercialise music downloads, reducing its own distribution costs and allowing it to run a profitable business while charging consumers less.'

Steve the pirate has a brother, he told me. His brother is 14. His name is David, but he prefers Dave. Everyone calls him Dee Dee. He lives in a north London council flat on an estate off the Caledonian Road. He lives with his mum. She's got herself a new boyfriend and works in the boozer down the road, behind the bar. Just part-time. Usually, after school, Dee Dee plays football with his mates in the shadow of the low-rise concrete block they live in. At seven he has his tea. Usually cooked by his mum, sometimes from the chippy. They do a lovely cod and chips there. Salt and vinegar, loads of it. The Codfather, that's the name of the chippy. If Dee Dee is buying for his mum and brother, he sometimes gets a sausage thrown in. Gratis.

Mum leaves for the pub job at 7:30pm sharp. Dee Dee waves goodbye. Then goes to his bedroom, ostensibly to do his homework. What actually happens is Dee Dee downloads and burns CDs. He spends hours doing it. New single releases – those go for 30, 40, 50p (50, 70 or 90 cents) at school the next day. He also makes compilations, sometimes to order. He sells those during lessons for up to three or four quid ($5 or $7). Occasionally, he will make an album to order for Steve to sell on his market stall. He'll do that for nothing. As a favour for his bruv. He's doing the same thing tonight.

For the last few years, Dee Dee and kids like him have been playing the British music industry for saps. They don't go to HMV or Virgin and splash out 13 quid ($22) for Madonna's latest. 'Why am I gonna pay. Why should I?' asks Dee Dee. 'My brother got this computer for me so we could save money. Anyway, I'm not hurting no one.'

The thousands made redundant by record labels struggling with rapidly declining sales in the last few years, the BPI, retailers. They'd all take issue with that. They'd like to get their hands on Dee Dee's gear. Probably Dee Dee himself.

He contacts peer-to-peer file-sharing groups like KaZaA, downloading new, sometimes unreleased tracks and burning them onto recordable CD-Rs. The IFPI (International Federation of the Phonographic Industry), the BPI's international trade body, is not a fan of KaZaA. It believes the majority of record companies' material on the peer-to-peer system is there 'without their consent'. And that is why KaZaA is at the middle of industry claims that it is infringing copyright – on a massive scale.

Dee Dee shows me around his cramped bedroom, a poster of David Beckham above his bed and boxes of new CD-Rs tucked beneath it. An old PC and an Apple, an iMac, sit on a cluttered desk, next to an external CD burner, Yamaha, scanner and printer.

'Where did you get the gear from?' I ask. At a guess it would cost this school kid well over three grand ($5,000).

Dee Dee ignores my question.

There are piles of newly minted pirate CDs crudely scrawled in felt-tip on white inlay cards. A box of pristine, white, blank CD inlays. DIY music. I spot a stack of *Evil Heat* by Primal Scream on his desk. There must be half a dozen copies, like the one I bought from Steve for £3 ($5). Dee Dee obviously supplied that one. A good little operation.

'Does your mum know about this?' I know the answer already.

'Oh yeah, I do her stuff. That's the great thing about it. I can do my own little compilations of stuff that I like. Mum, she likes the pop from the '80s, that was her time. And Kylie and Robbie Williams. I've done her a few albums. She takes them to the pub sometimes to play.'

'So where did you get the gear? Must have cost a bit.'

'Well, Steve got most of it. But, he doesn't know how to use it really. I was the one that learned,' says Dee Dee. 'I've got a mate who does this, too. He posts stuff up that he has and I can email him and swap files. We also swap stuff with other people, they might have albums we haven't got. I've done films too. Then you find out who's got what, you know. Some people are good with a lot of new techno stuff, R&B. There's a lot of rubbish out there, too. Really old stuff. There's quite a few good programmes around for finding what you want, though.' Dee fiddles with one of his pirate CDs.

'I started off with Napster. You know? Then the one that was really fantastic was audiogalaxy.com. That was fantastic – it had a centralised system where you could look up any record you wanted. There was a hell of a lot of it. You could download singles and albums and there were lots of groups. It had the facility to create groups and when you joined a group you could sends songs to others in the group. I also joined in a lot of private chatrooms.'

Dee Dee absently puts one of his CD-R copies in his CD player. I ask him where he is getting most of his tracks from now.

'There's always new ones. You get to know about new ones, talking to mates and things. Or maybe I'll see a username and send a message or put one of my own on a noticeboard.' The first track from Evil Heat starts playing.

I've got a new research document in my hand from Martin's office. The BPI commissioned it. It shows that Dee Dee is one of around five million people in the UK accessing music online. That would be good news, if they were all paying for it. Unfortunately, like Dee Dee, they're not. Some 73 per cent of young adults – 15- to 24-year-olds – say they log into file-sharing services. Here are some more stats: an average of 19 tracks a month are accessed by each downloader; 25, if they're hooked into a broadband service provider that can whizz the tunes down the line in seconds.

Now the really bad news, the bit that Dee Dee will be interested in: 57 per cent of those surveyed admit to burning onto disc. That means 2.5 million people creating, on average, 4.2 discs each month. Nearly a quarter of those people burning discs also say they make copies to give to friends; and 2 per cent – and this includes Dee Dee – admit to selling them.

'You're a two-per-center,' I tell him. Dee seems pleased.

'Shall I do one for you?'

Now, I'm buying into illegal music wholesale.

'Yeah, go on. I haven't got The White Stripes' *White Blood Cells*.'

'Coming up.' Dee zips into action. 'There was a time when I could get full albums easy. Now the Russians are the MP3 outlaws.'

Dee Dee bites his tongue as he fires up the iMac and manoeuvres the mouse around his mouse mat. I notice the mouse mat picture on is Michael Caine from the film *Get Carter*. Caine is pointing a shotgun.

'They'd post full albums on MP3, so I can probably find what you want on a Russian site.' He spends a few minutes scanning the Internet. I look around his room.

'Here we go. This will take ages. Shall we have a kick about outside? Who do you support? We're Arsenal around here.' I glance at the Beckham poster; Dee Dee sees me.

'Yeah, I like Man U, too.'

The problem is Dee Dee's mum won't invest in a broadband line and it will take about ten minutes for each track to come down the BT phone line rigged up to this council flat. It would take half the time with broadband.

'Yeah, I think each track is about two or three megabytes. Do you know how many are on the album?'

'No, but they're all short.' I pick up a football that is near his bed. Outside, kicking the ball to each other, Dee Dee adds.

'What I do is download tracks onto the hard disk, then burn them to CD. Then I use a scanner and printer to do the slips. My printer's only black and white. I want to get a full-colour one – they'll look almost perfect, then.'

The BPI say most of those downloading music, that's 65 per cent, do so because it is free. Fair enough. The worrying aspect for its record label members, though, is that a very high proportion of them, that's 60 per cent, do so because they want to try the music out for size. Get to hear it before buying. Maybe they can't find the track in the local record store.

Then there's the 24 per cent who regularly burn CDs off albums they think are OK, but not that great. Keep the download and the £13 ($22) and splash the money on a computer game, a few lagers or on the missus down at Top Shop.

About an hour later, we're bored of kickabouts. We go back to Dee Dee's bedroom. Almost immediately, the pirate CD rolls out of his computer. He plays the first track, 'Dead Leaves And The Dirty Ground'. Wow. Dee Dee skips onto track two, 'Hotel Yorba'. Perfect sound. He slots the CD-R back into its plastic case. I scribble 'The White Stripes/*White Blood Cells*' on a piece of card, hand it to him and he slips the card inside the case and snaps it shut. It took 56 minutes to record it and seven seconds to package it.

Not everyone is convinced by the new dawn of legitimate downloads. It's a small drop in the ocean compared to the number of illegal downloads on offer. And what does Dee Dee think?

'I don't know.'

I tell him he can now buy Billy Bragg and Soft Cell tracks from KaZaA. 'Buy them? Why would I want to do that if I can probably get it free? Anyway, who the hell is Soft Cell?' he asks.

'Billy Bragg and Soft Cell. Billy Bragg is sort of guitar and voice. Soft Cell, they did that record "Tainted Love". A duo, recently re-formed.'

'Never heard of 'em. My mum might have done, I suppose. I like Eminem, *Curtain Up*. I just downloaded that.'

Dee Dee is going to be selling more of his burned CDs at school tomorrow. There's no demand for Soft Cell among his class.

There is a solution. The music industry can supply its own legitimate online distribution services. But, Martin admits, it has been slow. The pirates got there first and people are now used to not paying for music downloads.

'We've been very slow in getting subscription models up and running,' Martin adds flatly.

But, the record business is fighting back. A few weeks after visiting Dee Dee, one of the majors unleashed its own right hook against the bargain-basement Internet operators. EMI launched an extensive online service. This makes tracks available as downloads prior to them being released, when they are sent to UK radio stations. And this doesn't mean just making the odd one or two tunes available as a download, which is how many companies had previously dipped their toes in the Internet market. Thousands of them are now available. A good chunk of the company's back catalogue. The new service allows surfers to download legally 140,000 tracks by 3,000 artists. Good deal, too. It costs £1 ($1.70) or less for a single track; about a tenner ($17) for a full album. The policy, according to EMI label boss Tony Wadsworth, is to 'make the digital sale more price-attractive than the physical sale'.

In March 2003, Madonna's single 'American Life' was offered electronically to US fans in the biggest paid-for download campaign. A few weeks later, BMG broke new ground in the UK. It issued an Annie Lennox single as a commercial digital download, eight weeks before its parent album hit the stores. 'Pavement Cracks' was offered for sale at £1.60 ($2.70) via digital distributor OD2. It was never made into a physical single release.

Then, in May 2003, the London labels were blown away by Apple. The computer giant launched its iTunes Music Store service in the US. All five majors are supplying catalogue, creating a repertoire of 200,000 songs, including hits by U2, Sheryl Crow, Sting, Eminem and Bob Dylan. Users can download a track for 99 cents (60p). Apple founder Steve Jobs promised that the service would be launched in the UK. In one fell swoop the Apple launch completely transformed the landscape because suddenly tracks by major acts or mainstream labels became available courtesy of a well-known and established brand. This wasn't another bizarre peer-to-peer group with a groovy moniker mixing upper- and lower-case letters. Mrs Carstairs, 43, Cliff Richard fan of Whitstable, would happily use Apple in the same way as Yuslef Hamed, 17, Ms Dynamite fan from

Brixton. As Martin Mills, chairman of Beggars Group, tells me: 'People trust Apple because it is not an existing player in the music industry. Also Apple Macs are a credible, minority player. They've got an artist-friendly feel, which makes people comfortable. And the iMac and iPod experience is very good.'

Almost at the same time, one of the independent record labels, Cooking Vinyl, linked up with KaZaA to offer downloads of records before they hit the stores. But, this time on a legit basis.

Kids like Dee Dee will have to pay for this content, rather than just picking up illegally uploaded files for free.

Giles Drew, head of new media at Richard Branson's label V2, tells me his company is jumping on board the downloading wagon. It is offering an Elbow track – not a single – months before it will become available on a forthcoming album. With a fast connection, he says, users will have it in 30 seconds; a few minutes, if their computers are slower. It's a strategy to test the market and the company's technology. 'We want to get the mechanics in place so we can supply the market with all our releases,' he says. 'Eventually all releases will be available as downloads. Artists will be freer to release music when they are ready. They can just put it out there without waiting for the record company in future.'

Drew also sees the digital future as a way of dealing with the singles market, which in the UK is dwindling. 'If it [the digital download] does work out well, then it is probably a cheaper way of doing a single. The singles market is not that healthy. Singles are largely promotional tools; there's not much money in them.'

However, persuading Londoners to pay for downloads when they have not previously could be a problem. Martin suggests an education campaign. And in May 2003 one arrived: pro-music.org. Launched as several, new, paid-for online music services were emerging, it is the legitimate music sector's latest strike against the spread of unauthorised music on the Internet. A new international initiative to promote legitimate online music services and confront the myths surrounding online music piracy. The website is supported by an international alliance of musicians, performers, artists, major and independent record companies and retailers.

The site includes the biggest international repository of information on the growing number of legitimate online music sites now offering more than 200,000 songs to consumers. It also features a step-by-step guide to the processes of making music and the teams of people involved, viewpoints on the piracy debate from a cross-section of artists, the media and the public, and answers to frequently asked questions about copyright laws for online music.

It is supported by London-based IMMF (International Music Managers' Forum), the IFPI (International Federation of the Phonographic Industry) and the IMPALA (Independent Music Companies Association), representing thousands of record companies. Pro-music has also drawn statements of support from a range of artists, as well as music companies such as MTV Europe and digital music distributor OD2.

Jay Berman, IFPI chairman and CEO, says, 'The success in the US of Apple's iTunes, which saw sales of over one million songs in less than a week, is proof that if it's done right music lovers want to get music in a way that rewards the artists and creators – that is, by paying for it.

'The point of this initiative is to arm people with knowledge. The pro-music.org site is an important resource for news and information about legitimate music online: where to find it, how it works, why it's important, and what the artists and creators of music think. Once they have gone through the site, we hope people will stop and think about the impact of their choices as consumers of music. And they can make their own minds up next time someone asks, "So what's the problem with getting music free on the Net?"'

Martin is also achieving successes on the legal front. The law is being stiffened up to put Steve and his fellow pirates out of business. A private member's bill in Parliament in November 2002 bought the custodial tariff for copyright offences in line with trademarks. Music pirates could theoretically draw a ten-year stretch in prison. That sends a strong message: that copyright theft is viewed just as seriously as if Steve were snatching a handbag in the street.

Music pirates have been jailed. An Asian pirate was handed a three-year sentence in March 2003 after being found guilty of 11 charges. Martin's anti-piracy unit was involved. It gave evidence, in some instances simply expert advice, in 671 criminal cases in 2002. Not all led to convictions. In reality, spells behind bars are rare for music pirates – many are just fined.

Trading standards officers, the primary force in fighting consumer crime, also do not yet accept copyright offences as a statutory duty. Martin believes that until that attitude changes, the battle will be tough.

'There is no overtime for trading standards officers in some areas. And when do markets and car boots take place? The weekend. So the criminals move around to different markets at the weekend knowing they won't be pinched.' Martin allows himself a wry smile.

'I call those free-trade areas.'

The record industry also has another solution at its disposal – a technological one. It can install anti-piracy technology on CDs. This would stop pirates from copying them.

'With the new Madonna album, you could have two or three codes,' says Martin. 'Once the hackers have cracked the first one, the record company will have sold x amount of units. Then they could trigger the next one.'

Work is already taking place to perfect systems. However, there is a problem. Some trials have shown that anti-piracy encrypted CDs do not play on computers. Many people like to play music while they work. They'd have to buy two copies. One for the hi-fi and one for the computer. The globalisation of the music industry means that CDs produced in England, with anti-piracy technology attached, may not work abroad, and vice versa. This rules out taking a CD to play in the hire car while driving through the USA. Some countries, such as Germany, also allow a certain number of copies of CDs to be made to give to friends and family. Thus, the discrepancies between copyright laws in London and Berlin need to be ironed out. As Martin adds, 'A technological solution would be dead simple – if it didn't have to accommodate the territories that allow copying.'

Outside the BPI, I head back over the Thames, north towards Parliament Square. I make a right turn at Whitehall and walk past Downing Street on my left. I'm mulling over what Martin has told me as I check out two Royal Scots Dragoon Guards, in full regalia. For some reason, the bearskins they are wearing remind me of Jack White's hair. Then I spot a record store. *White Blood Cells* is racked up at £9.99 ($16.50). I already have Dee Dee's copy. But I decide to buy the legit version. I throw Dee Dee's version away when I get home.

6 Electroclash

The streets are slick tonight. The lights along Old Compton Street are reflecting off the wet tarmac. It's quiet out. Business is slow for the bicycle rickshaws parked up on the corner of Greek Street.

I slip onto Dean Street and head north. A cab pulls up and a couple of suits dash into media haunt, the Groucho Club. A couple are making out in the doorway of a sex shop. I pass through Soho Square, a tiny patch of grass, and make a right.

Then I see the queue. Or at least the back of it. It snakes around the corner into Falconberg Court. All the way along the piss-soaked Soho alley and up to a small doorway protected only by a tiny red rope and a man wearing a pair of angel wings. It's a couple of hundred strong.

But, it's not just the number of people waiting this damp, cold Wednesday night in January. This is an extraordinary queue. There are gays, straights, mates, dates, bisexuals, transsexuals and misfits, fashionistas, art students, freaks and weirdos sporting mohicans, Sue Catwoman spikes, number-one razor cuts, dreads and dyed shags, and dressed in black masks, ski goggles, ripped T-shirts, fur and leather accessorised with zips, skulls, crossbones and – in one case – a tampon on a string. Not used.

There isn't an easy or accepted sartorial description for this look. Essentially it's brutal punk-trash-techno – anything basically, as long as it's way left of leftfield.

This is The Ghetto. They used to run a sex club called Skin here when blow jobs came before a drink. Tonight the sleazy disco basement club is hosting Nag Nag Nag. I join the queue, behind a 20-something girl in a pair of black fishnets, customised Converse sneakers and a ratty sheepskin waistcoat. I can't help notice that, apart from the fishnets, she is naked under the sheepskin.

It's going to be a long wait. I'm in the northeast corner of Soho in the City of Westminster. The modern-day boundaries are Oxford Street, formerly Tiburn Road, to the north; the south side of Leicester Square to the south; Charing Cross Road, previously Hog Lane and later Crown Street, to the east; and Regent Street at its westernmost point.

It was acquired by the Crown in 1530 and, prior to the 1666 Great Fire of London, which destroyed most of the city, Soho was grass. Fields and a few farm buildings. Sometimes it's called Soho Fields. But not often.

The last vestiges of these fields today consists of two pretty squares. Golden Square, which was previously known as Gelding Close and built in 1674, lies to the west. And by Charing Cross Road, Soho Square, originally known as King Square, was laid out in 1680. Two original buildings remain.

In Wardour Street, one of the main – and many – one-way streets (this runs north to south), there were about 60 cottages in the mid-17th century. Then Wardour Street was called Coleman Hedge Lane. Hunting took place on the fields attached to Westminster Palace and that is where the name Soho comes from – it's an ancient hunting cry.

The Soho of today was largely created after the fire and mostly by the 17th-century urban developer Gregory King, who began to build on the land northwest of St Martin-in-the-Fields to accommodate those made homeless by the disaster. Soho was within easy reach of the three royal palaces of St James, Whitehall and Westminster and Golden Square and Soho Square had many eminent residents up until the beginning of the 19th century. Dukes, duchesses, politicians, clergy – all lived in Soho.

However, from around 1800 the residents of these squares changed, and so too did the fabric of Soho. The working class moved in. They took over from the titled class. So did a new wave of settlers – refugees, fleeing from persecution in Europe. They included Germans, Italians, Russians, Greek Christians fleeing Ottoman persecution and French Protestants, Huguenots fleeing Louis XIV. The Huguenots built their own churches, St Patrick's on Soho Square and in Glasshouse Street. The Greeks built a chapel in Charing Cross Road. The Italians formed a social club, buying a property on Soho Square. Later, the Chinese would colonise Chinatown, centred around Gerrard Street and famous for its restaurants.

Many of the refugees were craftspeople, furniture makers, gunsmiths, printers, watchmakers, engravers, tailors and silversmiths. The tradesmen converted many of the properties for business use and also split them up so families lived cheek by jowl. This ethnic and artistic mix created a diverse cosmopolitan culture, alive to creativity and hedonism and an atmosphere of understanding and tolerance. These still characterise Soho today.

The dukes and duchesses moved out. Many left their Soho Square mansions, taking up residence in Mayfair or Belgravia.

Another group also moved into the area – prostitutes. The sex industry was established as early as the late 18th century, when Hooper's Hotel on Soho Square offered rooms for hookers to ply their trade. Leicester Square became home to bathhouses.

Sex and Soho have lived in each other's pockets ever since. Peep shows, bed shows, jazz mags, strip joints and 'models' available are all represented in Soho. But it hasn't always been a cosy partnership. In 1959, the government enforced a ban on street prostitution. The Street Offences Act imposed heavy fines and threatened jail time. The Act worked. Streetwalkers moved indoors and became 'models', leaving an explicit card on the doorbell and a red light on in the windows of apartments to signal they were ready to rent by the hour. Despite many more recent crackdowns on the sex industry, Soho is still one of the capital's notorious prostitution districts.

During the 18th and 19th centuries, Soho developed into a thriving commercial area. Businesses such as Josiah Wedgwood, Thomas Sheraton and Garrard started making furniture, tapestries, silverwaer, leatherwear, glassware, china. The cloth trade began in early 1777, when a tailor moved into a house on Golden Square. Crosse & Blackwell produced pickles, jams and canned goods in its factory on the northwest corner of Soho – now the Astoria music venue.

There was a meat market called Newport Market between Greek Street, Little Newport Street and Litchfield Street. In the 1880s, this was cut across by Shaftesbury Avenue, built to ease traffic congestion. Brewer Street was home to several major breweries. The area around Golden Square was known for its doctors and solicitors and, by the start of World War I, Soho boasted around 70 tailor shops.

During this time, many writers and artists made Soho their home. The landscape painter John Constable lived on Frith Street in the early 19th century. The essayist and critic William Hazlitt lived at 6 Frith Street, a site now occupied by Hazlitt's Hotel. The German revolutionary Karl Marx lived at 28 Dean Street, now occupied by the ritzy restaurant Quo Vadis. Casanova lived on Greek Street. Wheeler's restaurant on Old Compton Street was founded by one of Napoleon's chefs. The essayist John Dryden lived in the rooms above what is now the New Loon Fung Supermarket on Gerrard Street in Chinatown. The poet William Blake was born on Broadwick Street, and lived and worked for most of his life in Soho.

Soho was bombed during World War II and became a cheap place to rent a studio or apartment. By the 1950s, it had sealed its reputation as the main artists' quarter in the capital. Francis Bacon, Lucian Freud and Soho chronicler Jeffrey Bernard all drank at The Colony Room, where I met Joe Strummer, at 41 Dean Street.

During the swinging '60s, Carnaby Street, in west Soho, became the hub of youth culture, the centre of the developing pop and fashion scenes. The Beatles shopped in the street's boutiques, as did The Rolling Stones. Mary Quant sold the first miniskirt there. It was the inspiration for The Kinks's hit 'Dedicated Follower Of Fashion'. For a time, Carnaby Street was shorthand for fashionable. Not any more – the street is about chainstores today. But nearby Newburgh Street, which runs parallel to Carnaby Street, boasts some stylish boutiques.

When the Victorian writer John Galsworthy described Soho as 'full of Greeks, Ishmaelites, cats, Italians, tomatoes, restaurants, coloured stuffs', he could have been describing it today. It is a rich square mile, which has soaked up a mix of cultures. Anything can be bought and traded here. And it is – either in the street markets on Berwick Street or the advertising agencies and music publishing companies, which have made this locale their home. Today, Soho also has a strong gay culture and its numerous cafés, bars and pavement restaurants means it exudes a cosmopolitan feel – especially in the summer months.

But it is for clubbing, pubbing, eating and drinking that Soho is mostly visited. The area began to gain a reputation for entertainment in the 1920s, known for its night clubs in Gerrard Street, Coventry Street, Meard Street and Dean Street. Musicians came to work in Soho. Later, when their gig was finished, they'd go into Soho to play.

From jazz to punk, Soho has played its role as a host for different styles of music and the venues and clubs it is played in. In the 1950s, jazz came to Soho. Ronnie Scott opened his club in Gerrard Street, which he moved to Frith Street. Later, kids flocked to basement clubs, like the Les Cousins, at 49 Greek Street, to hear skiffle. Or they supped cappuccinos in coffee bars, like the 2Is at 59 Old Compton Street. This was a mecca for rock 'n' roll bands in the '50s. It opened in 1956 and helped launch the careers of Cliff Richard and Adam Faith, discovered by the famous impresario Larry Parnes. Marc Bolan and Led Zeppelin's manager Peter Grant both worked in the 2Is in the '60s.

In the '60s the Bag O'Nails in the basement at 9 Kingly Street was where Jimi Hendrix played his debut London gig and became an after-hours joint for many of the '60s rock stars. The Whisky A Go Go at 33 Wardour Street, now the WAG club, was also a second home for Pete Townshend and David Bowie.

The Marquee's most famous home was also in Soho, at 90 Wardour Street. It opened there in March 1964 and played host to every major rock act playing in the city: Jimi Hendrix, The Rolling Stones, The Jam, The Kinks, David Bowie, The Who, and The Sex Pistols, who were subsequently banned from the venue. In 1988, the club moved into a former cinema at 105 Charing Cross Road, before it was closed in 1996.

'Fuck You Til You're Groovy' – that's what they play in the basement at Nag Nag Nag. Down a narrow staircase, it's strip-club decor dressed up with punk: the faggot cowboys from Seditionaries; a picture of Siouxsie Sioux and Sex Pistol acolyte Jordan from notorious late '70s lesbian hangout Louise's on Poland Street; a poster imitating the Linder collage on 'Orgasm Addict' by The Buzzcocks. But, instead of 'Orgasm Addict', this says Nag Nag Nag.

'Nag Nag Nag' was the first single by Cabaret Voltaire and that's the point of this place – early '70s electronic dirge to 21st-century electrotrash, which is the bastard son and twisted daughter of early 1980s dance music, using New Order, Cabaret Voltaire, Throbbing Gristle and the disco of Donna Summer as its starting point before amping up the camp. Then the beats and bleeps are layered on thicker than the mascara on many of the boys down here. New York band Fischerspooner were the first band to champion the sounds; however, their career nosedived after the debut album and the scene is becoming more DIY again. Just like '76 punk.

I pay my four quid ($7), join the freakiest freestyle electrodisco in town run by a triumvirate of Jonny Slut, Fil Ok and a bleached-blonde Canadian DJ Jojo De Freq, who spins the sounds.

Tunes like 'Hooked On Radiation', 'Perspex Sex' by Freeform Five, a blast of early '80s New Order cut with Tubeway Army and melting into Fischerspooner. 'Sato-Sato' by early '80s German electronic duo Deutsch Amerikanischen Freundschaft slams out the speakers. Many on the dance floor weren't born when this was released.

That doesn't matter. Superclubs like Ministry of Sound have become less important to London clubbers, and tiny sweaty outposts like Nag Nag Nag have taken over the void. Already the place is packed. Pet Shop Boy Neil Tennant is at the bar and Boy George, sporting a black fedora and a Lone Ranger mask of make-up, is on the living-room-sized dance floor. George is in to relax, after his appearance in *Taboo*, the musical he wrote about the '80s, named after a club that his friend Leigh Bowery ran on Leicester Square at the beginning of that decade. George has taken the role of the Australian performance artist Bowery and is readying himself for the play's move to Broadway. 'It isn't a coincidence that Nag Nag Nag happened at the same time as *Taboo* started,' he says.

George is a regular at Nag Nag Nag, which draws a healthy crop from the world of art, fashion and music. Stella McCartney, Björk, Skin, Kate Moss, Mark Moore and Primal Scream's Bobby Gillespie have all made the trip to this basement. Although, according to George, they often don't stay.

'The celebrities that have been down walk straight out,' he laughs. 'Because there is no VIP area, so they walk in and it is a grotty little club.

There are no ropes, so they can't sit in the corner and be served champagne all night. So they come in and have their photograph taken and then walk out again. Kate Moss has been here once and every magazine is saying she is a top Nagger. But she's only been here the once.'

Hot US former boy band member Justin Timberlake, who is squiring his way around London, was also turned away from Nag Nag Nag. George explains: 'Justin Timberlake – we turned him away because he had too many people with him. We weren't being rude. I was embarrassed, I wanted to let them in, but the attitude was wrong.'

I hunt out Nag Nag Nag's Jonny Slut, formerly of goth outfit Specimen and a veteran club promoter after running the Batcave in the early '80s. He and his partners started Nag Nag Nag because he couldn't find a place he wanted to go. Inspired by the scenes in New York and Berlin and the electro of Fischerspooner, which sounded 'like nothing else around at the time', Nag Nag Nag was born. 'The music is important,' he says, adding that the aim was to mix kooky art students with celebs who probably should know better at their age. 'I want some flamboyance, crazy stuff. I've always liked punk, art-school punk like Cabaret Voltaire, where the name comes from. Stuff like Wire and Gang Of Four, that's been the music I've always listened to, so it made sense to start a club where I could play that music alongside the new electro. There's a connection between them.'

Electroclash may have failed in the charts, but it has spawned a new cult and also a place for the capital's biggest showoffs to dress up. It's brought glamour – albeit the DIY kind – sex and a dash of humour back to clubland.

Back on the floor, past the thin androgynous boys hanging by the cloakroom, George is still moving. Boy George, big pop star, big DJ. Born 14 June 1961 in Eltham, southeast London, his parents called him George Alan O'Dowd. George was a face on the club scene at the tail end of the '70s. This was the time of the short-lived and little-lamented New Romantic movement, with clubs like Hell, Billy's and Blitz. Mascara, lipstick, pancake make-up. Frilly shirts, jodhpurs, scarves, pointy boots. The boys used the ladies' toilets and the girls hung out in the gents. They shared make-up tips.

George was soon appearing in magazines – the newly launched *The Face* and now-defunct *Blitz*. George was photographed with his friend Marilyn. George and Spandau Ballet clubbing in Covent Garden.

He got a taste for performing – appearing with Bow Wow Wow. In 1981, he formed In Praise Of Lemmings after linking with Mikey Craig. Then Jon Moss and Roy Hay appeared to form Culture Club, mixing up a blend of white reggae and pop. By 1982 the band had a hit, 'Do You Really Want To Hurt Me?' It went to No.1 in the charts and George was all over Britain. A big media star, grannies loved him and so did all the kids. He would tell interviewers that he preferred a cup of tea to sex.

In 1983 came 'Karma Chameleon', but by 1986 – and after selling over 30 million records – the band split. George went solo, got himself a heroin habit, had a big hit in 1987 with 'Everything I Own'. He also became a vocal activist for gay rights, appearing on heavyweight political TV programmes such as *Question Time*.

George reinvented himself as a DJ. He plays clubs all over the world and compiles some of the bestselling mix CDs. From two-step to ragga, disco to techno, progressive house to Prada trance, George has got all the musical bases covered. He's been famous for two decades, but isn't interested in that. He's not impressed. He doesn't even miss Culture Club as a vehicle, nor the fame. 'They were not as experimental as I wanted it to be. They were not risk-takers, the band.'

Not that he regrets it, or getting out of the band earlier to concentrate on his successful second career as a solo act, or his third one as a DJ.

'I don't like being mercenary, that's all. I hate doing things for a business sense. I hate that attitude. It was, therefore, like there is no point doing this because they [the band] don't want to take it somewhere else, they want to stay where they are and they are happy doing that. They don't want to be threatened in any way or challenged in any way, so I have to do it and find out.'

George has got a lot of opinions, on everything. It's hard to stop George talking. He loves it. Chatting, gossiping, giving his opinion. I think he thinks it is part of his job and someone has to. After all, 'I think a lot of people in our business have nothing to say,' he suggests. He's not being outrageous or controversial because it is not hard to stand out in a music world populated by teenagers with no life experience, and public relation execs who try to control the image by glossing out any and every indiscretion. 'I don't do pregnant pauses, I'm not Valentino. Back then [in the '80s], I was more guarded with my thoughts, but as I got older I have got more comfortable. My views on things are not set in stone. I try not to take too hard-core a stance on anything because none of us really knows what is right or wrong. I have views about sexuality or religion or whatever, but I'm open to change if I meet someone who seriously challenges my point of view and puts across something that I think is, you know, true – then I may alter what I think. I say what I think and a lot of opinions are based on my experiences and that's all you can do.' Good. Sorted, that. Now what about this electroclash and the London music scene?

He clearly thinks electroclash and Nag Nag Nag is now. In an increasingly homogenised world Nag Nag Nag provides an antidote to £15 ($25) doors, designer fashion, superstar DJs cranking out house anthems and cocktails at £8 ($13) a throw. Even George thinks 'audiences need a change' from the superstar DJs like himself.

'They've got queues around the block to get in. The fact that people of around 16 or 17 are dancing to "I Am The Fly" by Wire is a sign that things are changing,' he says. 'There are young people out there who are growing up a bit now. They're not interested in Atomic Kitten. The whole electroclash is exciting. Because it has an air of acid house about it.'

He also believes the Nag Nag Nag scene will influence how music is made again, like the punk movement.

'People are doing what I am doing. They're not relying on majors, not relying on distributors, printing their own records. There is a whole different vibe going on and people are seeing that the mainstream businesses will not embrace alternative ideas – that's what's exciting about electroclash.

'It also has as a sense of humour. I love the stuff, like a tune "Fuck Me On The Dancefloor" – the music is fantastic. Someone is not going to play "Fuck Me On The Dancefloor" on the radio. No one is writing that record to get on radio.'

However, he concedes that eventually, like 'all great things', it will be assimilated into the mainstream, blanded out, made comfortable for the masses. Turned into product. Everything is – there's an inevitability about it.

'The whole process of manufactured bands. That's the problem now. If you go back 20 years, ideas travelled fast, but they travelled in certain circles. If a band in London, Liverpool or Birmingham were trendy, then you heard about it, but only certain people heard about it. Your mum didn't hear about it,' George explains. 'It was all very cliquey then. There was an underground network, but that has all been eroded now. Art is still avant-garde enough not to be in Woolworths and not to be assimilated in the same way as pop music. You don't see Picasso paintings in , do you? But you see pop records. People flog records next to vegetables now. It is the Americanisation of this culture.'

George even detects the hand of marketing and prepackaging behind the bands and groups who seem, on the face of it, cutting-edge. 'There are always things going on. You know what really annoys me? Someone says, "There is this band out." And I read about them and I go, "Who cares?" They are supposed to be underground, but they've got this great promotion and are being pushed [by the record company and media], and that doesn't really appeal to me.

'I got The Strokes album – I liked that song "Last Nite". To me, though, it is just old Velvet Underground; there is something about The Velvet Underground that is perfect. When Velvet Underground started, they had got this art movement – there was something about them that was perverse. The Velvet Underground had Andy Warhol. But the new wave of New York, what's new about it? It would be great if they were adding something to mix, but they aren't – they are just doing the same thing. There's nothing wrong with that. It's supposedly alternative bands that are not alternative at all. Is that all there is? Everything is just done by numbers now.'

He's pessimistic about the new generation doing something new.

Are young people more conservative?

'Oh my God, yeah. The art that you absorb – whether music or art or whatever – reflects the emotional condition of your culture.' George wants to see 'people who really give a shit, who believe a song can change your life, which it can. Songs can talk to you; something that will change your life.' In this bracket he puts Missy Elliott 'and a lot of R&B stuff'. He adds, 'I really love ragga, I love it. Not the polished stuff that gets on the radio, but I love the stuff that is really out of tune and the rhythms are really nutty, you know. You watch the way they dance to those records and it is so animalistic and sexual. There is something about that that I like because it is so anti-establishment. I know it's homophobic and stuff, but there is a kind of campness to it that I am sure they are not aware of.' He laughs. 'I saw these fantastic girls – you know, net T-shirts, big arses – they are kind of free, aren't they? They are uptight in other ways, but visually and physically they are kind of free and don't give a fuck.'

Also he believes the record and radio industry has a closed mind when it comes to established acts like himself. He doesn't get any radio play nowadays. 'I think people would [like me] if they were allowed to hear what I do. They are not. The mechanisms are not available to me,' he says. 'Unless everyone at Radio One is fired and someone comes in who likes me, then you have to adjust yourself. I'm not saying it was an easy adjustment. There were times when I put records out and I can't believe they were not playing this.

'I became really withdrawn. But by reacting like that you are confirming, almost accepting, what they do is right. I do take a lot of care of what I do musically. I wouldn't bother putting it out if I didn't think it was good. I wouldn't bother doing it, finishing it.'

Despite this, George thinks there is an upside in not being part of the machinery churning out records. 'I have thought for a long time things will change. Taking me out of that [promotional] routine allows me freedom.'

I head for the bar and order up a Schlitz – the only beer available – in a can. The girl in the sheepskin is waiting for someone to pick her up, or buy her a drink. I get her a Schlitz.

'Thanks.' Her name is Maria and she's from Salonica in Greece.

'Why are you here?' I shout above something that sounds like Kraftwerk's *Autobahn* but has been bastardised by a mixing team.

'I heard it is the only place in town. I hate those big factories where all the bridge and tunnel people go.' I guess she means people from Essex.

'This is do-it-yourself. I'm a student at St Martin's [art college] and there's nowhere to go in London on no money. Apart from here and one or two other places.'

She zips the pull off the can of beer, warming to her theme. 'I can come down here and no one is going to laugh at me, it's cool. There is no posing and no one takes any notice if a rock star turns up. They just get on with it.' I can still see George in the middle of a scrum of young men. One is wearing a Spider-Man mask and a thong. That's it. Apart from the studded leather dog collar around his neck.

'I guess,' I say. No one would look twice at a horse turning up for a night out with a zebra in this place. 'So where else do you go?'

Maria takes a long pull on her Schlitz and pulls a funny face. 'You know, there's this club called Death Disco.'

7 Plotted Up

Tim Abbot is kneeling on the carpet, his living-room carpet. He told me earlier in the evening – at about 2:30am – that it's the same carpet they specify for casinos on ocean liners. It's very thick, a nice pile. And very red. Tim chops his right arm downwards quickly. Playing the guitar now, air guitar. Suddenly he springs to his feet and screams into an imaginary microphone: 'They offered me the office, offered me the shop'. Tim is doing his Joe Strummer.

He races from one end of the blood-red carpet, falls to his knees, slides a metre or two and delivers the start of the second verse: 'They said I'd better...' Behind Abbot, propped against a wooden bookcase, is a picture of Alan McGee. A framed cover shot of the Oasis single 'Cigarettes & Alcohol'. Abbot is there, next to Noel and Liam, arms punching the air. Just like now, as he sings along to The Clash on his stereo at four in the morning: '...take anything they'd got.'

I take a hit off the spliff and root around the bookcases: a financial book, *Your Money Or Your Life*, Nick Hornby's *31 Songs* and a Samurai sword. And in the kitchen, by his Rangemaster stove, I see two pricey watches: an Omega and Jaeger Le Coultre. There are framed Manchester United shirts, signed by the squad, in the hallway. And in the toilet downstairs there's a pile of magazines, mostly *National Geographic*. The soap in the sink is a fancy make. It is still in its packaging.

There are also tens of framed gold and platinum discs. Primal Scream's *Vanishing Point* album is amongst them, a disc for Robbie Williams too, and something for UB40. Abbot used to work for Creation Records, the Scream's record label – he was the Managing Director.

He also used to manage the former Take That star, Williams, and the Birmingham-based reggae group.

Back in the living room I can hear 'Career Opportunities' is winding down. Tim slides back into view – on his knees.

A few hours earlier a BBC camera crew had been filming Abbot walk up and down his hallway. He'd been telling the presenter all about Oasis's millions. Oasis were signed to Creation. Only when the interview ended did he notice that his faded jeans were split at the crotch. Then he changed and we sat down with Ali and Robin Campbell at their DEP company offices in downtown Birmingham. Abbot was fixing up some sort of project with the UB40 boys, and I tagged along.

We cruise up to the meet in Tim's top-of-the-range Mercedes. He leaves his black Jeep Grand Canyon on the drive. We park up in the DEP garage. Outside there's urban decline; inside the garage are Mercs, Range Rovers, Land Cruisers, Beamers, a Jag. Ali and Robin Campbell are in the boardroom. Ali is in black track pants and big woolly jumper, and Robin's in black trousers, black jumper.

Robin points out of the DEP office windows, across the grim backstreets of Birmingham. 'They're going to rebuild most of this.' He sweeps his arm in front of him.

I look out at what was once the Victorians' industrial heart. Now it is body shops holed up in railway arches, pubs with no customers, greasy spoons. Ten, five, maybe two years ago, and the developers probably wouldn't have touched the place. But UB40 have single-handedly put it on the map, they've regenerated this run-down area. They've shown it can work. The creatives want to claim it now.

After the meet, Tim and I hit the pubs. But before I can line up the pints, Tim is in conversation with a guy – a big bloke.

'Yeah, sounds cool,' I hear Abbot saying. He pronounces everything with a Black Country twang, a sort of singsong voice – 'yeah' like 'yeeh'.

'Yeeh, awl-right, mate.'

'Proper' is his favourite word. He uses it all the time. His company, when he managed Robbie Williams, was called Proper Management. Proper and plotted. As in proper plotted up. If Abbot is proper plotted up, he is fine, sorted.

Two minutes later the big guy is back. Over his arm he is carrying a bright-yellow skiing jacket, almost Day-Glo. Red carpets, yellow jackets, Abbot likes his primary colours, but not in his wardrobe. He's dressed soberly: Gucci loafers, Paul Smith suit, crisp white shirt. He pulls out a score and the skiing jacket is his.

Abbot was a late starter in the music business. He did a bunch of other jobs before he joined a label, aged 29. Born in Birmingham, he was into counterculture at an early age. He'd been a skinhead at 12, Suedehead at 14 and into Northern Soul, glam, punk in '77, new wave. Abbot likes music. He also thought he was good at art. He went to college to get an education. His choice of course was marketing.

'It was a local college and I thought I was good at inventing adverts. Besides, I didn't want to do accountancy. It was a kooky thing to do then,' he theorises.

After a spell hanging out in Los Angeles in 1981, Abbot returned to the UK and got himself a job in London. The drinks group Pernod Ricard gave him his first job in marketing. His contribution to the marketing experience was half-price Pernod.

'It's, ah, um, it's an unusual, distinctive product that people could get pissed on. We developed that in the '80s disco,' he explains.

Next he worked for Levi Strauss, just as advertising agency Bartle Bogle Hegarty was rebranding the jeans as cool. Jobs followed for mineral water brand Evian, and by the mid-1980s Abbot was back in Birmingham running his own 'small- to middle-sized design and marketing outfit'. He did some industrial stuff. Then, as he was trying to put a marketing spin on conservatories while also running an acid-house club, up popped Creation boss Alan McGee at the end of the decade.

It was McGee who launched Oasis on the world. This is his history... McGee, a British Rail clerk with punk rock in his blood, moved to London in 1980. He had a band called The Laughing Apples, but they got nowhere. McGee met a bloke called Dick Green and they started a club called The Living Room, booking a bunch of bands. One of them was the Television Personalities, featuring Joe Foster. In the summer of 1983, McGee, Foster and Green started Creation Records.

They picked a bunch of bands that didn't trouble the charts too seriously. But, release number 12, 'Upside Down', was significant. It was by a couple of brothers from East Kilbride, The Jesus And Mary Chain. However, the band soon skipped to Warner imprint Blanco Y Negro.

In 1985, McGee put out the debut single from his mate Bobby Gillespie's Primal Scream. Gillespie, who liked Tim Abbot's record collection, had previously played sticks for The Jesus And Mary Chain. The band were going nowhere fast. Then DJ Andy Weatherall produced and Creation scored its first Top 20 hit.

The hits continued. Teenage Fanclub had *Bandwagonesque*, Primal Scream had *Screamadelica*, Ride had *Nowhere*.

Then McGee hit pay dirt. He was at a club in Glasgow, King Tut's. A Manchester band wanted to play – and they did. They played four songs, including 'Rock 'N' Roll Star'. McGee signed Oasis there and then. Liam and Noel Gallagher, the Gallagher brothers.

Britpop started. Invites arrived for Noel Gallagher and McGee to 10 Downing Street and champagne with the Prime Minister. Cool Britannia followed. 1996 became 1966 all over again, with Swinging London. Liam Gallagher and his (then) wife, Patsy Kensit, were on the cover of *Vogue*. It was Oasis versus Blur. Fashion, art, music: it was all happening in London. London was the number one city.

However, the drugs and booze took their toll on McGee. He ended up hospitalised, suffering from a nervous breakdown. It would take nearly two years for him to recover. Then the Britpop bubble burst. McGee also was having trouble working with Creation partner Sony, so he called it a day. He shut Creation, and in August 2000 floated the new label, Poptones.

McGee first met Tim Abott when he was in Birmingham for the night with Primal Scream's Bobby Gillespie and a 'selection of other madheads'. Tim's younger brother Chris was also working for McGee – he was running Infonet, a dance and techno label. The evening ended back at Tim's place. Gillespie clocked Miles Davis racked next to The Stooges in his record collection and McGee decided Abbot was a man he could use.

'For all his sins, McGee is a people person,' recalls Abbot. 'Alan said to me, "You should be in the music business." You know, I'm grateful for McGee. He is a risk-taker. He puts faith in people. He took a risk with me and my entrance into the music industry.' And then, revealing a level of self-awareness few in the music industry have, Abbot adds: 'I'm a maladjusted person, not accepted where I am and having aspirations to get to where I want to be. But not accepted there, either. In the corporate world, I was never going to exist.'

Abbot moved to London. He turned up at Creation Records in a Daks blazer and grey slacks. He was going to give the company a marketing audit. Probably the first music company – at least one that was independently owned – to have one. 'I turned up with this ridiculous in-search-of-excellence brief, so I was treated with suspicion for about six months. And then at the weekends we'd put our suspenders on and take coke,' he laughs.

At the time Creation had myriad labels with countless bands. McGee still hadn't seen Oasis. It had many different outside agencies working for it. Abbot dismissed some lines, some labels and some bands. Ideas such as an independent-rock radio station were also given short shift.

Then McGee phoned: 'I've just seen the band that will turn the company around.' He'd seen Oasis. Abbot became Managing Director of Creation. He began applying his marketing principles to Oasis.

'What has changed in the last 20 or 30 years is that we used to manufacture things and sell that to people. Now we find out what they want and supply that. That's how the Japanese managed to overtake companies such as Harley Davidson and Triumph. Funnily enough, Creation was always a manufacturing company. There was no research. Alan would go out and find the band, and I'd try and analyse the product or band and apply a lot of marketing laws, like you'd have with baked beans or for the launch of a washing powder. But with marketing, at the end of the day, you can't put a ribbon on a turd – you can't polish that.' Some of the Creation bands didn't polish up well.

But with Oasis, Abbot had more than a turd. The raw material was good. And he concedes Oasis would have had serious success regardless of his marketing acumen. However, he applied a few tried-and-trusted techniques, which may have supplied a few thousand additional sales. A clear message or key direction is essential. 'You need a cohesive strategy that runs through everything, from the band, through the management to the label,' Abbot adds. With the Gallagher brothers running Oasis, it was already there. 'They were a band of people, I always want to see people like that. The intellectual hooligan. The upper working class. Noel with his one-liners or quips, which are actually pretty good and funny. And Liam. Coupled with this, there was the political belief. They were our Rolling Stones and The Sex Pistols rolled into one.'

Sometimes, if it's not there, Abbot may need to create it. 'I sometimes ask, "Where is the mechanism?" A widget company will have a widget on the top of its letterhead and you need the same with a band. It can start with the name. He mulls over the name of The Suffrajets, a girl band he is currently working with.

'That's good, that is,' he says. 'We also have a band called Chester Road. It's the A5. Now, I don't know how that will play in America. But, then you get bands like Linkin Park. What does that mean to a kid in London? Nothing, but it works,' he argues. No one liked the name 'Oasis' at first. After a couple of hits, it didn't matter. The brand was up and running.

The typeface, the look, the image, must always be consistent. That means the video needs to be tied in with the in-store campaign and everyone from A&R through to promotion are pushing the same message. 'Marketing can start at A&R and pull through all the way to marketing. There should be a thread through the whole thing. A lot of bands, even now, they couldn't give a shit about that. They say, "Here's the DAT," and that's it.'

That may have worked for The Rolling Stones in the early '60s, 'But in this day and age you need to get the visibility. There is a lot of product, not just music, vying for the youth Euro. There is saturation. Marketing needs to break out and get the visibility.'

To find a way of breaking through the morass of other bands and information spewed out by Radio One, MTV and *Top Of The Pops*, Abbot believes true marketing should be qualitative, not quantitative.

That means tapping into some research. That means taking more drugs than the band, getting to know them, hanging out with them.

That's what Abbot did with Liam and Noel. He shadowed the band from 1993, through tours of America, Japan and Europe. That's what he does now, advising on haircuts and clothes.

'If you're going to be good, then you need to hang out with the band and only then can you communicate who they are. To find the visualisation of the band,' he says, then checks himself. 'Visualisation, that's a good word.'

Back at Tim's house, The Clash is still being blasted out of his living-room speakers. Abbot is tiring. It's about five now. He goes to lie down on a couch in the conservatory at the back of the house. This is where he keeps his giant tanks filled with tropical fish. Sometime, he watches the sun come up here and the birds feeding in his garden. Abbot is a twitcher. He has the books and the binoculars to prove it. I turn in also. But I'm keen to check out Tim's qualitative approach.

We meet up a week later. I clock him in the Keith Moon bar. This is the Astoria on Charing Cross Road. Teenage Fanclub are headlining and Abbot is in his element, conducting his qualitative research. He is scathing about record labels that apply the same marketing to a pop act as they use on a rock act. 'How can they do it?' he asks. 'It's not the same thing.'

Tim Abbot looks thirsty. I also notice the grey about his temples for the first time. I guess he's in his late 30s. He's actually 44 and has been through 'several' midlife crises. Those late nights with the Gallagher brothers may have taken their toll.

'Alright? Yeeh? Great. Get us a pint, will you?'

After losing a mint on Millennium Night promoting a club that didn't work out, Abbot decided to start a new company, Pool Side. It's a label and a management company. Sony helps fund it or, as Abbot says, 'they contribute to overheads'. Teenage Fanclub are putting a new album out on Pool Side: a best-of, *Four Thousand Seven Hundred And Sixty-Six Seconds: A Short Cut To Teenage Fanclub*. Abbot put the album project together. This gig is part of a tour to support the album. Abbot has known Teenage Fanclub for ten years. They released *Bandwagonesque* and *Grand Prix* on Creation.

I can hear Teenage Fanclub on stage, playing 'Mellow Doubt'. Abbot pulls out another Silk Cut and lights it from the one still in his lips. He takes a quick swig of the Stella Artois.

'I'd better just check on things. Awl-right?'

Sure, Tim. I take in the punters in the Keith Moon bar. Lots of late 20s, quite a few in their 30s. It's the Fannies – they've been around a while and the fans have grown up. Training shoes, Adidas, Converse sneakers, a couple in fishtail parkas. I sip my Jack and Coke.

The Astoria was built to make pickles. Crosse & Blackwell used it as the company's factory. The venue's first foray into the entertainment industry was as a strip club. Scantily clad ladies would sell cigarettes and then take their clothes off. More money could be made putting on entertainment for men and women. The next incarnation was as a music hall. Then as a theatre. Shows such as *Elvis*, starring Shakin' Stevens, and *John, Paul, George and Ringo…* were booked. Towards the end of the 20th century, the Astoria became the studio where satellite TV company BSkyB recorded *The Happening* and *Jukebox Jury* with the pianist, presenter and one-time Squeeze member Jools Holland.

Live music became its bread and butter in the '90s, with Nirvana, Black Sabbath, David Bowie, Metallica, Oasis, Prince, Eminem and The White Stripes all playing here. When U2 played in 2001, tickets changed hands on the black market for nearly two grand ($3,300).

In May 2000 it was acquired by the Mean Fiddler group. Mean Fiddler is a major London venue owner. It also promotes festivals like the Irish-flavoured Fleadh in Finsbury Park. Vince Power is the man behind Mean Fiddler. He started in 1981. He bought and refurbished a club in High Street Harlesden and called it the Mean Fiddler. It opened its doors at the end of 1982. Power ran Irish music evenings at the club and showcases for new bands. The Pogues, Eric Clapton, Johnny Cash, Paul McCartney, Christy Moore, Van Morrison, Roy Orbison, Shane MacGowan, Kirsty MacColl, Kris Kristofferson, The Black Crowes, Los Lobos and Nick Cave all played the venue.

He then bought more venues or opened new ones, and began promoting festivals. The Mean Fiddler group now controls a bunch of live music places in London. They include the Jazz Café in Camden, Forum on Highgate Road and The Garage in Highbury.

But, it hasn't been all plain sailing. Six months before meeting Abbot in the Keith Moon bar, the Astoria's licence was being reviewed following a series of incidents, fights and a shootout during a gig by the rap act So Solid Crew.

Teenage Fanclub are knocking out 'Alcoholiday'. I move into the main auditorium. Abbot has had part of the balcony annexed off for Pool Side and his guests. I flip a laminate in the direction of a security guy in a black bomber. He nods me in. Teenage Fanclub stumbled out of Glasgow at the start of the 1990s. More than a decade later they have some good Byrds-style gentle anthems: 'The Concept', 'Starsign', 'Radio' and 'I Don't Want Control of You'.

The show's over. Abbot has fixed an after-show party at Metro, just around the corner on Oxford Street. Drinks are drunk, smokes finished.

'Are we plotted up?'

Sure, Tim. We're plotted up, ready to roll. The Metro is a little club, almost bang opposite the 100 Club, with club nights on Saturday. On the way there's a little altercation. Someone forgets a bag. Someone gets pissy. He takes it out on Abbot. Abbot, not the biggest fella, slaps him and we follow on.

Up the stairs, then down some more, into a largish room with chairs stacked around the edges. Some of the Pool Side crew are there already, as well as some models, brought along to brighten – and enliven – the night. Someone hands around the nose.

The bar is on the left. There's a rectangular dance floor with a small stage at one end and a DJ booth at the other. The DJ is in a cage, like the cage in the first *Terminator* movie, when Sarah Connor is pursued by Arnie. There are giant speakers either side. The noise is deafening, literally. Tim and I get plotted up on the corner of the bar. I have trouble hearing Abbot's theory. He tells me he thinks the future of the record business is with production companies. This is the new model. 'The concept is low overhead. License material in. If you're also a manager, then you can bring in an act. It might be good to have a label to bring things in. The nuts and bolts, but not become a fully blown label,' he says.

I miss the rest of the theory and just nod my head. It sounds good, but we're both getting drunk, so most things do. We scramble out of Metro around 3am and find an after-hours club, squeezed between two Chinese restaurants, on Gerrard Street.

A few weeks later, I call Tim up to check out what he is up to. He went skiing, used the yellow skiing jacket sold to him in the pub, broke his leg and now he's in a wheelchair with a busted leg, and is going for keyhole surgery at the weekend.

'Yeah, it's a bit crap, really. After the leg op, I'll have to do some physio and then I want to massively get back and break a band.' His enthusiasm can't disguise flatness in his voice. But he's going to cheer himself up. 'I'm going to buy a Merc, top-of-the-range, sports coupé.' Abbot just made some money. The Teenage Fanclub album sold well. 'When I'm up, we should go down Death Disco.'

Abbot's old boss at Creation, Alan McGee, runs Death Disco. A club named after a Public Image Ltd single, the musical soundtrack is predominantly punk and its brothers and sisters: The Ramones, The Only Ones, Generation X, Pistols.

I'm at Death Disco tonight. It's being held at the Notting Hill Arts Club. McGee likes the place. He had his 40th birthday there and Joe Strummer, Courtney Love, Bobby Gillespie and designer Pam Hogg were there to toast him.

I arrive at Notting Hill Gate on the 31 bus. Just after nine, as the night turns cold. The bus stop is on Pembridge Road, just opposite The Gate Cinema, which opened in 1911 as The Electric Palace. It was the first London cinema to screen *Ai No Corrida* in 1978 and The Gate is screening another an arthouse movie tonight, with a little queue backing up from the door.

Two lanes of traffic on The Gate are now thinning out. A black cab pulls up and three women jump out, their Manolo Blahnik sandals clip-clopping on the pavement. Glossy manes, cute Lulu Guinness handbags, they've got the Notting Hill chick chic look down.

There's already a little bunch at the big wooden door of the Arts Club, a short hop over Kensington Church Street. As I get closer, I can see the look is predominantly choppy haircuts, skinny ties, suit jackets. A fiver ($8), and I'm in.

I go down the stairs and into the club. The circular bar Strummer stood at for McGee's birthday is right in the middle of the joint. McGee is standing by the bar tonight. With him is Chris Abbot, 34, brother to Tim. He's a manager.

On the walls, posters of skulls and crossbones with the legend 'Death Disco'. Over the far side, a tiny stage and a couple of banquettes with tables. It's waitress service. There are about 50 people already in the place and the DJ is warming up with The Only Ones' 'Another Girl, Another Planet'.

'Awright there, boys?' McGee asks. A Glaswegian, he has a strong Scottish accent.

Close-cropped hair, tonight he is casual – a pair of sneakers, jeans. He looks healthy considering the 'legendary substance abuse'.

He slips off to play some tunes. When he starts spinning the next record for the models dancing around their handbags and kids in black skinny ties and drainpipes, the record is 'Albatross'. It's over ten minutes, the longest track from *Metal Box*. I use the time to grill Chris, who helped his brother manage Robbie Williams.

At one minute past midnight on 26 June 1996, Robbie Williams held a press conference at the Royal Lancaster Hotel in Bayswater. At the time, Williams wasn't the major star he is now. He was seen as just another chancer. It was widely believed the talented one from the boy band Take That, the one who would carve a big solo career, was Gary Barlow.

A statement was handed to the press. 'I'm here tonight to celebrate my freedom,' it said. Williams was celebrating his freedom from former record company BMG. He was also poised to release a version of George Michael's 'Freedom'. Tim Abbot was sitting next to him that night. He had negotiated the freedom. He had been Williams's manager since the start of the year. He'd got him a new deal with EMI's Chrysalis label.

In the statement Williams continued, 'To be honest with you, I don't feel that I can really deal with talking about BMG and I don't want to give them any more of my time. If you've got any questions about anything else, I'll be happy to answer them and my manager, Tim Abbot, is here – he can fill you in a little more dispassionately about how we got to this point.'

Williams had met the Abbot brothers at the Glastonbury rock festival. Oasis were playing and the boy-band singer had come to hang out with them. 'This was the height of the Oasis,' says Chris Abbot. 'You couldn't get bigger or cooler at the time and Williams was just out of Take That. Robbie turned up, and we got on and had a laugh.'

Tim Abbot was Williams's manager for the start of his solo career. He attempted to graft a bit of rough on Williams's image by allowing him to hang out with Oasis. 'Here was this cheeky chappy doing his duck walk, and there was just something about him that was incredibly engaging,' Abbot says. 'I wasn't sure if he was going to be the next George Michael or the next George Formby. He was vaudeville, not rock 'n' roll.'

Chris takes up the story: 'What we did for Robbie, we took him out of BMG and negotiated a deal with EMI. That was a great deal. We put him in touch with top-end business lawyers, we gave him credibility when no one was interested. We saw potential and he was allowed to knock around with Oasis.'

With the Abbots at the helm, Williams's career began to ignite. However, the relationship wasn't plain sailing. Chris adds that Williams would often make rock star demands, which he or Tim found hard to swallow. 'Robbie lived in a cocoon world and was always protected. He wanted people to carry his bags. I'd say, "Carry it yourself, you cunt."' He laughs. 'That was our management technique.'

By October 1996, the relationship was all over. Williams claimed he wanted total artistic freedom. He terminated his management contract with Tim Abbot, subsequently hiring IE Management. Tim Abbot filed proceedings against Williams. He claimed £1.2 million ($2 million) in unpaid commission on Williams's three-album deal with EMI-Chrysalis. Abbot was furious and 'extremely disappointed'.

With a drink in his hand, Tim Abbot is the first to admit 'the Rob thing' was never going to work. He claims the label and everyone else associated with Williams wanted a corporate-style team. Tim doesn't do corporate style.

The pair eventually settled out of court before a potentially embarrassing High Court clash that could have revealed details of the singer's alleged drink and drug excesses and damaged the sales prospects of the former Take That singer's second solo album, *I've Been Expecting You*. At the time, the record was the most important in EMI's albums release line-up.

But that's the past. Tonight Chris Abbot has a new act he is managing. His band Moco are playing tonight. They're already attracting attention from a few labels, but Chris claims that all the 'majors are doing now is TV programmes'.

Despite this, Chris looks cheerful. 'Yeah, it's going to be good tonight.'

Moco are from Wigan. They've already put out a couple of tunes on brother Tim's Pool Side label. One song is called 'Where She Goes'. 'Everyone is all over it,' says Chris. Another is called 'Miss Manta Ray'. They are scoring a tidy bit of critical acclaim and getting a lot of radio play.

Chris wants to get a little action going from some A&R boys; that's why he asked McGee if Moco could play his club.

When Chris Abbot first moved to London, he worked in a hat shop on Old Bond Street. They made the hats used in the *Batman* films and *Raiders Of The Lost Ark*. Charlie Watts, The Rolling Stones drummer, and Jack Nicholson were both customers.

When he was about 18 or 19, acid house hit. He started working with Jeff Barrett, who was doing press for Factory at the time and later set up the label Heavenly. Then he met McGee. He started working for McGee, sometimes looking after Primal Scream. When McGee needed someone to visit them in the studio, Chris used to go down. Chris also started a small techno imprint, Infonet.

'I used to go to Detroit all the time to buy records and license them in. I'd take Alan along,' recalls Chris. He's gripping a state-of-the-art Nokia cellphone. Later, Chris teamed up with Tim to help out with Robbie Williams.

Now he is working with Moco. But the state of the British market is a worry for a manager like him.

'To be honest I'm getting more interest from US labels at the moment. I've just funded an album for them – it was about £10,000 [$17,000] of my own money. I believed in it and put money where my mouth is,' he adds. Chris has been busy in Sony's studios in Whitfield Street mastering the album. It's called *Fizzy Pop*.

'*Fizzy Pop* is the album and I'm trying to use it as a tool to get a deal in the UK or US. We've just done a video, too,' he explains. 'How you should try and think is to find a way to get funding to allow yourself to manoeuvre.'

Chris also has a fundamental problem with the state of the London A&R scene right now.

'What I am trying to do is get the A&Rs interested. It's always a good live show. So I'm saying, "Come down, see them. Tick box or fuck off."' Chris is decked out in a black jumper. Black sweater and thin needlecord jeans, tan colour. Now his mood is turning black, too. He looks around for the A&R executives who were promising to turn out tonight.

'A&R are redundant when they earn £75,000 ($125,000) or more a year and sign nothing. You have to do more than listen to music, you have to break bands and have an input. A&R executives in London hunt in packs. There's the joke:

'"How many A&Rs does it take to change a light bulb?"

Chris answers himself. '"I don't know. What do you think?"

'A&Rs do very little work. One of the things I can't abide. This is the only business where you can make an appointment, to see a band or have a meeting, and inevitably they don't show up. A&Rs don't return phone calls or emails. This is a business where we are supposed to help each other out. But that doesn't happen. I really don't understand why they are frightened to put their heads above the water. I've been in meetings and the A&R guy has said, "I've got to go now because I've got my gym induction." If you work for a major label, you don't know what the real world is about. If you don't like an act, have some balls to make a decision. Geoff Travis over at Rough Trade thinks Moco are good, but he says to me, "They're not for me. If you've got anything else, Chris, bring it to me." That's how it should be.

'We seem to have a policy now of signing things that everyone else likes,' he continues. 'Every A&R department in London wants something that sounds like every other A&R department. A&R in this country can't see further than the office door. Bands are about developing over two or three albums.'

The pattern at the moment is that the same record companies chase the same band.

I let Chris blow some more. 'Only to spend £30,000 [$50,000] on a one-off single deal. The shortsightedness of that is crazy,' rails Chris. 'Having a quick Top 10 record when it is much more important to sell albums.' There are bigger margins on albums. In fact, singles are essentially loss leaders for albums.

I think he's finished his A&R rant.

'In the UK,' he continues. He hasn't. 'If we don't raise our game creatively, we will be swamped by another US invasion. When the emphasis of media and record labels is all US-based, what chance do we have to develop in London? UK talent is fast becoming a test market for the US.'

He suddenly brightens. Moco appear on stage. A four-piece, there is a bassist like Joey Ramone, a guitarist with an afro, who looks like an inflated version of Jimmy Page, with the same guitar too, and a singer with a bit of attitude. I hadn't noticed, but the crowd just got bigger. It's now sardine time in Death Disco. Moco crank out the songs and the punters jump about. I retreat to one of the banquettes and get a Jack and Coke sent over.

When the band finishes, I catch Chris again. I want to quiz him on the manager's role. John Glover, chairman of the Music Managers Forum, told me the week before that he believes the manager's power is getting stronger. Conversely, the record company, with all its problems of online piracy, lack of singles sales and depressed market, is getting weaker.

Chris agrees. 'Yeah, the manager's role is changing at the present moment. The manager can't just be administration any more. He needs to take a bigger role.'

The bigger role Chris sees for London music managers is as the 'feeder breeder'. He believes the old-school manager, who simply look after their 20 per cent by cutting deals with record labels, TV shows and talking to promoters, is over. Band management of the future, he believes, should involve finding talent at an embryonic stage.

'What I am trying to do is sit with them, talk about visual ideas. We do everything. We are essentially a small production company. You need to get in early, have the vision to see things and then see them through by using the resources of labels,' he says.

The manager will put a team in place to develop the band, taking much of the risk away from the label. The label essentially becomes the cash cow and distributor.

'The new deal in the new industry', he explains, 'is that a record label should advance money to develop bands to managers or production companies. That will reduce the risk to everybody. No one gets caught with their pants down. It will allow the artist to grow and develop at a natural pace. We are the feeders, we are making it grow.'

8 The Investigator

There's an old adage in the music industry: "Where there's a hit, there's a writ." And where there is a writ, David Morgan might be behind it. Morgan chases record companies for his clients' cash. He's a royalty investigator. He audits labels and runs down executives who have been living high on the hog while the singers and bands once signed to their labels languish in unfurnished bedsits, seeing little or no cash from the hits that once took them to the top of the charts.

I'm surprised at the once-high-profile singers, bands and producers Morgan has represented. Their records are still played on the radio, packaged on new compilations or sometimes rediscovered and used in films or television advertising. That earns royalties, but sometimes they are simply swallowed by the record label or publishing company and never passed on.

Ironically, because they are cash-strapped, few artists have the means to pursue the companies through the courts. Some may not even realise the levels of money they are owed. Others, still working in the business today, are afraid of launching actions because they do not want to upset the apple cart – the people who employ them. The music business is notoriously gossipy and it is easy to gain a reputation as 'difficult'.

'The music industry is notoriously crocked. It goes back to the '50s and '60s,' claims Morgan. And, in Morgan's view, it isn't getting better. Listening to him, it's as if the cigar-chomping and cheating pop Svengali still rules the roost at record labels. 'Now you get independent producers coming along. They get in a young artist, maybe to do a vocal for a fee.

A lot of money can then be made if it is a hit, but the singer wouldn't see any more. These kids are so desperate to get their chance, they'll do it for next to nothing. If they knew what they were signing, if they knew that they were signing away millions of pounds, which could change their life, they wouldn't do it. But most haven't got that experience or a lawyer when they start out.'

Typically artists can expect to be cut between 12 and 14 per cent royalties on a record; the producer may take between 2 and 4 per cent; with the record company taking the rest. Some record labels have been known to pay the producer's royalty out of the artist's share. Ensuring that 12 to 14 per cent is paid is Morgan's job. Like a tenacious private dick, Morgan trawls through record deals, management contracts and royalty accounts, sometimes stretching back decades.

Just before I meet him, Morgan secured his biggest and most high-profile success to date. He negotiated a big windfall for Musical Youth, although many deals never come to light, to save the record company the indignity of explaining why it hasn't paid artists.

We're meeting in the Hilton Hotel in Holland Park, near Shepherd's Bush island. This is pretty swish, and quiet. Morgan uses it as his office and today he has a full load of meetings. I'm late. Morgan is on his second cup of coffee. He is wearing a striped shirt with his jacket off, folded neatly over the back of his chair and metal-framed glasses hanging from a cord around his neck. He's a cuddly-looking bloke. But, he's also a tough nut. You'd have to be, in his profession.

Morgan got into the music business in the '70s. He did pretty well, although there were a few close shaves. In 1977 he spent £100,000 ($170,000) recording a band, Fallen Angels. Morgan took the completed tapes to the producer Gus Dudgeon. At the time, the producer was hot. He was working with Elton John then.

'So, I went to see Gus, I think he was living in Cookham. I've subsequently calculated that the recordings would have cost around £1 million [$1.7 million] today,' adds Morgan. 'Gus said – and I'll not forget this – that they "sound like scrambled eggs".'

Morgan survived. He moved to Los Angeles, became Bobby Womack's manager, then made a killing a few years later with a dance hit mixed by Fatboy Slim. In the mid-1990s he had a phone call from Hazel O'Connor. The call took him into his new line of work. The singer was big at the beginning of the '80s, but Morgan claims had not been receiving a penny in royalties from a successful soundtrack album, *Breaking Glass*.

Morgan went to work. He contacted the record company and album's producer. Eventually he was able to cut a deal. 'It would have been bad PR for everyone involved if it had come out that everyone was collecting apart from the film's star,' he chuckles. That seems to be Morgan's main tool in his arsenal: embarrassing people and companies into doing the right thing.

That's what happened with Musical Youth. The five members of Musical Youth, aged between 9 and 13, were the biggest boy band of their day in the early '80s. They recorded the infectious reggae tune 'Pass The Dutchie', which was a global hit, selling something like five million copies around the world.

The superstar lifestyle followed. The band went on tour. They enjoyed five-star hotels, first-class air travel to the Far East, Europe and Africa. But, the '80s chart-toppers' dreams turned sour when the hits dried up. They were dropped by their label MCA (now part of Universal) and, following the break-up of the band in 1985, its members fell on hard times and some of their lives were ravaged by tragedy. Patrick Waite died in 1993, aged 24, and his brother Junior, 34, is now in a secure hospital.

Then they found out they weren't being paid royalties.

Morgan now claims the bands' lives were ruined by the record company because they were 'used and exploited'. He adds that nobody looked after the band's interests and, because they were children at the time, they were taken for a ride.

After launching his two-year investigation, using accountants and lawyers to hammer home his claim, Morgan points out that the 1982 chart-topper 'Pass The Dutchie' has featured on a string of bestselling compilation albums since the band's mid-1980s demise, and has been licensed to more than 100 projects (compilations).

The biggest-selling such compilation was probably *The Wedding Singer* – the spin-off album of songs released following the success of the 1998 Hollywood comedy romance starring Adam Sandler about a wedding singer who plays '80s hits. It sold around four million copies around the world.

Morgan estimates that the band should have been entitled to around £300,000 ($500,000) in royalties from *The Wedding Singer* alone. In total, he says that total recording royalties dating back to 1984 – the last time they received royalties – could add up to as much as £2 million ($3.3 million).

However, after the protracted negotiations between their record company Universal Island dragged on, the four surviving members of the group and Jean Waite, the mother of Patrick, finally decided to avoid an expensive court appearance and accepted an out-of-court settlement believed to be in the high six figures.

Sitting in the Hilton, Morgan reflects on the personal tragedy of those involved and says that, although band members Dennis Seaton and the Grant brothers are getting by, their lives could have been improved immeasurably if they'd been paid what they were owed by the record industry. 'They suffered. They really suffered. But, they've finally got money in their pockets again. This has taken two and a half years, when careers can come and go in a year.'

But there is happy ending. It's turned out good. Morgan tells me Musical Youth are re-forming. They will tour for the first time since they split. And, as part of the settlement, Morgan says Universal are also promising to release a greatest hits CD and DVD package, the *Twenty First Anniversary Of Musical Youth,* which will include hits such as 'Pass The Dutchie' and unreleased material such as a collaboration with Donna Summer, 'Unconditional Love', and Stevie Wonder, 'Watcha Talkin' 'Bout?'

They will also now receive future royalties on all their tracks.

Result.

We order up a couple more coffees. I can see Morgan is excited. He likes being the good guy. The man battling for the artists, the little guys, sometimes the big guys. But always up against bigger guys – the record companies, sometimes conglomerates.

He plays me a song on a tape recorder. The vocal is familiar. But not the song. 'But, it sounds like... I've heard it before,' I tell him.

We both listen for a few minutes. 'Yes, yes, I've heard it before.'

I'm mistaken. I haven't heard it. No one has. Well, apart from David and a few of his associates. It's one of three newly unearthed and unreleased songs.

'What do you think?' asks Morgan, his voice thick with an Irish brogue.

'I think it's pretty good.'

'Yes, I think he will be very interested to hear them.'

He – the voice on the tape, the singer of the songs – is a famous rock star. David Morgan is embroiled in the middle of a royalties dispute between him and his former producer, Gus Dudgeon. Dudgeon, one of the most successful producers working in London. But Dudgeon had a gripe.

Dudgeon produced a 1969 track that reached No.5 in the singles charts and launched the star's career. And he alleged he was stiffed on the production deal. However, Dudgeon's claim is vigorously contested by the singer's business advisers, who believe it has no foundation.

Dudgeon received a fee of £250 ($420) for producing the hit single, but believed he was entitled to 2 per cent of future royalties. 'We have no evidence that Gus was paid anything,' adds Morgan. He says he is asking the record company to remove Dudgeon's name from future packaging and material, because 'they have been exploiting his good name without reference to payment and have been doing so for over 30 years. No producer in the world would allow that to happen.'

Tragically, before he could see the claim through, Dudgeon died in a car accident. Morgan is now working for the Dudgeon estate. The three tracks, recorded around 1967, were unearthed while searching the producer's attic following his death. They include 'Waiting For My Man' and an instrumental.

'We're surprised at the quality of them, since they haven't been played since 1967,' says Morgan, looking at a sheaf of papers and notes on the table between us. Morgan likes to keep everything filed neatly. 'A lot of people, fans and the like, would love to hear them. See, he hadn't got his style together.'

Morgan also believes the tracks would be of more interest to the rock singer than him, but maintains he is not using them as a 'blackmailing' tool in an attempt to settle the case. Even though the Dudgeon estate is claiming ownership, it is unlikely it would be able to release the tracks without permission from the star. Morgan estimates the claim for Dudgeon could be worth several million pounds following extensive usage of the song on greatest-hits compilations and TV advertising.

The case hasn't gone legal yet. But a lot of strong-worded letters have been flying back and forth between the rock star's business advisers. Morgan looks like he has another battle on his hands to prove his client's claims. He looks like he is relishing it.

9 Punk Rockers At The 100 Club

Over two days in September 1976, The Sex Pistols played a festival at the 100 Club. On stage, Glen Matlock stood next to Johnny Rotten and played bass. The Clash, The Damned, The Buzzcocks, Subway Sect, Stinky Toys with Frenchy, and Siouxsie And The Banshees, also played there. Sid Vicious played drums behind Siouxsie one night. This was a new revolution – the punk-rock revolution. And Matlock was jump-starting it.

Nearly 30 years later, Matlock is back on the same stage, playing at the 100 Club again. But, there's no Lydon tonight, spitting out 'Anarchy In The UK' at a bunch of kids in safety pins and mohair. Lydon claims he based his stage act on *Richard III*.

Glen scoffs at that one. 'What do you think?' He tells me he thinks Lydon was more like Kenneth Williams from the *Carry On* films.

Glen is with his own band, Glen Matlock And The Philistines. The man who wrote 'Pretty Vacant', sitting in a Soho boozer on a buzz of Stella Artois and with Abba running around his head hasn't played the 100 Club for a while – for a long while. But, there he is up on stage, or the raised platform that passes for one, anyway. The Philistines are Chris Musto on drums, Terry Edwards on keyboards and Steve New, who played in Glen's post-Pistols band Rich Kids, on guitar. Behind them, a stack of Marshall amps and a big sign – '100 Club'. The place hasn't changed in over 25 years.

The Philistines play 'Ghosts Of Princes In Towers', the old Rich Kids song. Glen is singing, screaming into the mike. And the audience, a mix of youngsters and oldsters, press forward trying to get a view from behind the pillars. In 1976, the bike-chain-wielding Vicious threw a glass, which shattered on one of those pillars.

I ask one of the youngsters, a beautiful girl called Aisha, what she thinks. Aisha, a model, was born in 1981 and is wearing Converse sneakers, a pair of faded Earl Jeans and a top by Chloë. 'Yeah, this is punk rock, man. It's Glen Matlock of The Sex Pistols. Not The Strokes or Yeah Yeah Yeahs. The real deal, know what I mean?'

I guess so. I notice her friend, who is in his early 20s at a guess. He doesn't say anything, just nods. And when he turns to the bar I see he has painted an anarchy sign on the back of his army-surplus jacket and stencilled 'BOREDOM' underneath in white lettering.

Some of the old hands in the audience have kitted themselves in brothel creepers and vintage Vivienne Westwood. Glen might have knocked them out the gear when he worked behind the counter in Westwood and McLaren's King's Road shop Let It Rock (later Too Fast Too Live, Seditionaries, Sex and World's End).

There's a small knot of wooden tables at the far end of the basement, about 10m (10yd) away, and one guy is sitting there rolling a spliff on his bondage trousers. There's enough space to pogo. And some do.

'We did the the Pistols press conference [when the band re-formed for the 20th-anniversary concerts in 1996] here. I always liked the 100 Club because I just find it's very honest. It's been there for donkey's years. It has the same old room and real beer prices at the bar,' Glen says, off stage now.

Glen is 46, but passes for younger. He is propped up at the end of the bar, which runs along one end of the club. He's right: the beer isn't pricey. I buy a pint of lager and lime. Glen gave up the sauce about a dozen years ago. 'Yeah, I packed it in. I kind of had to,' he adds. 'I still can't get up in the morning.' Glen drinks non-alcoholic bottles of lager. He's sweating. 'I hadn't been down here for a long time. I went down a week before we did the Pistols press conference, and it was like a lunchtime session and it was very funny, all these blokes with goatee beards and jet-black jumpers, you know, a sort of jazz scene with all kinds of dancing.'

They still play jazz at the 100. It's on Oxford Street. Glen isn't a fan of this charmless artery, or 'the shoddiest street in the world' as he calls it. The club is just across from the Metro, and a stone's throw from Tottenham Court Road. During the 1976 Punk Festival, Pistols manager Malcolm McLaren operated his Glitterbest company from 119 Oxford Street. Just down the road, at No.165, was the first site of the Marquee Club, which started life in 1958 as the Marquee Ballroom. This is where Brian Jones was inspired by Muddy Waters to start The Rolling Stones. Just before the Marquee moved to its second location on Wardour Street in March 1964, Rod Stewart made his Marquee debut on Oxford Street.

In early 1962, producer George Martin, who ran Air Studios at 214 Oxford Street, also heard the first Beatles demos at the first HMV store. This was opened by Elgar, at 363 Oxford Street, in 1921.

Before punk, the 100 Club was already legendary. It has been promoting live music on the same premises since 1942. Originally a restaurant called Mack's, live music was first played here when the Feldman family hired the venue as the Feldman Swing Club.

Its rep grew. It became a regular haunt for visiting US servicemen. An early visitor was big-band man Glenn Miller, who appeared at the Club during World War II as bombs rained down in the Blitz. Still, it was safe in the 100 Club. Pretty safe, anyway. The club is in a basement a couple of flights down. Advertising at the time read 'Forget the Doodlebug – Come and Jitterbug'.

By 1948, the club's name had changed and it was now the London Jazz Club. The Feldmans stopped promoting, and new owners, the Wilcox brothers, inherited the address before Lyn Dutton took over in the 1950s. Dutton was Humphrey Lyttelton's agent and renamed the spot The Humphrey Lyttelton Club. It scored a major coup in 1956, when New Orleans trumpeter Louis Armstrong appeared. Then Billie Holiday turned up. Then, in 1958, the Humphrey Lyttelton Band had a hit with 'Bad Penny Blues', which kick-started the trad-jazz boom of the late '50s and early '60s – and spawned 100 bands, including Kenny Ball and Acker Bilk. The 100 Club also acquired a new name, Jazz Shows.

The arrival of The Beatles and The Rolling Stones, who played the Oxford Street Marquee in July 1962, soon ended the trad scene and the name of the club. In 1964, owner Roger Horton decided to dub the basement venue the 100 Club in a bid to attract blues and soul on top of jazz. Soon there was an invasion: Muddy Waters, Albert King, BB King, Bo Diddley, and their American soul cousins Jackie Wilson and George Jackson, all trod the boards.

The British blues and beat scene also kick-started here. Steam Packet, featuring Rod Stewart, Long John Baldry, Alexis Korner, John Mayall's Bluesbreakers, The Animals, The Who, The Kinks, The Pretty Things and The Spencer Davis Group – they all played the 100 Club.

The early '70s were rough times for the club, caught in strife-torn England and in the dead zone of glam rock and disco. But, when many clubs banned punk bands, the 100 Club saw an opportunity. It hosted its Punk Festival. It was £1.50 ($2.50) on the door – 7pm opening with late bar. The club became associated with the start of year zero. It could get hot down there, too.

'I remember doing an early gig at the 100 Club with the Pistols and it was really hot and sweaty,' recalls Matlock a quarter of a century later. 'We went to a club after. Bangs, I think it was, which was a club by the Astoria, a gay club there. And I put my hand in my pocket and thought "Oops, that is a bit lumpy," and it was my sweaty underpants that I had taken off after going on stage with a rubber suit with the band.'

A few weeks later, I call up Glen to invite him for dinner. Since I last saw him he's been in Spain, touring with the band. He's just got back from a jaunt in the States playing the Rock 'n' Roll Hall of Fame in Cleveland – an acoustic set, just featuring teenage Sex Pistol Matlock and a guitar. He has another band, Dead Men Walking, which also features Pete Wylie from Wah Heat. 'Everyone sings our best-known songs,' jokes Matlock. 'It's like The Spinners with swear words.'

I like Glen; he's got a good line in self-deprecating wit.

We meet at the Queens, a pub on the corner of Regent's Park Road. Just a few hundred metres away, on a cold winter morning late in 1966, The Rolling Stones stood on Primrose Hill. With the views of the whole of London stretching before them, the photographer Gered Mankowitz snapped the cover shot for *Between The Buttons*.

I'm early and get the drinks in: Jack and Coke and a non-alcoholic beer for Glen. I spot the movie actor Jude Law saunter by one of his local boozers with a factotum. With Notting Hill, this part of London is star central. The director Sam Mendes has a place down the road, so does Bush's Gavin Rossdale and his wife Gwen Stefani from No Doubt. The actor Alan Bates often takes lunch at Odettes across the road.

No one recognises Matlock when he arrives. He's in a black shirt from Linea, blue jeans, white trainers, and he's tied his jumper around his waist. He takes a swig of the beer. 'It's funny. I get recognised in unusual places. I remember I was hiking in the hills in Los Angeles, just north of Santa Monica. And this tour bus pulled up and a guy got out and said, "Hey, it's Glen Matlock from The Sex Pistols."'

Over the drinks, he tells me about the Cleveland gig, which turned out OK. 'The Rock 'n' Roll Hall of Fame it's like... I thought it was going to be naff, but it is really good. It's this big purpose-built building shaped like a pyramid,' he explains. 'It's all brand spanking new and must have cost millions of dollars to make. They've got some really good stuff, they've got Eddie Cochran's guitar; he only had one guitar that he played on all the records and it is there. It's something else.' Glen catches himself. 'Something Else' is the Cochran song that Sid covered post-Pistols. 'Ah, something else... They've got some Pistols things in there. Once a year they have the Rock 'n' Roll Hall of Fame award and the rest of the year they've got stuff on. Pop culture is their art, so they have other things on and I was the other thing on last week.'

Glen played a couple of Pistols songs and a couple of his own numbers. He also played The Clash's 'London Calling', Dedicated to Joe Strummer. 'I was bricking it. Really, if you go and play with a band, you've got a PA system and all that equipment and all the other guys from the band and all that noise to hide behind, but it was just me and an acoustic guitar.'

The Pistols re-formed in 1996 and again in 2002, and they've got some US dates lined up for 2003, but Glen doesn't expect his band will be playing the Rock 'n' Roll Hall of Fame in the near future. 'With The Sex Pistols, I didn't think it would last for ever and I kind of feel like I am in the *Blues Brothers* when we get the band back together,' he jokes. 'We're talking about a new tour this year, but I don't think John will be into all that stuff [the Rock 'n' Roll Hall of Fame].'

Glen didn't tell his old bandmates he was playing there. Steve Jones only found out when he called a guy he was trying to flog some vintage shirts to. 'This guy from Atlanta, he comes to see me play. He was talking to Steve Jones on the phone on the way up. Steve was trying to flog him some memorabilia and asked him where he was. And this guy says, "I'm heading to Cleveland, I'm going to watch Glen doing an acoustic show at the Rock 'n' Roll Hall of Fame."' Glen and Steve Jones are both Virgos, he tells me. They get on OK.

Matlock was born in 1956, in Kensal Green, London. He's been a Londoner all his life. He used to live 'Off the Harrow Road, so I haven't moved very far. Used to drink in the Mason's Arms up there.' His local now is The Warrington on Warrington Crescent.

His first records were by the Beatles and Kinks: *Twist And Shout* EP and 'You Really Got Me'. The Beatles connection would come to haunt him during the punk years. But his favourite band was The Small Faces.

One of Glen's first jobs was working in Whiteley's, the shopping mall in Bayswater. But, he slipped up with something and didn't want to go back. He knew he might strike lucky in Chelsea. He'd been hanging around a shop on the King's Road, so one day in 1974 he asked Malcolm McLaren for a job in Let It Rock pushing creepers to teddy boys. 430 Kings Road Chelsea, it is now one of Vivienne's Westwood's boutiques and it still has the Rock – spelled out in chicken bones – T-shirt in a frame on the wall. Westwood got the bones from a store across the road.

In the early '70s, on the other side of town, Steve Jones and Paul Cook were experimenting with a band. Along with schoolmate Warwick Nightingale, they formed The Strand in 1972. Jimmy Mackin and Steve Hayes helped out. Jones stole the equipment.

Jones was also spending his weekends in Let It Rock and soon Saturday boy Glen joined the band. Then a green-haired John Lydon walked in. He auditioned in Let It Rock to Alice Cooper – 'School's Out' was on the jukebox, which is appropriate as Glen tells it now. 'You know, it's kind of funny they've started having good stuff on Radio Two – about two years ago, I did the story of punk and then last year they did the Alice Cooper story and got John to present it,' he says.

Initially the Pistols worked on '60s covers – The Who's 'Substitute', with a couple of Glen's favourite Small Faces songs. The first gig was on 6 November 1975 at Glen's college, St Martin's College of Art at 107 Charing Cross Road, supporting Bazooka Joe, named after a gum and featuring a pre-Ants Adam Ant. Glen used to go to the college. The way he tells it now, 'the main reason' that the Pistols formed was because there was nothing to do that was of any interest to them. 'We thought we'd make something ourselves.'

The debut Pistols gig was cut off in its prime – someone pulled the plug. But soon the band was gigging all over London and the Home Counties. Then they played the 100 Club Punk Festival and a month later signed to EMI ('EMI'...'unlimited supply'). 'Anarchy In The UK' rolled off the presses a few weeks later.

On 1 December, the band appeared on the *Today* programme, and were interviewed live. The Sex Pistols swore, '...you dirty fucker, what a fucking rotter'.

The host, Bill Grundy, was outraged, 'Well, that's it for tonight. I'll be seeing you soon. I hope I'm not seeing you again...'

Matlock looked about 15 years old. Some geezer was so annoyed at primetime cussing that he kicked in his TV set. The following day, the tabloids were full of it.

The scandal prompted EMI to drop the band and promoters cancelled all but three of the subsequent Anarchy tour dates with The Clash, The Damned and The Heartbreakers (featuring former New York Dolls Johnny Thunders and Jerry Nolan, Walter Lure and Billy Rath on bass).

But Rotten and Glen weren't getting on. Glen left the Pistols in February 1977 and Sid Vicious took his place. There was a rumour that Glen might join his mate Mick Jones in The Clash. But Glen formed The Rich Kids with Steve New, Rusty Egan and Midge Ure.

He got the name from Cocteau's *Les Enfants Terribles*. They had a couple of hits. 'The Rich Kids', the debut single, was released in January 1978. The first 15,000 copies were pressed on red vinyl. It was the group's biggest seller.

We finish our drinks at the Queens and saunter down Regent's Park Road towards Chalk Farm. Ritzy Regent's Park Road – Kate Moss does her shopping here. Glen stops to admire watercolours in a small art gallery. 'There's some good things about London that don't change,' he tells me. 'There's a kiosk right next to St Martin's. The original St Martin's on Charing Cross Road, where I used to go and we played our first gig. It's the only place I've seen on my travels that sells Sobranie Cocktail cigarettes. Because when I was at art school the girls were sent there as a kind of finishing school and they were all from the Cadogan Estate or their dads owned the Cadogan Estate, and they used to smoke Sobranie Cocktails and they're still there.'

The doors to Lemonia are flung wide open, the noise from the busy restaurant rattling across the street. It's busy with well-heeled architects, ad execs, financiers, designers, and now a punk rocker. Glen goes for a starter of hummus, I want taramas, and a drop of ouzo too, just to get lubricated.

Glen's in a philosophical mood. He's answered questions about The Sex Pistols until he is blue in the face. The Pistols is something he is proud of, 'but it also is a bit of a millstone'. He's in a new band now, still writing songs. It's a mixed blessing, the history. 'Oh, the early days of the Pistols, I kind of trot that out parrot-fashion nowadays,' he says, picking over the hummus. 'I put a slightly new twist on it, but on the other hand I feel because of all the Sid stuff and what he did and what I did, I kind of feel I have to blow my own trumpet, because no one else is going to do it for me, you know?'

Yeah, I guess. Sid gets the glory.

Even now people come up and tell Glen what punk meant to them, how it changed things. Maybe it changed their lives, but he is more sanguine about it changing the face of London and the music industry. The way he sees it, nothing really has changed. There are still boy bands, girl bands. Maybe the haircuts have changed.

'You turn on the radio and hear something and it is S Club 7 or Atomic Kitten. That is kind of alright because there has always been stuff like that around. It's only annoying when that is all there is.'

Now Matlock wants to be recognised for the songwriter he is, but the weight of history weighs heavy. It's tough to break out from being a member of the most notorious band in the world.

'I don't feel I have a career. The Pistols thing...it's a double-edged thing – people only want to really know you for that. In later years, I think I have written some of the best songs I have ever written, but it's always overshadowed by the Pistols. That's a frustration. I'm a songwriter. I'm not even a bass guitarist; I'm a songwriter. As people get older they don't stop what they used to do, and when you are doing your stuff and it is not seeing the light of day that's difficult.'

That's part of the problem of the record industry, he feels. It pigeonholes. Once a punk rocker, always a punk rocker. 'Rather than ex-Pistol, I would rather they say, "There is Glen Matlock. He wrote that fantastic song that they are playing on the radio all the time." But Ray Davies [of The Kinks] wrote some amazing stuff and he isn't getting played on the radio, either.'

And the new bands, which are taking the Pistols and repackaging it for the 21st century – do they deserve the radio play?

'Like The Strokes? Yeah, they're alright. They're good. I don't want to sound too much like an old bloke, but I've heard it all before. It's alright. You know, Marilyn Manson is a poor man's Alice Cooper and he is a poor man's Screaming Jay Hawkins. Only Screaming Jay Hawkins is original.'

Glen digs into his moussaka. Now he puts his own music out on his own label. He gave up trying to get another deal. 'These days you can make a record and make it pay for itself if you do a few gigs,' he explains. 'You can earn a living. It's all down to the Internet. You could never do that before.'

One thing he doesn't think has changed is London. Maybe the days of playing strip clubs on Brewer Street is over, but Matlock isn't lamenting that. 'We had hired the El Paradise for the night. They had all these little footlights and John smashed them and this Maltese bloke stood at the front and stared at John for three numbers,' says Glen.

A few weeks later, Glen was in the barber's on Denmark Street when the same guy turned up after his protection money. 'This stocky Maltese bloke turns up. He put his arm up and I could see he had a gun in his holster and the barber was doing my neck with a cut-throat razor at the time.'

However, he still says there are nuggets to be found. His old haunts are still pretty much intact. 'I love walking around London and it has become much more of a 24-hour city,' he says. 'I've still got my little round. If I need new guitar strings, I go down Denmark Street and it is still exactly the same. Not exactly the same, but pretty much the same.'

The Sex Pistols rehearsal space at 6 Denmark Street is still there, too. 'Me and Steve lived there. I found it in the *Melody Maker*. There was a Greek bookshop out the front, which isn't there any more, but the building is exactly the same. And I found out recently that my nan was born in there. Amazing. In that same building.'

The musicians' café on Tin Pan Alley where Glen and John used to while away many an hour is also still open. 'The La Giaconda is still there. When we were skint, me and John used to go there a lot.

'I'd say, "How much have you got?"

'And he'd say, "Enough for two jam sponges."

'We used to go to Bar Italia too, and that's still there. Have an espresso and a line of speed.'

We both glance around at the braying architects and designers ordering up souvlaki. 'I think London is kind of more poncy now, though. I can do poncy, but it is only as good as the people who go there. The trouble with poncy sometimes is it fills up with too many poncy people.' We order up two espressos apiece. That'll be enough to keep us awake tonight.

The Buzzcocks supported The Sex Pistols at the Lesser Free Trade Hall in Manchester. Glen Matlock played bass on that night in 1976. Tonight – nearly 30 years later – the Manchester band are still together. At least, Pete Shelley and Steve Diggle are. They're playing the Shepherd's Bush Empire tonight. It's a stone's throw from the Hilton, across Shepherd's Bush Green, in between Shepherd's Bush and Goldhawk Road tubes.

I hit Holland Park Avenue. Rush hour is over, but the traffic is still backed up on Holland Road: commuters trying to make it out of London on the Westway before *Coronation Street* is over.

As I pass the grim shopping complex, the Concord Centre, on my left I can see the lights of the Empire over the green expanse of common. I cross the Goldhawk Road – Local Shepherd's Bush band The Who played the social club at number 205 in their early days.

There's an enormous Australian pub next door, but the Empire still retains a glimmer of its original grandeur. Since opening a century ago in August 1903, the Shepherd's Bush Empire has been a landmark and player on London's music and entertainment scene.

In January 1995, live music and restaurant operator Break For The Border bought the Empire from Andrew Marler, who had converted the venue into a live music hall. It pressed ahead with a £2 million ($3.3 million) restoration, and in January 1998 the newly formed McKenzie Group agreed terms to purchase it and Brixton Academy.

The McKenzie Group is one of the leading venue operators in London. It runs the Empire, the Brixton Academy, and in June 3002 it bought the Marquee Club in Islington. I want to talk to McKenzie Group Managing Director John Northcote about the live scene in London and whether venues are doing the right thing by their customers.

And what are his plans for the Marquee, one of the most famous London venue names? After opening in 1958 as a jazz club, the Marquee introduced R&B to London and attracted everyone from The Yardbirds to The Sex Pistols. For a few decades, it was a cramped and sweat-drenched Soho dive on Wardour Street. However, it closed in the mid-1990s, with the original site turned into a fancy restaurant. In 2002, Dave Stewart's Artist Network group relaunched the legendary name on the site of a £4 million ($6.7 million) venue in an Islington shopping mall, complete with Michelin-starred chef in the accompanying restaurant and 'industrial Moulin Rouge' decor. However, punters, more used to burgers and fries, and their rock 'n' roll a little bit dirtier than a shopping development, stayed away. The club fell into administration in early 2003.

Joe Strummer, lead singer of The Clash, who tragically died just before this book was started

The original Fridge opened in 1981 and was the first venue to book acts such as The Eurythmics and The Pet Shop Boys

Notting Hill Carnival, a celebration of Caribbean culture and the biggest street carnival in Europe

Dingwalls, opened in the late '70s and now considered to be one of the most popular live-music venues in the capital

The 100 Club. This venue has hosted every style of music since opening in 1942, from The Sex Pistols to The Humphrey Lyttelton Jazz Band

Boy George: Club-goer, singer in '80s pop act Culture Club and now reinvented as a DJ and creator of the successful musical *Taboo*

Once a magnificent theatre in the middle of Brixton, the Academy has been transformed into one of south London's premier stages

Buskers on London's Underground network are part and parcel of the commuter's journey, despite it still being largely illegal for them to practise their craft

The Astoria started life as a Crosse & Blackwell factory, but the likes of Black Sabbath, David Bowie, Oasis and Eminem have enabled live music to became its bread and butter since the '90s

Musicians taking part in a traditional Irish fiddle session, a common sight in Irish pubs across north London

The Electric Ballroom, which started life on Camden High Street as an Irish ballroom in the 1930s and opened as the Electric in 1978

John Peel, one of London's most influential DJs, credited with discovering hundreds of bands and the only remaining Radio One DJ from the original line-up

Glen Matlock, the Sex Pistol who wrote many of the band's classic songs and was famously replaced by Sid Vicious

Opened in 1990 and now part of the successful Mean Fiddler operation, the Jazz Café has established itself as one of the city's top soul and R&B venues

As one-third of the fabulously successful '80s production team Stock, Aitken and Waterman, Pete Waterman has worked with everyone from Kylie Minogue to Dead Or Alive

Ronnie Scott's, the most famous jazz club in London, which moved to its present location on Frith Street in 1965

Denmark Street, aka Tin Pan Alley and, in the '50s, the heart of London's music business, home to offices of publishers, managers and record labels

Despite this, Northcote is bullish about being able to put the venue back on the live circuit by September 2003, although the Marquee brand will not be reused and is remaining with the administrators. 'The live scene is tough at the moment, but we are doing our best to make it less so,' says Northcote. He should know. He's been around long enough. He first opened The Borderline off Charing Cross Road in 1988, helping to take the bar, restaurant and venue to become a fully quoted public limited company by 1993.

When I catch up with Northcote, he is recovering from a late night up with REM at the Brixton Academy playing in front of nearly 5,000 fans. 'It's funny, I remember putting REM in front of 250 people at The Borderline in the early '90s. They called up and said, "We're Bingo Hand Job", which I wasn't too impressed with. Then they told me it was REM. It was one of those gigs that now thousands of people claim they were at, but of course the place only held a couple of hundred.'

After his Borderline experience, Northcote linked with Ian Howard to create the privately owned Mckenzie Group in January 1998. The shareholders of McKenzie Group include Red Stripe lager brewers Charles Wells and leading UK music promoters SJM Concerts, Metropolis Music Ltd and MCD Management Ltd, which helps when Northcote is looking for bands to put into his venues.

The first step for McKenzie Group was to buy out the Brixton Academy and Empire from Break For The Border. In June 2000, Northcote became Managing Director, with Howard assuming the role of chairman of the group.

In November 2000, the group embarked on a major venue-opening programme at the Birmingham Academy. In October 2001, it launched the third Academy brand in Bristol, and in March 2003, after a £3 million ($5 million) refurbishment, a 2,500-capacity venue in Glasgow. With seven concert venues now stretching from Glasgow to Bristol, Northcote's group attracts through its doors more than two million people each year to watch bands.

Northcote tells me he has plans for future developments, with new venues opening in London and nationwide. His strategy is to eventually have a range of different-sized venues in each major city similar to the model in London – with the 800-capacity old Marquee (rebranded as an Academy venue), 2,500-capacity Empire and 5,000-capacity Academy.

This means he can operate the old Marquee for up-and-coming bands, club nights and dance events. This will dovetail with the two other, larger, London venues, which host bigger bands who may have developed their audience at the smaller venue. 'It's great to be opening a small venue again. It gives me the opportunity of once again being involved in new talent and emerging artists,' he says. 'The core task is new talent, which is exciting for me, because without new talent coming on board there will be no live music industry.'

The Buzzcocks are out on stage. It's a beautiful little theatre retaining the opulent design and grandeur of its early years.

I'm up on the balcony, which is supposed to be haunted after a man fell to his death from the roof at the turn of the century. However, Shelley and co would give any ghost a sleepless night with the barrage of noise their amps are feeding the audience with tonight. The band has a new album out, which is called *Buzzcocks*. And they're selling it well with this performance.

The Manchester group's high-octane guitars, bass and drums produced three classic albums in the late '70s, *Another Music In A Different Kitchen*, *Love Bites* and *A Different Kind Of Tension*, before they split in 1981. However, in 1993 Shelley and Diggle found a new rhythm section with Tony Barber on bass and Phil Barker on drums. They haven't looked back since.

Barber produced the new album, and the punksters rattle through a couple of new songs tonight before treating us to some old favourites such as 'Harmony In My Head' and 'Ever Fallen In Love With'.

Since Soundgarden opened it in March 1994, the former TV theatre has been inviting bands on stage for a decade now. Northcote has seen Blur, Radiohead, Johnny Cash, Sheryl Crow, Primal Scream, Lou Reed, Iggy Pop, The Sex Pistols, Manic Street Preachers, The Smashing Pumpkins, Tricky, Massive Attack, Air, Death In Vegas, Moloko, Groove Armada, Zero 7, Destiny's Child, Elton John, The Who, Oasis and The Rolling Stones all grace his stage.

It has hosted the Mercury Music Prize, MTV's Five Night Stand, the UK DJ Championships and Comic Relief. Jon Bon Jovi even set a record here, when he sold out a 2002 show in just eight minutes flat. And now The Buzzcocks.

So what's the secret of running a successful venue?

Northcote doesn't need much time to bat this one back. It's not rocket science. Just getting the details right.

'In the old days, a live music venue meant a stage at one end of it and a bar at the other, with a surly bouncer outside who was always giving people grief,' he says. 'Now people expect a lot more. The music venue experience has to catch up with what cinemas did a few years ago, which was smarten up their act.'

And when he says 'a lot more', Northcote means that venue operators like himself have to address issues such as attracting the right act for the right customer.

Then there are the basics. The view, the sound, level of comfort, toilet facilities – 'whether there are enough' – and those staffing issues are also paramount to the venue operator. 'We always make sure the doormen know what sort of venue we are operating. If people like a venue, they are going to keep going back, again and again.'

And, it seems, the devil is in the detail. Northcote isn't planning on making radical changes to the old Marquee in Islington. But in its first guise it boasted a 160-cover bar and grill run by an award-winning chef. This, concedes Northcote, is not a priority for rock 'n' roll fans. That will be reduced in size and the food 'downplayed', which probably means fewer grilled aubergines and more burgers and fries. Standard gig fare.

I buy a hotdog outside and stand on Shepherd's Bush Green waiting for The Buzzcocks' fans to pour past me and down into the Underground. Over a century ago, this spot was rural. Shepherds used to rest their flocks on this little patch of grass on their way to market.

The arrival of the railways in the borough was the catalyst for development. The extension in 1864 of the Metropolitan Railway to Hammersmith via Shepherd's Bush from Paddington started these changes. As a result, the second half of the 19th century saw a massive increase in population in the area, accompanied by a huge house-building programme.

Industry also moved in, and in 1913 the country's first daylight studio opened in Lime Grove. In 1960, the BBC also sited its TV centre just up the road from the Empire . By this point, the Empire – designed and built by prolific Victorian architect Frank Matcham – had been on the site for more than 50 years.

The venue was built for the theatre manager Oswald Stoll, and opened on 17 August 1903. The first performance was The Fred Karno Troupe. It was a music hall with weekly variety revues for the next four decades and then, in 1953, the BBC bought it and converted it into a studio and theatre. Max Bygraves and the Tiller Girls provided the entertainment in the early years under the banner of Variety Parade.

Later the Empire played host to all the top TV shows of the '60s, '70s and '80s: the kids' show *Crackerjack*, Esther Ranzten's sideways look at life, *That's Life*, comedian Tony Hancock running his skits in *Hancock*, Terry Wogan's comfortable chat series, *Wogan*, and the rock show *The Old Grey Whistle Test* with whispering Bob Harris introducing bands and The Damned smashing up the studio saying, 'We're a punk band.' So are The Buzzcocks.

10 Paddy's Night

It was Paddy's night in the drunk tank. Tonight that's The Stag's Head. And the craic is mighty, as they say. That's Dermot Fitzgerald saying it. 'The craic? Ahh, get yerself here. Wot'yer havin', fella?' Dermot is from Yougall in County Cork and he's had a dozen pints. That's what he is telling everyone, anyway. Behind him is a photograph of James Joyce; above him, a stuffed Stag. 'I've drunk 12 pints and I'm pissed, so there. You want a Jam'son, fella?' Sure. Since you're asking, Dermot.

This is St Patrick's night in The Stag's Head on Hawley Road, NW1. The Guinness is flowing; Jameson's, too. There must be 200 crammed into this old bar with black-and-white photos of the streets in Kinsale. And they're all drunk. It's ten, but I doubt they'll be turning out soon. This is as Irish as it gets in London. A little piece of Cork, a slice of Limerick and a hefty slug of Dublin. Bert, the landlord from the old country, behind the bar; his son Connor, too. Connor's just back from Ibiza. He likes dance music, but tonight he's behind the cause. He's got a green top hat on.

There's a quartet in the corner. A couple of them play every Saturday night, but tonight is special. They've enlisted two new players. They're pulling the stops out, playing a fiddle, a flute, a bodhran and a button accordion. They launch into a slow but loud set. The strains of 'Carrickfergus' clash with the drunken banter, singing – not to the same tune – and shouts. The door bursts open, and two guys in full Irish football strip stagger in.

'Bert, Bert,' they chorus. 'Two pints of Guinness.' And collapse across the pool table on which a girl, wrapped in a tricolour with a giant green plastic shamrock perched on her head, is dancing a jig.

St Patrick's Day is Ireland's greatest national holiday as well as a holy day – the anniversary of the death of the missionary who became the patron saint of Ireland. Celebrated with parades, speeches, dinners, dances and piss-ups like this one. Green is the only colour – that, or a shamrock.

St Patrick, or Maewyn, was born in Wales about AD 385 and well into his teenage years was raised as a pagan. At the age of 16, he was taken prisoner by a group of Irish raiders and sold into slavery. He turned to religion, becoming a devout Christian and finally escaping to Gaul, where he studied in the monastery under St Germain, Bishop of Auxerre. Eventually he became Bishop of Ireland and was successful at winning converts, which often brought him into conflict with the Celtic Druids. He established monasteries across the country and set up schools and churches to help convert Ireland to Christianity. The shamrock, the traditional icon of the day, stems from a tale that Patrick used the three-leafed shamrock in his sermons to represent the Father, the Son and the Holy Spirit. His mission in Ireland lasted 30 years before he retired to County Down. His death on 17 March AD 461 has been commemorated as St Patrick's Day ever since, including tonight.

When the first immigrant Irish came to London in the mid-19th century, they settled in Camden Town. They brought the St Patrick's Day tradition with them. After the famine had devastated their country, they came to London looking for work; many on the canal – they became navvies, named after the navigation canal – that cuts a jagged path right through the heart of Camden. After work finished on the canals, the navvy became synonymous with building work, the casual labour found on sites today.

Pubs like The Stag's Head became an integral part of Irish social life. It was where fellow immigrants met, fought, laughed, swapped tales, played music, picked up tips about where work could be found and often got paid. Friday evenings were a big night. Payday Friday. With a few pounds in their pocket, a navvy stood the ganger man a drink – or two, or three. Later, the pub acted as a bank for men, who didn't have a national insurance number, passport or anything to say that they existed, except for the buildings they erected. Come Monday morning, the navvy asked the ganger man for a sub, an advance to see him through the week.

I ask Dermot what the pub means to him.

'In the old days, when I first came here, the pub is where you escaped the overcrowded rooms you shared with any number of compatriots. The pub was where you could keep warm and forget what you'd become and remember what you'd left behind you. Music and these guys' – he points to the foursome in the corner bashing out a tune – 'were part of keeping those memories alive. I still come here because I like the music. The tunes are my life.'

Most of those who emigrated came from poor rural areas, mostly the west of Ireland, which had strong music traditions. As well as Paddy's night, they brought the sessions with them. The session is literally an impromptu gathering of musicians, who play tunes, sing songs and get a crowd tapping their feet. The pub is generally the favourite place to break out the instruments, but a front parlour, a wake or the street have also witnessed many sets of reels and jigs.

Dermot introduces me to a serious young man at the bar. His name is John McGinley. A librarian by day, musician by night. McGinley plays sessions in Irish pubs across north London, mostly in Camden, Kilburn and Kentish Town, but sometimes as far out as Muswell Hill. But not tonight. He's enjoying the craic. Irish pubs are where the craic is. This indefinable quality – the craic – is what makes an Irish pub. And has unmade all attempts to package and market it. London has seen more than its fair share of faux-Irish pubs with a number of chains of Irish theme pubs, complete with hay rake and flagon of Murphy's.

'They were sorry attempts to market a Disneyesque idea of the craic in the same way that McDonald's tries to sell the idea of nutrition. You've either got it or you haven't,' declares McGinley.

The Stag's Head is one of the few places that has. According to McGinley, it is an institution with the London Irish and their friends who appreciate a good pub. Dominic Behan's bitter anthem 'McAlpine's Fusiliers' captures some of the essence of this. 'The craic was good in Cricklewood/And they wouldn't leave The Crown/With glasses flying and biddies crying/Sure Paddy was going to town'.

As McGinley jokes, the crack is still good in Cricklewood, but now it comes in the form of little rocks.

McGinley is from Dublin, from the Ranelagh district. He's a thick-set young man, 27, but he's sensitive. When a couple of punters start arm wrestling at the bar, McGinley turns his back. He pitched up in London just over four years ago and lives in the East End. 'You know, most of us are Catholic and the music can get stuck in a rut – you play the same songs and tunes in the same ways over and over again. So I found it exciting to come to a place like London, where there are people from Ireland, France, eastern Europe. It's a real melting pot, if that doesn't sound too much like a cliché. And where you get a melting pot like that, you also get ideas for music.'

McGinley plays the guitar, but never in a session, and the fiddle. 'So I've incorporated a lot of the sounds that I hear on the streets into how I play. It sounds stupid, but I can hear a lot of Indian influence in my fiddle playing now, because I live quite near Brick Lane and I think hearing that music floating out of restaurants has just seeped into what I am doing.'

He's even bought some Indian records to play along to at home. 'At the risk of sounding pretentious, I was looking for another kind of tune that I could adopt and use. But it's only like a groove, a different beat. When I play my fiddle, it doesn't sound like Indian music, it sounds Irish,' he says.

McGinley also takes time out to introduce me to the main instruments that are accepted at a session. They are the fiddle; the melodeon accordion, or variations like the concertina; the uillean pipe; the flute; and sometimes the tenor banjo. Pianos were once popular as backing instruments, but are seldom used now. There's not one in the Stag.

The melodeon is a single-row instrument, which has a naturally rhythmic sound and has been absorbed into traditional music worldwide. Any two- or three-row diatonic button-key accordion ('accordion' is the generic name for the family of bellows-driven free-reed instruments with chords as well as melody notes) can be called a melodeon. The melodeon was developed from the harmonica early in the 19th century, in the border area between Saxony and Bohemia. The earliest instrument is believed to be the Aeolidicon, made by Eisenach in Hamburg in 1800. The melodeon fingering system has remained remarkably unchanged and is very similar to a harmonica on the right hand, with a different note on the push and pull of the bellows, and bass notes and chords on the left hand.

The uillean pipes are a purely Irish instrument, which date back to the beginning of the 18th century. They probably share some common ancestry with Scots lowland pipes and other bellows-blown pipes, but are played sitting down and are no louder than a fiddle or accordion. The design of the uillean pipes, with three drones and three regulators, stabilised around the start of the 19th century.

However, they nearly became extinct and were only saved by the efforts of musicologists in the United States and Ireland, who helped promote the instrument through the early part of the 19th century and up to the 1960s. They are now enjoying a revival in Ireland, but are still rare instruments.

I tell John that they look like bagpipes and earn a withering look. 'They're nothing like bagpipes. Can you see anyone wearing a kilt here?' he asks, scathingly. 'The bagpipe is all about parades, and I think was a military instrument. The uillean pipes are a social instrument. There's also a great difference to the way they are played. There is a real skill to uillean pipes, different techniques come into play. Like a guitarist, I suppose. Players don't usually learn from sheet music, but by ear, so they create their own versions of tunes, which can vary enormously.'

The tin whistle is also called a penny whistle or just plain whistle. This is an end-blown fipple flute, which utilises the six-hole, simple flute fingering system. The tin whistle is a version of an instrument that exists in various versions in other cultures, but the instrument is most identified with Irish music.

'There's a lot of seriousness about the session,' McGinley tells me. 'You could break out the wrong instrument in the wrong pub and you'd be in a whole heap of trouble. No one will take a guitar player seriously, for example. It's not seen by the purist, the traditionalist, as the real thing. You can never have a violin, either.' McGinley glances over towards the quartet. 'Ah, that's a fiddle, never a violin.'

McGinley isn't so convinced about the bodhran, the Irish drum, held in one hand and beaten with a tipper by the other. 'Ah, you know. I'm not so sure they should be playing it. It's Irish alright, but it's a bit of a joke, isn't it? I've got to hand it to the lady there, she's doing a grand job with it. That's a good rhythm she's got going.'

Master fiddlers, who were hod carriers during the week, played for fun and for drink at weekends. Eventually, Ireland lost many of its musicians and sometimes its music. During the great folk explosion of the 1960s, music scholars from Ireland visited London, New York and Boston to record some of the music before it was lost for ever.

'There's a grand album, *Paddy In The Smoke*. Get hold of that, because it is one of the records that captures the sound of London weekend pub sessions,' McGinley tells me.

'There are still lively sessions in pubs across London like this. Young Londoners with Irish parents are going to classes and workshops to learn the traditional instruments. The fiddle, the bodhran, the melodeon, the tin whistle and sometimes the uillean pipes are being mastered by young men and women who may never have been to Ireland.'

McGinley claims that the music is being passed on from generation to generation – jigs, reels, slides, polkas, and every style of traditional dance music as well as the slow airs, such as 'Carrickfergus', 'My Lagan Love', 'Danny Boy', 'She Moved Through The Fair', 'The Lark In The Clear Air' and 'The Dawning Of The Day'.

'Funnily enough, the whole *Riverdance* phenomenon has given new life to traditional Irish dancing, and I know that when they were kids the Gallagher brothers from Oasis were dispatched by their mother to learn Irish dancing,' he explains.

Some London pubs may have sunk into joyless rooms where people gather to watch endless sports in silent, slack-mouthed awe or noisy homogenous-styled casinos. But, while the Irish strive to keep their traditional music alive and boozers like The Stag's Head host it, there will be forever an Ireland in the capital.

11 King's X

King's Cross is a good location for a music video. There's lots of atmosphere, as the directors call it – cobbled streets, railway arches, narrow little passages. It's Dickensian, especially at night. I climb out of the tube. It's about 9:30pm. I'm heading for St Pancras Chambers, the Gothic red-brick facade in front of St Pancras railway station. Video director and editor Chris D'Adda of Solid Film Company is using the location to shoot a short film.

D'Adda has struck upon a stunning backdrop for his film. Formerly the 300-bedroom Midland Grand Hotel, which first opened in 1873, the interior is spectacular. Also, spectacularly derelict. However, many of the original features are intact. Victorian wallpaper and baths are salvaged for the film. The crew, wrapped up warm in their parkas, are setting up a new shot. There's a lot of waiting around, but not much talking. The actors shift about. An assistant has a quiet smoke. D'Adda whispers a few instructions to his team, and they take their places again. 'Action.'

The film is about a man with an illness. He is bleeding through a hole in his stomach. He sends away for a miracle cure on the Internet. It arrives at a price: his girlfriend has to sacrifice one of her eyes for the treatment. Cut. As the cameraman stops filming and the actors break again, I wander over to the back of the building. Beyond it, lit by powerful lights and stretching as far as I can see, is the Channel Tunnel link.

It's a massive construction site, running north, past Victorian tenements and giant Victorian gasholders, St Pancras Old Church and St Pancras Gardens. These contain the Soane Mausoleum, a memorial built by Sir John Soane in memory of his wife.

D'Adda is getting ready to set up another shot. He learned his trade in music video. He directed 'Faster' for the Manic Street Preachers. The single got to No.16 in the UK charts.

When a single is released, the record company goes into marketing overdrive. Promos or music videos are an important tool in that process. They give a pop star's best side. They present them in the best light. And videos get bands shown on TV – there is lots of opportunity for that. There are around 20 satellite music channels in the UK alone, all catering for different styles of music. MTV has over half a dozen: MTV, VH1, MTV Hits, MTV2. Dance, rock, soul. Sky has three channels. And then there are the music shows on TV. Most, like the BBC's *Top Of The Pops*, concentrate on live performance, but occasionally they show videos.

I corner Dave Knight, editor of *Promo*. *Promo* is all about the music promos – who's making them, who's in them. Knight's offices are on Blackfriars Road. We hit a café – I have tomato and basil soup, Knight gets a toasted sandwich. He gives me the short history of pop videos.

'The Beatles, you could argue, created video. They made films for a single because they didn't have time to turn up for a show. Originally, that's how they came about. They were produced so a band didn't need to turn up and tour,' he says.

That's now changed. Now videos are produced as part of the whole package. Most high-profile, proper single releases have videos,' he tells me. 'They help sell the single. And they are important because people watch MTV and many other music channels.'

Knight adds that the video can also help the record company and band. 'They are controlling the image. To show themselves in a certain way,' he says. Sometimes, especially with dance music, the band doesn't appear at all.

With the arrival of the DVD format, music video couldn't be better placed. DVD is now more important to music fans than the VHS format. 67 per cent of all visual sales were bought on DVD in 2002. Less than 40 per cent bought music on DVD in 2001. And, although the music sector is still modest – 2.7 per cent of the overall DVD and VHS market – over 3 million units were shifted in 2002. British Video Association Director General Lavinia Carey tells me that music is a big success for

DVD because it lends itself to it. 'There can be so much more information. There is all the behind-the-scenes stuff, lyrics, interviews with the band and camera angles,' she says.

With household DVD penetration reaching around 30 per cent, she also expects the product to become mass-market by the beginning of 2004. One result of this will be to widen the range of artists and titles available.

Despite this, there is a problem with music videos. Because of the state of the record market, there is pressure on promos. Sales of singles are declining so there isn't the need to make videos. Knight elaborates. 'Just now, it makes the making of videos problematic. Companies ask, "Why spend all this money on videos?" Budgets are being cut.'

He adds there is also a lot of 'desk jockeying' going on. 'There are less videos being made with full-on production, camera crew, hair and make-up. Kids now make a lot of music in their bedrooms and that is the same with videos. You know, the digital world has turned everything upside down.'

A few weeks after the shoot, I catch up with D'Adda again.

He ran an office in the same Camden building as Blur's former record label Food, directing videos for London's indie scene.

Now, when not filming, he works almost exclusively from his Hampstead home, just off Hampstead High Street, NW3.

Hampstead has a place on London's music map as a residential outpost. After success, the salubrious streets of this leafy north London borough are where the London record industry moves to spend their cash. Sting and George Michael both passed through. Pink Floyd's drummer Nick Mason still lives here in East Heath Road. Boy George, too, in a Gothic pile in Well Road. Before the Pistols became notorious, Johnny Rotten also squatted with Sid Vicious at 42a Hampstead High Street, not 100m (100yd) from D'Adda's gaff. And early in The Rolling Stones' career, Mick Jagger and Keith Richards shared a flat at 10a Holly Hill, just around the corner from the Holly Bush pub.

A little further south, at 100 West End Lane, the former site of the Moonlight Club puts Hampstead on the venue map. The Moonlight was a must-play venue in the late '70s and early '80s. Joy Division played it, just a month before the death of singer Ian Curtis in May 1980. So did The Stone Roses.

D'Adda has a beautiful modern house, tucked down a quiet side street. He has spent the last year renovating it himself. D'Adda, tall, early 30s, is good with his hands. He has built an edit suite in one of the rooms on the first floor and created a little recording studio too, on the second floor. He keeps his guitars and amps up here.

Today he is putting the finishing touches – applying lacquer – to two gigantic speakers downstairs in the living room. They stand at one end of his living room opposite an original Hammond organ and an old, rather regal, Silver Cross pram. It used to be his. He thinks he can make a few hundred selling it on eBay.

He's busy working, too. The latest project is editing down 32 hours of video for Nick Cave. It's a studio performance, and Mute, Cave's record company, wants to include it as an enhanced feature on the singer's new album.

We troop up the spiral stairs to the well-kitted edit suite. Tannoy speakers, TV monitor, latest Apple computer. On the whitewashed walls, rare framed film posters. *Convoy* with Kris Kristofferson. *Rumble Fish* with Mickey Rourke and Matt Dillon. *Dance Of The Vampires*, one of D'Adda's favourites, starring Sharon Tate and Alfie Bass. D'Abbu loads the video tape and Cave and his band, The Bad Seeds, flicker onto the screen. They're running through 'Fifteen Feet Of Pure White Snow'.

D'Adda started his career, like many video directors, as a runner. Although that nearly didn't happen. Videos are canned all the while. 'The very first job I was supposed to do was to be a runner on an Elton John video. But I got a call on Sunday night. The shoot wasn't happening,' he jokes. 'That happens a lot in the music video world. It's not unusual for a video to get pulled at the last moment.' Sometimes the record company will reduce its risk by releasing a single before filming a video. If the music stiffs, forget the promo.

D'Adda graduated to sweeping floors at studios – fetching the tea for the second assistant director, that sort of thing. Then he got a break. Pressing 'Play' and then 'Stop' on the DAT machine that bands would mime to during video shoots. Sound playback. That got him more jobs. He would call up contacts – the focus puller, clapper loader, camera operator, director of photography, lighting cameraman – on call sheets, to see if they needed help on their next shoot.

Eventually he began filming. Shooting videos for unheard-of bands for little or no money. He put himself a show reel together and sent it out. That led to work for well-known bands for quite a bit of money. Video shoots nowadays can typically cost anywhere between £5,000 ($8,000) and £100,000 ($170,000). Some big names will spend much more. Radiohead may spend £250,000 ($400,000). The most expensive video is believed to have been Michael and Janet Jackson's 'Scream'. It cost around $7 million (£4 million).

The production company will take between 15 and 20 per cent of that, with the director pocketing around 10 per cent. Normally the record company, which sets the budget, will pay half; the band or artist, the rest. The director will receive 50 per cent of his fee as an advance, and the remaining 50 per cent after delivery.

The process: a video commissioner at a record company will send out a tape of the track they want a video for. That will land on half a dozen directors' desks. Each director, usually working for competing production companies, will then listen to the track hundreds of times. Then they formulate a treatment. D'Adda digs into his desk drawer, pulls out a file marked 'Treatments' and flicks through the hundreds of neatly typed pages.

'They might just be a few paragraphs or a few sides of A4 paper,' he adds. He pulls out rejected treatments for the Manic Street Preachers' single 'A Design For Life' and Sleeper's 'Inbetweener'. D'Adda's treatments are extremely detailed: right down to where band members are standing, what they do, what they play, when the chorus comes in.

Sometimes the record label may provide a brief. Perhaps they want the film to be 'narrative-based', without the band featured in the video. Maybe they want a celebrity in it or strictly 'performance-based'. Like 'Faster'. 'Directors often reuse or recycle ideas they had on other videos because so often they have been turned down on other jobs,' he adds.

The directors submit their treatments. The record label, the band and the band's management read them. Then, crunch time.

Some treatments will fall by the wayside. And, if no treatment is a clear winner, two directors may be pitched against each other. More information and new ideas are thrown back and forth. Some directors may storyboard the script at this stage, give themselves an edge like that. This may go on for weeks, until a director prevails.

'You want to score the job, so sometimes you can be churning out two or three different treatments for one band.'

Then full production starts. A crew is rounded up and locations, usually specified in the treatment, are scouted. Then the shoot starts. Finally there's an editing process – the record company approves it or orders a few changes, and then the video is screened.

Back in King's Cross, D'Adda is reading though a page of dialogue. He has a fundamental problem with the process of music promos. He believes they have simply become commercials for bands. Bands just accept that the video is something they are required to do. The creative process is being eroded. 'A lot of bands are not really interested in videos,' he says. 'They have no idea what they want. What I can't understand is why they don't get the director and put them in touch with the band, so from the start they are working together. Because in a lot of cases the video ends up being personal to the director and not the vision of the person who wrote the song in the first place.'

I call Knight. Put D'Adda's thesis to him. Knight has another theory. That the crisis in video is a generational one. 'Music promos have been around for a generation or more. It is not a fad. And it is more and more commercial. But the creativity is suffering. Some people have been making videos for nearly 20 years. Some go off and do adverts or make feature films, but many come back. You can have a long career and make a good living from promos. There's only a finite number of videos being made, so there aren't that many people breaking into the industry. A lot of directors have been around for a generation or more, and if no one new is coming into the business, then the creativity could stagnate.'

Record companies are also less inclined to take a chance on an untried director. 'The established directors will deliver on budget and on time; no one needs to take a risk. But that's what is needed sometimes,' adds Knight.

I leave D'Adda and his crew filming. On the street outside, I look right, up the Euston Road. Next door to St Pancras Chambers is a piece of brutal architecture – the British Library, built in salmon-pink brick to match. It's closed. I turn left, down the Euston Road back towards King's Cross.

The winos are out and the hookers. I cross York Way. Two blocks north, the warehouses around Regent's Wharf have been converted into smart apartments. The snapper David Bailey has a place there. And the inventor Sir Clive Sinclair. But here, at the intersection of Euston, Gray's Inn and Pentonville roads, King's Cross doesn't look quite as salubrious. There's a couple of adult mag shops – *Asian Babes* and *Penthouse* are the speciality. There's a strip joint at the southern end of the Caledonian Road. In a pub, The Flying Scotsman, I can hear the music. Can you believe it? Madonna's 'Like A Virgin'. I duck inside – there's sawdust on the floor and a big wooden bar. The girls, who perform on a wood stage in the saloon bar, collect change in pint glasses. A good tip is 50p (85 cents).

Along Pentonville Road and at the junction with Gray's Inn Road, are endless fast-food places – quick Greek, fast pasta, fish and chips, hamburgers, hot dogs. Legend has it that this King's Cross is the site of the battle between Boudicca and the Romans in AD 60. For much of its history the King's Cross area was rural, largely unpopulated. It was also known as Battle Bridge, an ancient crossing of the Fleet River by the Gray's Inn Road.

However, in 1836, a monument to George IV was erected at the junction between Euston Road, St Pancras Road and Pentonville Road. This led to the name change – to King's Cross. By 1845, the monument had been demolished, but the name stuck.

The main feature of King's Cross is the Regent's Canal, which runs through it. The canal was built to link the Grand Junction Canal's Paddington Arm, which opened in 1801, with the Thames at Limehouse. Architect John Nash was a director of the company formed to build and operate it. It was opened in two stages, from Paddington to Camden in 1816, and the rest of the canal in 1820. It cost £772,000 ($1.3 million) – twice the original estimate.

At King's Cross, Battlebridge – one of the many basins on the canal – was built and opened in 1822. It is now the site of the London Canal

Museum and old warehouses converted for media and design companies, which began moving into the area in the early '90s.

The canal was nationalised in 1948, becoming part of the British Transport Commission. This was split in 1963 and the British Waterways Board took control. The last horse-drawn commercial traffic was carried in 1956, and by the late 1960s the canal's commercial use had ceased.

The canal is now a leisure facility. Joggers run along its towpath, up to Camden and beyond. A nature reserve opened at Camley Street in the early 1980s. And boat trips ply their trade between Camden and Little Venice (in west London), where the canal meets the Grand Junction near Paddington.

I stand near the old George IV monument. Right in front of me is the Scala. Iggy Pop played here and Mick Rock took the photographs, which appear on *Metallic KO*. The venue, formerly the King's Cross Cinema, was opened just before World War I. It was originally used to manufacture aircraft parts and then, after 1918, as a place to demob soldiers.

Finally completed, the King's Cross Cinema opened in April 1920 – it seated 1,390 people. It was bombed in the war and totally refurbished as The Gaumont in 1952. In 1962, The Gaumont became the Odeon and it stopped showing mainstream films in 1970. In February 1971, it began a short-lived project – the Cineclub – screening uncensored adult films. After just four months, the Cineclub was gone and the King's Cross Cinema was back.

However, in addition to the mainstream features, the venue also became a rock venue at weekends. Iggy Pop, Hawkwind, Gary Glitter – all played it. A local petition by local residents stopped this in 1974. A year later, the cinema closed, following a spaghetti western double bill of *The Good, The Bad And The Ugly* and *A Fistful Of Dollars*.

In 1980, a new extraordinary life began. The King's Cross cinema became a Primatarium – an audiovisual exhibition to highlight the problems facing the environment. Again, the project failed. In 1981, the cinema was taken over by the Scala Cinema Club. It had been forced to move from its original premises on Tottenham Court Road. The Scala was renamed – again. The cinema club screened independent, arthouse films: Andy Warhol all-nighters were common, Paul Morrissey's *Bad*,

Godard's *Weekend* and Alex Cox's spaghetti western *Straight To Hell*, starring Joe Strummer. All watched from a high-banking terrace of seating. It became London's best repertory theatre, but by 1993 the cinema club went into liquidation. Just before closing, it had illegally shown Stanley Kubrick's *A Clockwork Orange*. The resulting legal action was the last nail in the coffin.

The cinema closed again.

However, in March 1999 it was reopened again, this time as a night club and music venue. It's a popular spot that London labels use for their showcases – putting new bands in front of the media to see how they perform.

Underneath the Scala is a snooker club – snooker and pool. The door to the pool hall is open when I walk up Gray's Inn Road. I take a peek inside. A girl in hot pants has the black to pot. She does it. She holds her cue aloft in celebration. Her opponent, a geek in glasses, slinks away.

I ask her for directions to the Water Rats.

The pool girl looks up and points with the cue.

'Down there, mate. It's about a five-minute walk, tops.'

'Thanks.'

I head south on the Gray's Inn Road.

Oasis played their first London gig at the Water Rats. I can't miss it – a pub, pub rock. A band is already in action. The huge bow window that forms the front of the pub is covered in bills for forthcoming attractions. Kicker are on in a few weeks. Tonight it's Paleday doing a half-hour set on the pub's tiny stage. I almost fall over the bar on the way in. They're a funky two-piece, light pop, but I haven't got time to check them out.

I'm meeting Warren tonight in the Water Rats. Warren Bramley. He has a record label with his partner Tony Wilson, who put The Sex Pistols on his show, *So It Goes*, in the '70s. He also set up Factory Records, which counted Joy Division, New Order and Happy Mondays among its stable. Tony Wilson wears clothes by Comme des Garçons.

Warren doesn't wear Japanese designer gear. He is wearing a woolly hat. He's from Barnsley. Warren knows a bit about A&R. That's his job for his and Wilson's record label Red Cellars – as in the 'red cellars of pali Kao'. I'm not sure I get it, but Warren helps to explain. 'It's in tribute to Factory. It seemed right to have a reference to situationism.' I still don't get it, but I get some pints in. 'As Tony once told me, "In music you don't give up your day job," so if we think the time is right, and the band are right, then we may start releasing music. At present Red Cellars is the best label never to put out a record.'

Right.

In the meantime Wilson is back presenting on TV. Bramley is managing director of Four23Films, a production company that boasts clients including Virgin Records and Ninja Tune.

Bramley is as pessimistic about music videos as D'Adda. 'In the last few years, the majority of video commissions appear to have been about playing it safe, keeping within the one postal district when choosing production companies, keeping budgets high to guarantee a result, painting by numbers, no shock, no surprise, no controversy.

'The early videos on MTV and Max Headroom were made by people coming sideways to the industry, killing themselves to deliver, within nonexistent budgets, nothing less than a mini-feature film. They treated the music firstly as a soundtrack, striving to find cinematic moments, small jewels of imagery, some conjured up, some contrived, some by sheer fluke, all of which would go perfectly with the song.'

In the evenings, like tonight, Bramley and Wilson go hunting for the next Joy Division. It means standing in sticky bars like this. They got pretty close to signing The Music early on. However, the hotly tipped rockers plumped for Virgin before putting out the creditable debut album *The Music* in 2002.

Bramley gives me his life story over the first pint of heavy. Born in 1975, he grew up during the miners' strike. The first member of his family to pass an O level at school, he explains. 'You have three ways of getting out of Barnsley: either join the army, join a band or go to university.'

Bramley chose university, where he studied Law. 'But, I wasn't sure I wanted to be a lawyer. To quote Kedar Massenberg, chairman of Motown, he said, "I didn't do a Law degree to become a lawyer, I did a Law degree to become Clive Davis." I like that. Unfortunately, I wasn't that far-sighted.'

But he did get into music, at Wilson's label, Factory. 'I was asked to speak at a business conference recently to talk about the business-planning process we had at Factory. It was the first time I'd heard the term "business planning" and Factory in the same sentence,' jokes Warren, staring at the band strumming away. 'But during my time at Factory you were always encouraged to be creative. If you had an idea, you were encouraged to try to make it happen.'

He tells me that he likes Bill Drummond's theory. Bill Drummond from the K Foundation. 'He has this theory that if you need a good idea you just have to go down to the pub with your mates, because they'll have some stunning ideas and the thing is that not one of them will do anything about it. So steal those ideas.'

After Factory, he became general manager of In The City, the UK's annual music convention, which showcases over 500 bands, DJs and artists, over five nights, in more than 50 venues. It's been in Manchester, Dublin and Liverpool, and helped uncover the unsigned Coldplay, Stereophonics and Muse.

OK, so what about A&R? Currently, Warren and Tony can't agree on whether to sign a band. Wilson thinks they're good, Bramley has his reservations; something to do with the guitarist, the way he holds his guitar. It can be as simple as that – not the right image. 'And, most importantly, it's not what's now, it's what's next. If it works, it's obsolete or. as Woody Allen said, "If you've seen a bandwagon, you've already missed it."'

It's a feeling, then? A gut reaction to what is on stage.

Warren ponders that while he sips his pint. 'Yeah, I guess, mate.'

I wonder if finding a successful band can be as simple as that when Bramley delivers something else.

'You know what? The best A&R tip I ever got was to go to a gig, ignore the band and find the guy or girl who is dressed most uniquely.' We both look around the Water Rats. Most of the crowd is in jeans, trainers and T-shirts.

'Look for someone that really stands out from the crowd, unlike anybody else in the venue.'

No, no one like that tonight.

'And then follow them home, stalk them, because you may have just found the first signs of a new youth culture.'

Just then, as the band begins to pack up for the night, a girl with matted long hair, secondhand double-breasted suit, with the trousers snipped off at the knees, hovers into view. The bar's closed and she's off. I glance at Warren. He shrugs. The girl certainly isn't dressed like anyone else in the Water Rats, but I'm not convinced a new movement is in the offing. We don't risk it. Warren and I finish our pints and wait for her to leave.

12 Piano, Double Bass And Drums

It is raining when I hit Soho. I go down Frith Street, right on Old Compton Street, past Bar Italia, the Italian café. It's open late for a cappuccino or you can watch Juventus versus Roma on the big screen at the back. A row of red Ducatis and Harley Davidsons are lined up outside, with their owners posing next to them in leather. I slip past the bikers and their birds across the street. A neon sign above a narrow doorway advertises Ronnie Scott's club, the jazz club – the most famous jazz club in London, England, Europe and probably the world.

Chalked up on the board is tonight's big attraction, Kenny Garrett Quintet. I slip inside and it's like slipping back in time. It's cosy in here, like a '50s club with black-and-white photos of the acts who have played the club in the past. It's like a roll call of jazz legends – modern jazz, jazz fusion, Miles Davis, Ella Fitzgerald, Dizzy Gillespie, Sonny Rollins, Hugh Masekela, Roy Ayers, Diana Krall. All big names.

There's a thick velvet curtain between me and the main stage. I pay my £25 ($42) and I'm through. The place opens out into a nice little den, with low ceiling and low lights and the stage straight ahead. I'm meeting Don here. I'm not sure Don has a surname. I'm not absolutely sure Don is his real name. But I know Don plays double bass. Also, I can't miss him. Don is 6ft 1in (183cm) without a hair on his head. Born in Jamaica, he started playing bass for a reggae outfit in Kingston. Then he got older and, he says, wiser. Jazz – in particular, Miles Davis and John Coltrane – began to push King Tubby, Scientist and Lee Scratch Perry to the back of Don's record collection. I squint through the cigarette clouds drifting up from the little round tables, dressed with white linen. No Don.

There's a bar on the left. Don's not there, either.

The maitre d' appears. 'Yes, sir?'

'I'm meeting a friend,' I say, peering past him. 'I think I'm first.'

'Smoking or non-smoking?'

I'm guided to one of the smoking tables right by the bar. I notice there are two levels. My level extends in a semicircle all around the club and is elevated, by one step, above the dance floor in front of the stage. The dance floor is crowded with tables, tonight in prime position. I order a Jack Daniel's and Coke.

Ronnie Scott opened his first jazz club in a basement around the corner from here in Gerrard Street. That was in 1959. The tenor sax bought into the idea of a club after a trip to New York and jazz haunts like the Three Deuces in the late '40s. Scott got to hear the Charlie Parker Quintet with Miles Davies at the club and then skipped next door to blow his instrument with Dizzy Gillespie.

With the help of an ad in *Melody Maker* marking the opening performance by Tubby Hayes Quartet, Scott and his mate Pete King turned 39 Gerrard Street, a former taxi drivers' rest room, into jazz Mecca. At a time when the scene in London was almost nonexistent, and picking up an import by Dizzy or Charlie was the equivalent of a week's rent in a Shepherd's Bush bedsit, the club was a hit.

But not initially with American jazzmen. The Musicians' Union operated a ban on jazzers visiting from across the Atlantic. Scott and King fought the ban and won. The deal with the Musicians' Union and the American Federation of Musicians meant the Tubby Hayes Quartet played the Half Note Club in New York, and Zoot Sims was booked for a four-week residency at Ronnie Scott's.

Other American jazzmen followed: Johnny Griffin, Al Cohn, Stan Getz, Sonny Stitt, Benny Golson and Ben Webster.

By 1965 the place was jumping, and the pair moved the club to Frith Street, buying next door in 1968 and adding an upstairs room. The booking policy also widened from jazz, allowing visits from artists such as Tom Waits and Jack Bruce.

Unfortunately, Scott isn't around to watch tonight's performance. He died tragically in 1996.

I don't know much about jazz. That's why I invited Don along. He knows his stuff. I also called up the boss of Universal Classics and Jazz to give me a steer on the current health of the jazz scene. Bill Holland's company runs the Verve label. Bill looks after the Salford-raised opera singer Russell Watson, and his jazz label has stored up a fine roster, including Diana Krall, Natalie Cole, Wayne Shorter and jazz violinist Regina Carter. Bill's excited right now, because he has just signed a new 23-year-old jazz player, Jamie Cullum. 'There is something about jazz that people find scary,' says Holland. 'They find it too intimidating when there are all these improvisations.' Holland says he has watched performances at the Royal Albert Hall when people have walked out a few minutes into a song when the singer or musician begins to improvise. 'Real jazz, it's a step too far for a lot of people. They just like the simple melodies. To become mass-market, you need to sing material with a recognisable tune.'

For a record seller like Holland, there's a problem. He needs to sell jazz; to make it approachable, while keeping the purists happy. The credibility of an act will go straight out of the window if it becomes 'too sugar-coated' and his record company ends up with 'smooth pop with a touch of jazz'.

Garrett takes the stage. A hush comes over the audience. The knives and forks stop clattering. I hear a wine bottle plink against a glass.

'I'm Kenny Garrett,' announces Garret, alto sax at the ready. One, two, three, blast – he knows his chops. Garrett is an alumnus of one of Miles Davis's later groups. This sax playing is almost hypnotic, blues-tinged, careering for minutes into long, long improvisations, then snapping back into precise, rapid-firing style. It's individual and he has seemingly inexhaustible funds of invention. It's sparkling stuff.

Garrett is one of the most distinctive saxophone voices to emerge in the 1980s. Born in Detroit, he is a product of the flourishing jazz scene in the city. But he also took on board soul to gospel. Like his contemporaries Geri Allen and Regina Carter, he came under the influence of inspirational trumpeter Marcus Belgrave.

In 1978, Garrett was offered a slot in the Ellington Orchestra and just years later moved to New York to play with the Mel Lewis Orchestra and the Dannie Richmond Quintet.

Garrett released his first album, *Introducing Kenny Garrett*, in 1984 on the Criss Cross label. During the mid-1980s he was also recording with Art Blakey, Freddie Hubbard and Woody Shaw. Then, in 1986, Miles Davis called. The ensuing five-year partnership was a turning point in Kenny's life and career, and it was his work with the trumpeter that brought Garrett's work to an international audience for the first time. Kenny says Miles's genius was getting the best out of musicians – not controlling them, letting them be free. Garrett sounds free tonight.

Since parting with Davis, Garrett has collaborated with a huge number of other musicians, including former A Tribe Called Quest member, Q-Tip. 'What I'm appreciating now is some of these young hip-hop artists really trying to become better musicians. It's all about sharing.'

Garrett listens to hip-hop a lot, and Asian music. He's studied Japanese and this helps him create his musical style.

On record there's some kind of Japanese melody. It's in the music, it's sometimes hidden, but he always has that influence in there somewhere. 'We can go in any direction-free style, bebop style, whatever style,' he says. That's what Kenny Garrett's music is about, being free. And getting all those influences in there.

It's a good night so far. Garrett adds, 'My thing is I want people to be entertained. I don't play tunes just because they're on my latest CD. In live performances I kind of combine all the CDs. Sometimes people request songs that are not in the set-list, so we just play them all.' No one at Ronnie Scott's calls out for a song.

Not a bad little à la carte menu at Ronnie Scott's – nothing too fancy. Don slides into the seat next to me. He leans in close and whispers above the horn on stage.

'Hey, sorry I'm late. Someone tried to mug me.'

'What?' There's not a mark on Don. My bet is that the mugger came off worse.

'Tried to steal my watch right off my arm,' he adds, flashing his Breitling chronograph. He examines his massive right fist under the light from the table lamp. His knuckles are reddened, slightly grazed. I was right – the mugger didn't stand a chance. 'I hope that doesn't bruise up or stiffen, man.' He clenches the fist. 'But it don't look too bad.'

A waitress drifts near. Don spins around and waves his other hand as she passes. 'Miss, can we get a bottle of house champagne right over here, please? I'm thirsty.' He whips up the menu. 'Mmmnnnn-mmmnnnnn. Man, I'm hun-greeeeeee.'

I order up a fillet steak – medium rare – mushrooms and French fries, followed by New Orleans bread pudding with bourbon sauce. That'll hit the spot. Don goes for Arizona-style spicy potato wedges with sour-cream dip, vegetarian club sandwich, Greek salad and a platter of cheese and biscuits. I guess the mugging made him hungry. Veggie, too. On stage, Kenny is still leading the band into all sorts of places. I get my ear bent about Don's theory of jazz.

'You know, jazz. It ain't that different to what I was doing with my reggae sounds. It's a feeling, man. You go from one room to another and feel your way around the vibe,' says Don. 'Maybe you pick up a mellow feeling if the room's cold, slow down. Pick it up quick if you running down the stairs. Get filled up in the kitchen and you lets it blow.'

I still don't understand jazz. That's no explanation, just a feeling. Maybe I should forget the explanation, just go with it. Kenny rolls out another long improv with fast, note-spraying pieces ducking and diving over torrential piano figures and pumping chords. The percussion is pushed right to the very edge. The music is urgent and intense, then relents and we throw him a short burst of applause.

'So, I guess it was really around the early '80s, maybe earlier. I think that was the time of a big renaissance.' Don speaks slow and elongates his words for effect – 'renaissance' becomes 'ray-nay-sonce'. 'Maybe it was my man Winston. Mr Marsalis. Dude like that. The whole thing had peaked, man. Before then, everyone was blowing their horns like it was an uptown 1930s jazz joint. It wasn't worth a dime. Soul was the thing then; maybe what I was doing with my reggae thing. Jazz before that was fusion for old birds. Then in the last decade or so your vibes, man, Kenny Garrett and cats like that started doing stuff that really put the boot into jazz again. Made people sit up and take notice.'

I'm not listening now. Either you like it – and get it – or you don't. I'm beginning to hang with the Garrett tunes. I don't think I've made it in the kitchen yet.

Hamish Birchall has. He's a jazzer and looks like one, too, with scarf and glasses, black jacket, dark-grey trousers and sensible shoes. Birchall isn't a trainers sort of man and he has the skitty, forgetful, ethereal way of a musician. We fix to meet at the Jazz Café in Camden.

The Jazz Café was set up by Jon Dabner on Camden's Parkway in 1990. It became part of the Mean Fiddler organisation a couple of years later. It's not just about old jazzers, though. The Jazz Café was an early supporter of acid jazz and it has attracted a new crop of improvisers.

Alongside the live music programme, the Café has also developed a strong club culture, staging nights such as Messin' Around, Deep Funk and monthly jazz-dance session Hi Hat. As the Jazz Café celebrates its first decade, it is seen as one of the most stylish and relaxed venues in London, treading a middle path between club and performance space.

Birchall hasn't played Ronnie Scott's club or the Jazz Café. He's typical of many London musicians – jazz musicians – living hand to mouth. Birchall is a drummer. He plays in a trio – piano, double bass and Birchall on the sticks; the most popular jazz unit. His name is with several London agents. When they want someone to play, they might call him up or they might call someone else. Now 99 per cent of the work he gets is private functions: a wedding, bar mitzvah, a party.

He also does a lot of corporate work: a company is hosting a function to drum up some new business, and Birchall is drafted in to play in the boardroom, but not too loud because he can't overshadow the chairman's pitch. 'That pays reasonably well. My last gig was a commercial bank,' he says. Birchall calls playing for City boys a gig.

'They can be very enjoyable. Usually people book you because they like that sort of music. Sometimes we play in bars, but I don't like them because the bar staff have been known to put the jukebox on.'

Birchall supplements his income with a second job. He works for the Musicians' Union, based in Clapham. He is their expert on licensing reform – the government's plans to reform entertainment played in London venues, pubs, clubs, restaurants and wine bars with a new piece of legislation known as the Licensing Bill. This will affect all venues where live music is played. He isn't too happy with the way the Bill is being drafted.

Under the new proposed legislation, all licensed premises in London (and the rest of the country), of which there are around 100,000, will be required to apply for a music licence allowing them to put on bands. This will entail a one-off, lifetime fee of between £100 and £500 ($170 and $800), depending on factors such as size and location, and will enable live music to be performed on the premises. On top of that, every year an additional charge of between £100 and £150 ($170 and $250) will be applied, which covers inspections by local authorities.

Birchall fears that some licencees will not apply for music licences and will be discouraged from putting on entertainment because they fear licensing authorities will impose unnecessary and costly conditions to their licences, such as requesting expensive adjustments to venues. Small folk groups could wither and jazz trios will not be welcome in the local boozer if it hasn't an entertainment licence.

He and many other musicians are also critical that the Bill appears to penalise live music specifically. They question why a live music licence is needed at many bars and clubs that have TV screens attracting large, noisy crowds. A licence isn't required for screening a England versus Germany football match. Birchall believes the real problem is that it is a Bill primarily about licensing, 'and that has an uncomfortable relationship with music'. He is also pessimistic about music minister Kim Howells' confidence in local authorities. He says, 'Our experience of local authorities is that they routinely enforce the letter of the law. Any loopholes will be a gift to some jobsworth.'

The Bill will also effect Birchall's livelihood. At the moment, he and a mate can set up in any London pub. It need not have an entertainment licence. This is the two-in-a-bar rule. Two musicians of any kind are allowed to play – singer and guitarist, pianist and vocalist, drummer and bass. Any two musicians, but not three. Even if someone drinking at the bar joins in, the council can shut the boozer down. Birchall's trio couldn't play. The two-in-the-bar is an exception under the current law.

Live music supporters have been attempting to push through amendments to the Bill. They want to exclude music played in churches, hospitals, prisons or museums. Also, they do not think a licence is necessary if the music is acoustic, semi-amplified or 'incidental', such as a piano player in a hotel foyer.

Birchall is also pushing for venues with a capacity of around 200 people to be exempt if the music event finishes before 11:30pm. It will be a major feather in his cap, and a huge boon for live music, if he can get the government to swallow that. He's got support in high places, including from his boss at the Musicians' Union, John Smith, who says, 'There is already a plethora of laws and regulations that control the playing of live music, including fire, health and safety laws. Without an appropriate exemption for small events, this Bill will be a severe deterrent to grassroots music performance.'

Simply Red's Mick Hucknall also believes the government should exempt small venues from the music licensing regime. 'No musician wants to compromise fans' safety, or the public at large,' he says. 'But their interests should be fully protected by health and safety laws. Musicians rely on these small venues to kick-start their careers. They can ill afford additional unnecessary bureaucracy.'

Birchall is also relying on Tory shadow Culture Minister Baroness Buscombe in the House of Lords to push the government on this.

They have had some success. Amendments made to the Bill opted out churches, schools and colleges from a requirement to have a licence to perform music. The government is also adding a further amendment to the Bill to make it clear that entertainers who unwittingly play in unlicensed premises will not be committing an offence. Previously, regardless of whether they had a role in organising the entertainment themselves, singers or musicians could have been fined if the premises were unlicensed. Kelly Wiffen, research and parliamentary officer at Equity, says the group welcomes this move after listening to 'our concerns'.

Birchall has also managed to persuade Howells and the government to allow incidental playing of music without having to apply for an entertainment licence, like a jazz trio in a hotel lobby. There has also been some concession on unamplified music.

The two-in-a-bar is not all that has altered in London. Things have changed on the jazz scene in the capital since Birchall moved down from Oxford two decades ago. Birchall, 45, has always had a passion for drums. He bought his first kit when he was a teenager. He'd saved some cash from working at an airport catering company.

'The jazz I was listening to then. Well, it was Kenny Clark, Art Blakey, Buddy Rich. I like some pop, stuff like T Rex, but somehow it just didn't grab me like jazz. You know, you're just drawn to something, something grabs you. That's what the drums were for me,' he adds.

Birchall screwed up his exams and worked as a pizza chef in Oxford. He worked in a car plant for a year, worked in a ironworks, did a bit of gardening. But he continued to play drums. He laughs. 'I think I was probably the middle-class equivalent of the New Orleans jazz guys who were roofers or something and played the bars in the evening.' Not as romantic in Oxford.

Then he got work in a country and western band. 'You have to be flexible' doing two or three gigs each week. One job took him to France, Belgium and Denmark. He was drumming for a show, *Holiday On Ice* – Birchall did a big drum roll when a performing dog jumped through a hoop; rolls and crashes when a juggler did a big trick. 'That was a strange percussive journey,' grins Birchall, through gritted teeth. 'A great adventure.'

Then he tipped up in London. A straight job here, drumming in bands there. He worked on the *Observer*, then a band looked like it would work out. But it didn't. 'When I came to London in 1983, I found myself playing a lot of straight-ahead jazz, trad jazz from the '20s and '30s. We played a few restaurants. Bertorelli's near Rathbone Place. The Barbican, Royal Festival Hall foyer. Then we got a gig at Smollensky's on the Strand, playing every night of the week,' he says.

Then work started drying up. People didn't want to hear jazz so much – not in restaurants, anyway. The '80s became about design and minimalism and that didn't fit with a bunch of jazzers whacking out a tune over the penne. Better for a sophisticated restaurant to serve up some sparse Japanese chime music to go with their tiny portions. 'That's been the pattern since – part-time work gigging, hustling for everything, a lucrative gig here, nothing the next week,' he says.

Jazz trios also take up room. That's fewer tables for paying customers. Far easier to have a multi-disc CD player under the bar. Throw in a few jazz classics and no one will know the difference. And the CD is played by Miles Davis, who is surely better than the musicians hired in for £50 ($85) a player each night? That's also £150 ($250) each night the restaurant has to find. Over a grand ($1,700) a week. That's a lot of overheads for a struggling restaurant or bar with competition springing up all over. The jazz band is going to get the axe before the bar staff or waitresses.

'The problem with jazz is that it is not theatrical like pop. You can go to Ronnie's on an average night, there's a lot of tables that are not focusing on the gig. It's good at atmosphere if there is a nice warm, informal setting.'

Also, quite simply, jazz went out of fashion. 'It's incredibly hard to earn a living here. Incredibly tough. A lot of jazzers rely on teaching to make ends meet,' explains Birchall. And, unfortunately for Birchall and a lot of jazz-heads like him, it hasn't come back. It's not in vogue – not in London, anyway. Meantime, Birchall is still on the government's case about the Licensing Bill.

13 Groovy Government

The London music business gets into bed with a lot of partners: TV, radio, fashion. But, its strangest bedfellow is the UK government.

In the last few years the industry has developed a close working relationship with ministers and their departments.

It works both ways. Politicians get a bit of gloss. When Cool Britannia ruled in the late '90s, Prime Minister Tony Blair invited some fun people for champagne at Downing Street. Oasis's Noel Gallagher and the band's label boss at Creation, Alan McGee, were among them. In return, the music business gets a government minister on side. The government can get things done. It can help sell music abroad. It can help stop the pirates.

But there is sometimes tension at the heart of the relationship. The music business can stand on its own two feet. It is wildly successful. The music industry is one the UK's biggest and most culturally significant creative industries. Composers, producers, managers, music publishers, artists, concert promoters, record companies and online music entrepreneurs combine to produce a dynamic, vibrant industry. It is the third largest market in the world for sales of music and second only to the US as a source of repertoire. It is estimated that Britain may account for as much as 15 per cent of the global music market. It doesn't need grants. Unlike other industries, it doesn't need subsidies. So it doesn't like being told what to do. But it does occasionally need government help.

The government minister with responsibility for the recording industry is DCMS (Department of Culture, Media and Sport) parliamentary undersecretary Kim Howells – music minister, for short. I call up his office to fix an appointment. But, before visiting the DCMS offices off Trafalgar Square, I want to examine the issues. I arrange to meet Stephen Navin in Hampton's Wine Bar on Whitcomb Street near Leicester Square. It has little square tables, bistro chairs and a good wine list.

Navin – that's what he calls himself on his answerfone message: 'Navin here...' – is the music industry's man on the inside at the DCMS, the conduit between the London labels, trade bodies and the corridors of power.

Or, as Navin explains, 'My formal role is music industry adviser to the DCMS. I'm attached to a part of government. The music industry, being so large, obviously is dealt with by a lot of government. With the government, I ask, "Are we doing enough? Can we do more? Where does the government begin and end?"

'Particularly at the moment, there are a lot of issues hitting the statute book. I've always described my job as a sort of a bridge between what I thought were two states on either side of the river. On one side of the river I thought you had the government, and on the other side I thought you had the music industry. It isn't as simple as that. We know the music industry is made up of a huge number of differing groups – sometimes they work together, sometimes they have differences which separate them, whether it's publishers, labels, performers, managers, retailers. The government has great difficulty dealing with such a disparate organisation. It prefers something simpler to deal with.'

That's Navin. He knows what's going on. But, he has frustrations, too. 'I've no idea how long I'll be doing this job for. They've got me on a couple of months' notice. Nothing comes to pass very quickly. No one reports to me and I can't make decisions. I can make suggestions. The industry needs to link up a lot more. I'm only valuable at the DCMS because I'm pushing out a different message from the institution. The fun of this job is, don't be sucked into this, don't become a civil servant. You need to have balance.'

Most agree that Navin is the best qualified for the job. A smooth operator, he's been around the London music business a long time.

Navin is 52 – in his own words, an 'old fart'. His father was Irish, his mother from the northeast of England. He was educated at Trinity College, Dublin, where he studied French and Spanish. He likes French music, holds an Irish passport, feels 'more British than Irish', but would support Ireland in a rugby match, has a house in Shepherd's Bush, a place in Wallingford near Oxford, and still runs a home in the west of Ireland.

He was at college at the same time as Chris de Burgh and the fifth member of U2, manager Paul McGuinness. He was at Virgin in the very early days and says he tried to sign U2. He worked closely with Richard Branson. Branson brought him back to work at his record label V2 when Navin left his post at BMG. He takes a philosophical view to most things. 'I hop around. There is a lot to do with this job, and it's exciting. The fun is getting hold of people and shaking them around a bit.'

There is a historical reason for Navin's office in the DCMS. In 1997, when the Labour government came to power, the (then) culture secretary Chris Smith believed he didn't know enough about music. 'Music was an industry he felt the government didn't really know much about. It was an extremely important industry – economically, culturally and educationally – and I think he was messianic in his approach.' But, there are dangers. 'The industry has always resisted government involvement because government and creativity don't go hand in hand,' Navin tells me.

We catch a couple of large glasses of Chardonnay.

Navin elaborates: 'This [the UK recording industry] is important for this country and it could become a lot more important and we can help ourselves become a richer government by fostering this industry. Before, I think the industry was nervous of government. We wanted free trade, not too much interference. Yes, government is civil servants and the essence of government is regulation. It doesn't necessarily mean constructive support. In France the [music] industry welcomes government support. Perhaps because it's not doing very well and needs support. I think the British government said, "This industry can take care of itself. Let's give them copyright support, but not overdo it." So there's been a mutual mistrust and a mutual respect. Each party getting on with what it does. Now the government believes music is very important to the economy as traditional manufacturing slides towards oblivion. The government has an obligation to support those industries that do sustain jobs, wealth, tax, VAT generation and education. What they've done is still to be mapped out and be worked upon. But the enthusiasm is there. The enthusiasm is even more real because it's driven out of self-interest.'

Navin adjusts his glasses and we call for a couple more drinks. Belgian beer is on the menu – two Chimays.

'So many issues affect the industry as whole,' Navin tells me. 'And there are a lot of issues we agree on. But it moves slowly.' To help speed things along, Navin is examining the possibility of setting up a think-tank. 'My problem with government is it is not connected up. Number 10 [Downing Street] could do that. They can say to civil servants, "Get the dream team to identify the issues and find a way for the right government department to be involved,"' he adds.

A group called the MIF (Music Industry Forum), set up in 1997 and comprising experts from all areas of the music business, has met with the DCMS. They have identified four strategic areas where the government, specifically Howells and his department, can help. One of them is exploiting the opportunities afforded by new technologies; simply the sale and distribution of music online. It is predicted that worldwide sales of music in this form could reach around $4 billion (£2.5 billion) by 2004. This presents significant new opportunities. It also presents threats – namely, piracy.

The government can help. 'Piracy is a complex one for the government to deal with,' says Navin. 'There's commercial piracy, which is relatively easy to understand. But then we have file-sharing, which is difficult for the government to deal with at some level. There is a whole piracy spectrum. At one end you have pirate behaviour, thievery, connections with organised crime. So you think that's bad, people are being ripped off. Then you edge across through CD burning. Then across the spectrum to digital piracy – where should downloading fit in with the laws? What do we know about that? The government has not done research into that. Music and technology – where does it meet up? What role does the government need to play to give value to copyright? If copyright means anything, it should be treated with respect. It's the heart and minds argument – can the government be involved in creating an environment in which you deliver to the customers what they want? At the moment they want free music. Will a 15-year-old ever pay if he's getting it free? There's a lot of education that needs to be done, a lot of PR needs to be done.'

Navin also believes that laws do not work in cyberspace, nor record companies trying to control websites by investing in them and trying to control them vertically. 'You can't constantly have laws that say "No". You want to find ways of saying "Yes", and the government should be at the epicentre. We want to have best practice across the Internet environment in terms of education and training. I think that's where we have to push the industry.'

The government also has a role promoting music abroad. The UK's performance at increasing exports and exploiting world markets is good: the UK has an estimated world market share of around 10–15 per cent, second only to the US. The market share in Europe is thought to be as high as 30 per cent. Developing markets in Asia, Latin America, India and eastern Europe will be important sources of demand in the future. The DCMS is currently exploring how it can best maximise music's export earnings, particularly in relation to the US.

As we sit supping Belgian beer, support for a New York-based UKMO (UK Music Office) appears to be gathering momentum within government circles. The idea is to have someone in New York permanently batting for singles and albums being made in London to help break artists in the US.

There is definitely a problem. Over the past few years there has been a worrying decline in the hit rates of UK acts in the territory that accounts for around 40 per cent of the world's music sales. In some weeks in 2002, there were no British acts in the *Billboard* Top 100 singles chart – the first time that has happened since 1963. Of the 40 top-selling US albums in 2002, none came from London.

Navin realises the problem. 'The whole radio situation in North America is obviously a barrier to those who can't afford to pay for it. The complexity and immensity of doing business in North America, sadly, is a problem. How do you move up the ladder? You've got to be radio-friendly – getting your music spread across the country is very difficult'.

There is behind-the-scenes lobbying to get the UKMO off the ground. Various government offices are being pressed to support it. But the process has been slow. It's about money and who will run it. 'One thing about the civil service is that it's impeccably honest and it's one of Britain's great assets. Therefore, the desire or non-desire to spend money is extraordinary. Hesitancy is profligate. There is an opportunity here and it doesn't involve a huge cost, bearing in mind the industry and the government are partners in it. It's like all investment: you have to be prepared to lose it. We need someone to run it who can attract talent and become a conduit, and if it fails we will have lost only a few hundred thousand pounds.'

Navin believes the government and Howells are in favour of UKMO, but that the project needs a good business plan. 'At the moment there's no business plan that has been approved by anybody. From my perspective, I could write you a business plan on this card and it would probably be as valid as a 50-page document I could spend tens of thousands of dollars preparing. At the end of the day it's all about the person who runs it, because you've got to have a piece of luck and be prepared to lose some money. We need to find the right person. In that marketplace in NYC, that person could become a magnet and a transmitter.'

Further progress on UKMO was made after I hooked up with Navin. Howells met Baroness Symons, the Minister for Trade and Investment, at the Foreign and Commonwealth Office. They discussed the level of funding the government can give the project, expected to cost around £350,000 ($600,000).

The DCMS parliamentary undersecretary asked Symons to look at opening government purse strings to help fund the UKMO, which would then trigger commitments promised from other music industry groups. Another potentially crucial element for funding is the level of assistance offered by the Brussels-based EMO (European Music Office), which helped Sweden, Norway and France establish music outposts in the US in 2001. The European Union 2003 draft budget set aside 2 million euros (£1.4 million/$2.3 million) to finance 'pilot projects' and the UKMO would be eligible for some part of that. An EMO spokeswoman says the share allocated to music is still unknown, but confirms it is helping to lobby for UKMO funding from the EU.

This activity prompted AIM (Association of Independent Music) CEO Alison Wenham, a vociferous campaigner for UKMO, to tell me that 'a lot is contingent on the government, but I would be bitterly disappointed if we haven't made a strong case.'

Then Howells and Symons penned a joint letter to the UKMO sponsors – the BPI and AIM – suggesting the music industry should nominate a representative who could initially take a six month placement in the government's diplomatic office in New York. The move would give the music chief an opportunity to assess the market and time to draw up a proper business plan for the UKMO.

The MIF has also identified a role for the government in helping to improve creativity, enabling songwriters, composers, performers, managers and record companies to continue to tap into the capital's cosmopolitan culture, the vibrancy of the live music scene and to discover and invest heavily in new talent.

The future of the music industry depends on new talent, but how talent is discovered and developed could have much to do with the way new government legislation is framed. Currently three important pieces of legislation are occupying Navin, which could impact on creativity and the diversity of music available in London: the Copyright Directive, the Communications Bill and the Licensing Bill. The latter two – in draft form – are being batted back and forth between the House of Lords and the House of Commons.

He says, 'Those are what I take back over the bridge when I turn to the government. I pick up the input of the industry and pass that back to government. And when I look to the other side of the river I see different states. There is one leader, Tony Blair, but within the Italianate principalities there are different interests – the DTI [Department of Trade and Industry], the DCMS, the Treasury, the cabinet office itself.'

The Communications Bill will impact on the diversity of music offered by radio stations in the capital. Unless the government introduces safeguards to ensure that commercial radio owners broadcast a wide choice of music in their programming policies, conceivably radio broadcasters could pipe a diet of bland pop 24/7. Both listeners and the music industry would be poorer.

Another pan-music industry group called the MBF (Music Business Forum), which counts the BPI, AIM and managers' organisation the IMMF among its members, is currently lobbying the government to make amendments to the draft Bill to ensure that radio licences won on the promise of broadcasting folk music or country music are adhered to and that there will be a diversity of music available to Londoners.

Navin says, 'I've been involved with the Communications Bill. From the point of view of the industry, it is vast piece of information across the whole spectrum of broadcasting. Musical content is critical, particularly in local radio.'

However, in the first salvo of an increasingly concerted campaign to safeguard diversity of music on radio, musicians – including DJ Paul Oakenfold and Mr Scruff – claim the Communications Bill will produce blander programming. They quote a NOP poll which found some 72 per cent of people would support measures to encourage local radio stations to cover local music.

Frances Lowe, Director General of British Music Rights, which promotes music interests at government level, also says there is concern that no mechanism to safeguard diversity of music on radio exists if licences are renewed. She says, 'If there is any further consolidation of radio, there should be safeguards to ensure radio does not become bland.' She adds that the concerns extend to public service broadcasting. The organisation is briefing other politicians to debate the issue in Parliament in a bid to get the equivalent safeguards the government is providing for the TV industry applied also to music.

Lowe adds, 'We want to see that if there is a change of ownership, there will still be a commitment to programme new original music.'

Navin, who has signed the Official Secrets Act, offers an insight into how legislation is dealt with at the DCMS. 'There are not many places to have meetings, so I go to the canteen, which is near the entrance to the smoking room, and many conversations are sparked off there. The Licensing Bill team are good smokers, the Communications Bill team are not such good smokers. I tend to seek out special advisers linked to the ministers. I'll go to the second floor, where the ministers are.'

The Licensing Bill is also a complex piece of legislation, which has far-reaching consequences for the music industry and musicians based in London. Navin explains, 'The Licensing Bill is an area where the government and the music industry can work together to deliver something we're in favour of.'

But, already the draft Bill is attracting flak from Birchall and others. 'With licensing, the government has so far had a difficult war with this Bill. It has possibly not thought it through, but it's thinking it through a lot more now. We've spent a lot more time thinking, "What are we trying to achieve?" We've always been trying to achieve an environment where local pubs and clubs and places of entertainment should be encouraged to have live music. One of the things we have to make clear, one purpose of the Bill, is to stimulate interest in music. For venues, we want to make it easier for them to get a licence to put on live music.'

Navin will also sit on a committee to draw up guidance notes on how the Bill should be adopted by local government when it is passed. 'If the Licensing Bill goes through with improvements, I'm going to sit with a team of people, looking at the guidance notes to be given to local authorities, and from my perspective I would like it made clear that the purpose of this Bill is to promote live music and entertainment and people should not be frightened. There are a lot of good things about the Bill. There's a balance. The balance with the Licensing Bill would be one in favour of live music and also to benefit those working in it... Everyone should understand the importance of live music. I think live music could be great for tourism. Think what it can do for publicans. We should be proud of our musical heritage.'

That's the government and music industry working together. It isn't all plain sailing, and as I negotiate an appointment with Howells there is another flash point. The squares in government do their best to shoot themselves in the foot.

The furore starts when Home Secretary David Blunkett describes some rap and garage lyrics as 'appalling'. He told a BBC Radio Two show he believes there is a link between what producers behind rap and garage music sell in shops and violence on the streets. He said, 'We need to talk to record producers, distributors and those who are actually engaged in the music business about what is and isn't acceptable.'

The debate was ramped up by the music minister. Howells suggested on a BBC Radio Four programme that rappers are glorifying gun culture and were partly to blame for the deaths of two teenagers, Charlene Ellis and Letisha Shakespeare, who died in a Birmingham drive-by shooting. Howells singled out south London's So Solid Crew, describing the act as 'idiots' who glorify gun culture and violence.

The ministers' views go down like a lead balloon in London's black music community. Urban labels, promoters and PRs condemn Howell's suggestion that lyrics are helping to promote violence. The BMC (Black Music Congress) suggests there is no evidence to prove a link between rap lyrics and violence. 'If you are a grounded person, then when you hear Eminem talk about killing, not everyone will imitate him,' says BMC founder Kwaku. However, Kwaku accepts that at present it is 'hip to be hard' and he suggests that many acts use more profanity in their lyrics than they would in real life to up the ante and help sell more records. 'We need to create environments where record companies are open to artists who say more than just guns,' he adds, accusing many labels and radio stations of simply promoting the more commercial – and often US-derived – gangsta rap.

Some in the black community also believe the music business should have a responsibility to encourage alternative acts to gangsta rap, help promote more positive lyrics and also assist inner-city communities. In Brixton, I speak to Charlie Parker, founder of Fas Fwd. He believes the major record companies have a responsibility to put more money and support back into the communities where urban records derive, to give lyricists the skills to turn the negative images they see into more positive messages. 'We need to put some learning on the streets,' he adds.

Privately, the BPI chairman Peter Jamieson is also annoyed. Blunkett and Howells aren't being helpful. Music is now getting the blame for social ills. The BPI is offering to meet the Home Secretary to address the issue of gun references in lyrics. Jamieson tells me, 'The government wish to meet, we have to step up to the plate. We are bound to help in any way at all.' However, Jamieson stresses that it might be more useful for the government to tackle the root causes of crime, suggesting that the negligible increase in hip-hop and rap album sales in the UK between 2001 and 2002 (from 4.2 per cent to 4.4 per cent) cannot account for the 35 per cent rise in gun crime in the last 12 months. 'I would suggest the availability of firearms is more relevant,' he adds.

He has penned a letter to Blunkett, which contains a sting in its tail. It says, 'It might be wiser to regard some of these songs as news bulletins from the streets. They tend to reflect a problem rather than create it. Various social issues and the sheer availability of guns would appear to be more appropriate targets than singling out the recorded music industry as a convenient scapegoat.'

Navin also sees the folly in the government's stance. 'We're all agreed that music is powerful. It has the ability to move people to good or evil. It has an extraordinary effect on people. And so it should. Kim Howells and the guns thing... The great thing about Kim is that he shoots from the hip. It's a very easy debate to lose. You start talking about censorship and the government is on a hiding to nothing.'

However, Blunkett's agenda changes. Criticism of rap lyrics gives way to asylum seekers. He leaves the music industry scratching its head after offering no proposals for moving the guns-in-music debate forward. No summit is being mooted. A spokeswoman for the Home Secretary says, 'There is absolutely no indication that [there will be a meeting with] the rap music industry or other musicians.' Probably more disappointing for the music industry is a lack of communication from the DCMS or Howells.

After my briefing with Navin, I have a long list of questions for Howells – guns and rap, for one. Then I am thrown a curve ball. Just as I nail down a meet with the music minister, his office tells me he will not answer questions about hip-hop lyrics. No guns and rap. Howells doesn't want to discuss it. He won't talk about anything else, either. No Communications Bill, no UK music office. However, he will discuss one issue. At least it is a big one. The really juicy bit of legislation, which is getting under the skin of Birchall and the live music community – the Licensing Bill.

The DCMS offices are at 2–4 Cockspur Street, just north of the heart of government in Whitehall. I'm given a identity badge and wait on a black leather sofa in the lobby with marble floors, big columns. Ten minutes later, I'm on the second floor, ushered into a large office with an oatmeal carpet, yucca plant and downlighters. Howells has his suit jacket off, white shirt, red tie. He sits on a green couch opposite me, under a picture of Stonehenge. His press officer and five advisers take up positions around him, all sitting in comfy armchairs. Sandwiches, coffee, water and orange juice are on offer. Howells bites into a sandwich. He is hungry.

Initially, he is also defensive. His department is sponsoring both the Communications Bill and the Licensing Bill. It's hard work. And now he is being stung by criticism that he hasn't taken advice from musicians or the Musicians' Union on licensing.

Birchall and the Musicians' Union are well-known to Howells. They have had their spats. Howells has accused the Musicians' Union of being pedantic, adding that 'it thinks a postman whistling will need a licence'. He also denies they aren't being consulted. 'The Musicians' Union has sat around that table,' he says, pointing to the round wooden table laden with our lunchtime snacks. 'I'm open to meet anyone.'

However, Howells accepts that music venues are not trouble spots. 'Most problems and violence are not associated with music venues,' he says. They are associated with areas where there is no mix of venue because the clientele feels intimidated by 100,000 18- to 24-year-olds who get plastered. The parts of the city with least problems are where the music venues are.'

But he says they still need to be licensed. However, he is keen to assure me London musicians and venue owners will not be penalised when the new legislation is brought in. Already his office has published a leaflet to 'set the record straight on some of the most pervasive myths being circulated about the Bill'. An aide passes me the list. Among those 20 myths singled out are:

- spontaneously singing 'Happy Birthday' will NOT be illegal;
- spontaneous pub singalongs will NOT be licensable;
- carol singers, going from door to door, or turning up unannounced in a pub and singing, will NOT be licensable;
- a postman whistling on his round will NOT be licensable.

Howells says there was a need for it because of the untruths being perpetrated. 'I am very interested that the guidance that goes out to people ensures them music venues are not jeopardise3d. There will be adequate protection for performers. People were coming up to me and saying, "Does this stop me from singing 'Happy Birthday' to my grandmother in a restaurant?"' says Howells, shaking his head and taking another bite of his sandwich.

Under the previous law, a pub could also skip a music licence if only two musicians performed at one time – the so-called two-in-a-bar rule. There has been a lot of misinformation about whether that will continue. Howells nails that for me. 'If there are two singers in a bar at the moment, [they can] continue with that arrangement. I want to ensure the Bill is enforced with a heavy dose of common sense on the ground. I hope the music world, local authorities and the industry will take the opportunity to help shape the guidance and make sure this happens.'

Howells also deflects concerns that venues will have to suddenly make expensive alterations to comply with the Bill. He adds that venues will still be subject to health and safety and the new Bill will add no additional costs. 'We've just seen two appalling accidents in the United States [where concert goers were killed], and I am not going to be the minister who is responsible for allowing that to happen here. Not for one person, let alone 100-odd who died, or whatever,' he says.

More importantly, Howells believes the new Bill will save venue operators nearly £2 billion ($3.3 billion) over the next decade, which can then be pumped back into promoting more music in London and the rest of the country. 'What we have been able to do is look at the costs and we believe it will reduce the costs very substantially. Costs to the venue, cost of obtaining the licences, and so on. That is a big saving. We arrived at £1.9 billion [$3.2 billion] over a period of ten years and I think in the end that is the most important thing of all. I'd like to see us go beyond that.' He adds, 'We want to try to encourage local authorities to treat music well and hope they see the importance of music and creative expression, and that it shouldn't be seen as a burden or something they've got to put up with, but ought to be seen as a way of developing the economy.'

Howells also offers an olive branch to his critics by saying he wants musicians to help Navin provide guidance to licensing authorities when they enforce the Licensing Bill. 'We are absolutely determined that local authorities are not going to take advantage. We've thought long and hard about this...which is to say "try and understand the creative industries are phenomenally important right across the country".'

Warming to his theme, Howells says, 'We want live music to flourish in this country. That's our endgame. The Bill has been drawn up to deliver it. We must make sure the new licensing system is delivered with common sense on the ground. The music world has a key role to play in making this happen. We have produced a flexible Bill, which I believe strikes the right balance between freedoms and protections. I am confident we can go on from here to produce supporting guidance that realises this aim.'

After about an hour, I am escorted from the room and parked on the busy road outside Trafalgar Square. I call Birchall. There have already been some developments. The House of Commons slung back the Lords' recommendation that venues with fewer than 200 people should be exempt from the Bill. Now the Lords has failed to keep the ball in the air. It looks like the Bill will become law, with only the concessions already won by Birchall and his supporters. 'Yes, I'm disappointed,' says the jazz drummer. 'But we've achieved quite a few victories and the job is now to ensure that we have a say in how the guidance notes are drawn up, so that local authorities don't crack down hard on live venues.'

However, there has been success from the MBF. In the same week, the House of Commons made amendments to the Communications Bill to ensure that the concerns from the music business over diversity of music on radio are met. Radio will still play jazz. Birchall has got to dash. He's got two gigs this weekend.

14 Electric Avenue

'Want some weed, man?'

Now I know I'm in Brixton. It's like a mantra. I come up out of the underground on Brixton Road and the dealers pounce.

'Want some ganja? Skunk? Weed?'

'Not tonight, brother.'

I turn left towards Electric Avenue so named because it was the first street in the area to get electricity. A century later, Eddy Grant wrote a song about it.

Here's a gypsy and she wants to tell my fortune, let me know what the future holds. I know it – a drink and The White Stripes at the Brixton Academy down the road.

I find the pub. There's no sign, but I can hear some reggae coming from the back room. Inside, it's dark, very dark. There's a candle, actually hundreds of them. Imported Guinness in bottles is the only drink on offer. There are crates of the stuff holding up a makeshift bar. I order up the stout. A half-pint glass comes with it, but the barman, a black man missing his two front teeth, doesn't pour.

'Two pounds [$3.30].'

I absently pick at the label on the bottle. I notice the sell-by date passed by half a year ago. I don't tell the barman. It's not a fight I'm going to win.

John Peel had a fight a few weeks back. John Peel, the DJ, was in the middle of a fight when I called him. Not fisticuffs, nothing like that. Peel was sitting at his home in Suffolk – Peel Acres, as he calls it –

talking on the phone. 'They told me I couldn't play the single,' he explains. He was talking about *Elephant* by The White Stripes. 'They sent me the record and when I started playing tracks they told me to stop. It was embargoed. So I'm not playing it at all.'

By 'they', Peel meant the band's record company and the team of lawyers, accountants and PRs employed to ensure the new album from the Detroit band gets maximum marketing and play-list impact. Peel felt he'd been slighted and wouldn't play the album or tracks from it, including the soon-to-be-released single 'Seven Nation Army'.

'I don't take any notice of what the BBC management tells me to do, so I'm not going to do what they tell me. I'm sending the record back to the accountants,' he told me. I got the impression that refusing to play records is about as near to fighting as it gets in the radio business.

But then it wouldn't have been a smart move alienating the 63-year-old veteran DJ. Some think the Radio One stalwart is the most influential DJ at championing new music in the UK today. He was one of the first DJs in London to champion Jack and Meg White of The White Stripes before they broke big.

And Peel's got a good track record at discovering bands. Maybe not discovering them, but at least playing the records no other DJ will touch until they've achieved platinum sales and the greatest-hits album is available in . When his colleagues on Radio One were playing hoary old chestnuts from the Electric Light Orchestra and Genesis in 1976, he invited punk group The Damned in to record a session. Most groups have recorded sessions for Peel when they were at the top of their game or on the cusp of breaking big time: Joy Division, The Fall, Syd Barrett, Pulp.

There used to be little joshing and banter when his radio colleagues ended their programmes and handed over the microphone to Peel. He tells a story of once waiting in the Radio One car park with the intention of beating up a fellow DJ. He lost his nerve.

'So how do you want to do this?' he asked me on the phone.

'I don't know,' I replied. 'Maybe I can pop into the office, watch you do the show.'

He suddenly brightens. 'Come to a session. We've got a bit of scene happening up in Bury St Edmunds and these two bands are playing Wednesday – Dawn Parade and The Exiles.'

'Sure.'

But, first Jack and Meg. They're playing two sold-out nights at the Academy, another McKenzie venue, one of Northcote's places. I finish the beer and get back onto Brixton Road, under the railway bridge and head towards the gig.

Brixton suffered two major riots in the last two decades and remains bedevilled with drug problems. It's always had a colourful, but edgy character. However, in the last few years the borough has sucked in long-overdue investment, which has seen a slew of swanky bars and restaurants open and help transform the area.

Tensions between the police and local community have also eased dramatically since 1981, when the Metropolitan Police's heavy-handed stop and search (so called 'sus') campaign, Operation Swamp 81, was in full swing. The result: lots of innocent black kids hassled by the cops, frustration, mistrust, violence, a major riot on Railton Road.

The Romans built the Brixtonians their own road, the road I'm walking on, Brixton Road. But in the 11th century the area was called Brixistane, literally 'the stone of Brihtsige', a mound of stones used as meeting points for the local community.

Largely, Brixton, as it eventually became known, remained agricultural and totally undeveloped until the Industrial Revolution in the 19th century. The first development started after 1816 following the construction of Vauxhall Bridge, the nearest crossing point over the Thames.

Some of the oldest buildings in Brixton are on Acre Lane, leading to Clapham west of here. St Matthew's Church was built in 1812 and the Trinity Almshouses in 1822, which preceded a massive transformation of Brixton between the 1860s and 1890s, when railways and trams linked Brixton with the centre of London.

Electric Avenue got its name in 1880 and the middle classes moved into the large three- and four-storey houses built along

Brixton Road. However, by the early 1900s the homes were broken up into boarding houses and the white collars were supplanted by blue-collar families, many working on the markets in the area – or in theatres in the West End.

Between 1910 and 1915, at least nine cinemas opened in Brixton, including the Palladium, which in the '80s became The Fridge night club. Some were situated in railway arches and later closed on safety grounds; however, the Ritzy on Brixton Hill survives.

By 1925, Brixton had the largest shopping centre in south London, a thriving market and a popular greyhound track opposite Max Roach Park, just a few minutes north of the Academy. This venue was originally a movie theatre called the Astoria and billed as Brixton's Wonder Theatre when it opened in 1929.

The venue's first feature was (appropriately, considering the venue's latest incarnation) *The Singing Fool* starring Al Jolson. Queues for the opening show, watched by the director Alfred Hitchcock, started at 8:45am and by noon two queues completely encircled the building.

The main feature of the entrance is a massive semi-dome and a circular, marble-floored entrance hall, whose ceiling was originally painted to represent the sky. Five pairs of doors give access to the inner lobby, which has two staircases leading to the upper vestibule and foyer, the latter giving access to the balcony.

Originally, the auditorium was designed to give the audience the impression that they were sitting in an Italian garden. Effects machines projected clouds onto the sky on the dome – sun during daylight hours, soft moonlight and twinkling stars at night. The proscenium was also flanked by tall cypress trees and two towers; the one on the right concealed the organ chamber.

In the first month of its opening, 175,000 people visited the Astoria, but dwindling audiences and modern cinema multiplexes helped close the venue in 1972. With the stalls downstairs removed to provide a dance hall, the Astoria was renamed the Sundown and began a new life as a rock venue.

The future of the building looked bleak in 1974, when planning permission was sought to demolish the Grade II listed building and replace it with a motor showroom and petrol station. Fortunately, for tonight's White Stripe fans, development plans failed and it became an equipment store used by the Rank Organisation.

The Astoria reopened, briefly, as a rock venue in same year as the 1981 riots. However, by 1982 it was closed again. It was reopened again in 1983 following a major restoration and the Academy's success grew throughout the '80s. The dramatic interior was also used as the backdrop for video shoots by Wham! and Boy George's Culture Club.

In the late 1980s, dance music was becoming a phenomenon and Brixton Academy became the first UK venue to be granted a 6am licence. Northcote and his partner, Ian Howard, bought the venue in 1995 and have overseen a complete £500,000 ($835,000) refurbishment to return the Art Deco building to its original grandeur.

In the 1940s and 1950s, West Indian immigrants mostly settled in Brixton, bringing with them their own rich culture, which has given the area a colourful and eclectic flavour. These cosmopolitan roots are reflected in its market, which started outside on Atlantic Road during the 1870s.

The market became an important focal point for the black community, and still serves up West Indian specialities such as flying fish and breadfruit. Today, the market has expanded to the outdoor market selling secondhand clothes on Brixton Station Road, the fruit and veg market running the length of Electric Avenue, the Granville Arcade and Market Row covered markets, which host everything from a Caribbean bakery to a fishmonger, and Reliance Avenue, which mostly sells clothes.

The memory of the riots has had an adverse effect on visitors, but, with increased local investment and new shops and bars opening almost every week, the area is becoming a must-stop destination for tourists and music fans.

The ticket touts are out in force tonight, standing outside the Academy on Stockwell Road barking their offers.

'Come on ladeez and gents. Pair of tickets. Only a ton [$170].'

One of them – stocky, cropped hair – waves a ticket for the show in front of me.

'What about it, mate? C'mon, do us a favour.'

A guy behind me can't wait to get his cash out quick enough. He's paying more than three times the ticket price. The White Stripes need to be good at that price.

And they are.

'Hey London, it's good to be back home,' shouts Jack White before launching into the band's bluesy, garage rock. The faded grandeur of the south London venue lends itself to the sound as The White Stripes pick their way through a set-list culled from *Elephant* and their three previous albums. They also pull off a couple of covers, 'Jolene' and 'I Just Don't Know What To Do With Myself'.

Peel is still smarting from his White Stripes spat when I catch up with him. It's pouring with rain in Maida Vale around the corner from Delaware Road, site of the BBC studios. Peel has used the studios for the last couple of decades to record sessions for his programmes. He had tried to give me directions on the phone, but couldn't remember the address. We agree to meet in a restaurant. Peel always dines there pre-session.

He is sitting at the back of the otherwise empty restaurant. He's in jeans, faded blue T-shirt and has a skull ring on his finger that Keith Richard would be proud of. The ring is the only giveaway that somewhere inside Peel there is lurking a little bit of anarchy. He's a collector of rare coins and rare records. He's 63, although he claims he doesn't feel it. With salt-and-pepper beard, he's polite, mumbling, shy, a little doddery and he rarely makes eye contact.

'Seven Nation Army' is on the playlist of practically every radio programme in the country. But Peel still won't play it. He's sent his pre-release copy back – with a note. 'It's a shame,' he tells me. 'The first time I played their records a couple of years ago, they came to the studios at Peel Acres and I was talking to the chap, telling him how I'd seen Eddie Cochran in Liverpool four days before he died. At the end of the session, The White Stripes played an Eddie Cochran tune and Gene Vincent track.' That day in 2001 they also played 'Dead Leaves And The Dirty Ground' and 'I Think I Smell A Rat'.

Peel seems genuinely upset, because he obviously has great affection for the band. 'Well, British bands wouldn't do that [play a track by an old rocker]. They won't go further back than the Oasis second album. They won't acknowledge influences beyond that. But, The White Stripes did and played it. Again that's probably because British groups couldn't play Eddie Cochran. They wouldn't think it is hip.

'What I like is how bands like Fleetwood Mac would introduce you to the blues. You wouldn't know the song, but then you'd check back and find out. It's the same with The White Stripes. People will hear them doing and find out about Robert Johnson.'

He picks at his Thai starter. Peel is amusing company. At one point he claims his only literary ambition is to write a book on Finnish woodsheds. Clearly, it'll never be written and a few weeks later it's revealed in the press that the self-styled 'D-list celebrity' is about to spill the beans on his early marriage to a teenager in Dallas and having carnal knowledge of the feminist thinker Germaine Greer. He is about to write his memoirs. The £1.5 million ($2.5 million) advance must be a big persuader.

Once cult listening for thousands of students in slug-infested bedsits, Peel has bloomed into something of a national treasure and has broadened his broadcasting range to present a programme on Radio Four about ordinary folks and their ordinary lives. It's compulsive listening for millions of ordinary folk.

Happily married to Sheila – nicknamed the Pig – for nearly 30 years, John was born in Heswall near Chester in the northwest. After completing his military service in Britain in 1962, he went to the USA and Texas to seek adventure. He became an 'office boy' trying to sell insurance to people who liked his accent more than the policies he was offering.

But then The Beatles hit big and Peel, the chancer, spotted his main chance. He played up his acquaintance with the moptops – he had none, but knew they were from Liverpool. This was enough to bag him a job working on WRR Radio in Dallas, where callers would ring in to find out personal details about Paul McCartney and John Lennon. Peel would play for time by cuing up the next piece of vinyl before researching the answer. Bizarrely, the pop king also found himself at the press conference held just prior to JFK assassin Lee Harvey Oswald being gunned down himself by Jack Ruby.

He met his first wife as a 20-something DJ in Dallas and for the next three years moved to various radio stations in America – one in San Bernardino, and one in Oklahoma, which he was fired from.

On returning to Britain in 1967 he used his connections – his mother's next-door-neighbour – to help him secure a job at Radio London with the celebrated show, *The Perfumed Garden*. Having worked in California, the bosses thought he was too cool to audition. They put him straight on air without and he has been there since.

He soon joined the founding team behind Radio One, establishing himself with the late-night programme *Top Gear*. He discovered Roxy Music when Bryan Ferry sent him a demo of what would become the band's debut single, 'Virginia Plain', and later was one of the first DJs to give exposure to punk and reggae when the alternative being fed to the nation was prog rockers Yes and Rick Wakeman. Peel now believes pre-punk dawn was the worst period for music.

Peel's shows are two hours long, broadcast from 10pm on Tuesday, Wednesday and Thursday nights. He seems impatient to start his show tonight. But first I get an impression of how the BBC used to operate when he first arrived. 'Everyone, even the staff on the door or the guy looking after the car park, used to talk with demob accents,' he recalls. 'This one chap, he'd always ask me for records,' he recounts, adopting a ridiculous postwar accent. "Do you have any records, Mr Peel ?"'

'So I say, "Yes. Er, yes, OK. What do you like?"

'"Well I like most things, Mr Peel, but no darkies."

'"OK. Well, what then?"

'"I like Diana Ross."' This tickles him.

Forty years of broadcasting hasn't faded his enthusiasm for the music or discovering new unsigned acts. Something makes him want to find and play new music, not stick with The Beatles. Why? He can't explain it. One of his producers got 'stuck in a time, but I suppose that's OK'. He adds, 'I'm 63, but I don't feel like it.' That doesn't really explain it. Peel reaches for his insulin and injects himself at the back of the empty restaurant.

Peel is probably at his most comfortable cataloguing his thousands of pre-release records or behind a microphone. That's where he belongs. There's a streak of dogged anti-bullshit about him, which comes across in his shows. He likes to champion the underdog. That's probably why he supports his local football side, Ipswich Town, alongside lifelong team, Liverpool. 'I remember when Richard Branson set up his Frontline label and the reggae guys came and recorded for him for about a week, and a week later went and recorded the same song for someone else,' he chuckles. 'That's the chaos of the music business and I love that,' he says.

In fact, it seems Peel has a total disregard for most of the apparatus of the music business. If he had it his way there would just be a band and an audience. 'You can feed in all this good music in at one end and it comes out at the other end, and all the people in between I could take a baseball bat to,' he jokes. 'The music just comes out the other side unblemished.' Then he plays it. It really is as simple as that.

A few days later, I visit the Yalding House offices of BBC's Radio One – the nation's favourite, as it once was – in central London, just around the corner from Broadcasting House in Portland Place. Now, the station has sadly slipped behind Radio Two in the ratings, as more and more commercial stations have bitten out chunks of its audience and older listeners have transferred their allegiance to Two.

In the mid-1990s, Radio One had a makeover. The older DJs, the dinosaurs, were shipped out and a new team of hip gunslingers employed to man the mikes. Peel was – and still is – the only survivor from the original team.

There is a picture of the station's 48 DJs today posted up in reception. Some are half Peel's age. Perched on vinyl seats, four pluggers, waiting to persuade producers of the gold that they're carrying in their hands, anxiously wait to pitch their new releases.

Peel's producer, Louise, guides me over to her and Peel's den in the large open-plan office – all strip lights, air-conditioning pipes and curvy Formica desks – which houses the specialist DJs.

Their workstation seems to be total chaos. On the desk, beneath the Technics turntable and Denon and Sony audio equipment, copies of London listings magazine *Time Out*, a copy of the *NME*, heaps of new CDs, some unopened hopeful demos from unknown bands recorded on obscure labels litter the table.

'To Mr John Peel', reads one. Beneath the table is a mess of bags and records in brown cardboard carriers. Behind Peel's chair, his Liverpool scarf.

Louise is 29 and dresses like her and Peel's listeners: denim skirt, Adidas white trainers, black top. In a typical week Louise and Peel are sent probably 100 CDs, around 5 per cent of which are demos by kids. 'Some are well presented with great artwork,' explains Louise. 'Some are just bits of crayon.'

Remarkably, Louise and Peel have a system. This is it: unlike most producers at the stations, whose shows are guided by playlists, they don't meet pluggers. They've also phased out attending the weekly playlist meetings, where the head of music and other producers bring in their favourite tunes to formulate the A and B and C lists, which decrees the number of spins a track will get throughout the day on each programme.

Louise tells me the role of specialist shows like Peel's is to find the new raw talent that will eventually find its way to the playlist meetings. The bottom line is, they decide what goes in the Peel programme. Not the station's management, no other producers, no one else. 'With this show, it's about what John likes. He hasn't got an ideal listener in his head. We've got listeners who are 13 and some are 30. John will only play a record because he like it, not because it has had good reviews. John doesn't give a shit about the whole promotional thing, but he doesn't lose interest in bands just because they become popular.'

However, it can be tough on them both sorting out the wheat from the chaff. They both listen to records almost every minute of the day, when they're driving to shows, driving home, in the office, at home, anywhere. 'It's a constant battle to keep up with records that come in,' she adds, running her eye over the hundreds of unopened parcels stacked on their desks. 'It's very lucky if the demos get a listen. With the best will in the world, we can't listen to everything.' On the drive up to Peel Acres, Louise and Peel will toss

CDs they don't like into the back seat. CDs felt worthy of a play on the radio get stuffed into the door pockets.

At the office, Peel puts elastic bands around the CDs he likes and passes the bundle to Louise. They are booked in for a play on his show. He usually does his scripts a week in advance, but often there are late changes. 'A record that comes in the post Tuesday could find its way onto the show that night,' says Louise.

At 9pm the pair go to Studio Y1 to listen to more records and prepare for the show. It's over at midnight and Peel stays overnight at a hotel around the corner. On Wednesday lunchtimes the pair go record-shopping. They have a regular route around Soho, but sometimes travel to Notting Hill to check out the Rough Trade shop or up to Camden.

Before the session in Maida Vale, Louise and I visit a local liquor store and ship a few packs of Carlsberg lager to the studios around the corner to keep the invited audience happy. They're mostly listeners who've won competitions. 'We never set very hard questions,' says Peel, readying himself in the DJ booth. 'Usually just things like "What is the new album called by so and so?"'

The kids at the studios don't look like they get out much. They could probably name every album released that year. Some of them will have made lists. Woollen hats, T-shirts, baggy jeans, but clean-cut types, their mothers know where they are most nights.

Technicians are setting up for the bands when the air is suddenly cut with Peel's dulcet tones. It's the start of his show. Peel might have been thinking about his blues conversation with The White Stripes. He cuts straight to Elmore James for his first record.

15 Producer And Beggar

The first record of a market being sited in Borough was in 1014, when King Canute built a bridge across the Thames. Five minutes after knocking on Pete Waterman's Borough High Street office door, just down the road from the market, I accuse London's – scrub that, England's – most successful record producer of being like Canute. Not the market builder, but the deluded King Canute who sat on his throne futilely ordering the tide to turn.

Waterman doesn't want to turn the tide on the Thames a few hundred metres north of here. But I tell him it sounds like he wants to hold back the progress of technology. The inevitable march of progress. Waterman doesn't like this. Waterman, the man who discovered Kylie, isn't having it. He stands up behind his desk and shouts. He looks angry and sounds angry. He's furious. There's a lot of cussing in there. But it's too much of a pantomime performance to be really threatening. No, no, no, he is saying. He knows he can't stop technology, but he wants to stop its unfettered use: principally, its use to download music for nothing. Free. Gratis. This is one thing Waterman can't tolerate. Taking music without paying for it. He wants to lock up these downloaders. The freeloaders who steal music, and that means students. He wants to put them all in prison. Fill our jails with future captains of industry.

'What's the worst crime in Britain?' he shoots the question at me.

'Murder? Rape?' I venture.

No way. Not in Waterman's world. 'It's copyright theft,' he rails. I argue, but am overruled. Pete is still standing, prodding the air with his fingers. The air is blue with swear words. 'And you know what?' – no, Pete – 'It's the government's fault.' I shake my head in disbelief. His argument is that, because government is responsible for education, it is ultimately responsible for universities. And these seats of learning are complicit in letting the students get away with it, with downloading music for free. Ergo, the government is turning a blind eye to crime. I shake my head again.

The producer who discovered Steps wants the government to confiscate the computers students use on campus to download music. I talk about priorities. The war on terrorism against prosecuting a war on kids in combats trying to exist on a baked-bean diet and a meagre grant. Pete's not buying that, either. 'It's the law and they are breaking it. And that leads to more serious crimes.'

The thing about Pete Waterman is that he has been in the music game for a long time. A very long time. He's a senior statesman, a veteran. There isn't an award he hasn't won. As a writer and producer he has reached the pinnacle of pop – top of the charts – more often than The Beatles or Elvis. He is a master at knowing what the music-buying public want and then giving it to them.

He has built his reputation on dance records, bought by gay men and teenage girls. Pop and pap. Pappy pop. But they sell by the millions. He's a council member at the BPI, sitting on the body's chart committee. He regularly holds master classes and has spoken in the Houses of Parliament, addressing a cross-party music group. He told them what's what. He likes to tell people what's what. He is about to tell me what's what.

He wants to tell me there is no clear road for young producers in London to get a foot on the career ladder. Typically, Waterman isn't just going to complain about that. He's going to do something about it: he's launching a massive new studio complex on the South Bank to encourage young producer talent into the industry.

'The advantage to being in this for 30, 40 years. Well, there is an advantage and disadvantage,' explains Pete, running his hand through his white hair. It's slicked back. He's 56. 'The advantage is, I've seen everything before. The disadvantage is that you can get jaded.'

But, he doesn't get jaded. He keeps himself busy, does Waterman. He's always at it. He produces records. Not everyone likes his records, but he doesn't care. He makes a lot of them. He's made a lot of money making them. He's made a lot of stars making them. He's on TV – he does a show called *Pop Idol*. He sits with a couple of judges and tells young kids if they've got any talent. Some of them have. A lot haven't. Pete doesn't pull his punches and they now call him Pete Slaughterman because of it. He tells them straight – no bullshit from Pete Waterman.

Waterman was born in bomb-ravaged Coventry in 1947, next to a railway line, which is an important detail. His old man worked in an aircraft factory; the electricity was turned on at teatime. Young Pete sold coal to neighbours from an adapted pram. An illiterate school-leaver – he only learned to read properly when he was in his late 30s – Waterman took a job on the railways in his teens. He was a railway fireman. He stayed for 18 months, stoking, oiling and cleaning before he heard The Beatles.

The Liverpool group got him interested in music and he started out playing records. A DJ before DJs were invented. If he had his way, he'd tell you he invented DJing. Then again, who has been around long enough to argue the case? Maybe he did. He started playing records at parties in the late '50s and by the time The Beatles came on the scene had a reputation as the guy with the big record collection.

He played more records, sometimes obscure ones sourced from US military bases, at more parties. By 1964, he was working in jazz clubs and hanging out with – and lending records to – the bands of the day: The Pretty Things, The Yardbirds, The Graham Bond Organisation. He was knowledgeable, was Pete. He knew all about The Doors, Jefferson Airplane and The Byrds, too. And people liked having him around. In 1968 Fleetwood Mac booked him as a compere, to host their shows.

The same year he hooked up with the giant club group Mecca to become house DJ and began fooling around with Motown Records. He'd been an early fan of the Chicago label and at the end of that year Motown boss Berry Gordy sent him a test pressing of Marvin Gaye's 'I Heard It Through The Grapevine'. It became one of his favourite records.

By the early '70s Pete was known as the Motown DJ in Britain, but his staple diet of obscure records dried up when Motown moved to Los Angeles. He turned to the new sound coming out of London – glitter rock. He began playing Gary Glitter, Sweet and Mud records in his DJing sets. He hosted the first Bay City Rollers tour. He also turned to the new sound coming out of Philadelphia, the Philly sound. Record-company promo staff visited his clubs. They saw they were full of kids. So full that some kids were turned away.

Then, late in 1973, he had an epiphany. He thought he could make music. He visited Gamble and Huff in Philadelphia and began assisting on the sessions, working with Tom Bell and Linda Greed and The Three Degrees. This was a turning point. Waterman was no longer simply playing records, he was helping produce them.

Soon he was in Jamaica. He met Bob Marley, Lee Scratch Perry and Peter Tosh. He also took time out to make his own reggae record. It cost him just $80 (£50) to do that, and become a bona fide record producer in the process. He found his calling, did Pete.

In mid-1974 Waterman returned to work for CBS to break the Philly sound open. He also got a job at Radio One – no-slouch Pete. He hosted the *Soul Show* on Saturdays, just about the time his listeners were settling down to their PG Tips and salmon paste sandwiches. Teatime with Pete on the radio, playing his favourite Billy Paul record.

CBS then brought him back to work on breaking the Philly sound, working with The Stylistics, George McCrae and the Hues Corporation. Then he heard a sound at a record convention in January 1975. It was Silver Convention's 'Save Me'.

Disco was born. Pete had a hand in that, too – hand-in-everything Pete. By the end of 1975, London and the rest of the world had the disco diva Donna Summer and disco kings The Bee Gees and a thousand discotheques playing their music. Next, Waterman was working with King Disco himself, John Travolta, on the classic disco movie *Saturday Night Fever*.

Times changed and Pete changed with them – 2-Tone arrived in Britain, brought by Pete's home-town boys from Coventry, The Specials. Pete was on the ball. He became the band's manager – for a while. Then, rockabilly with Matchbox. Then, electronica with Soft Cell. Then, he joined Elton John's Rocket Records. Then, in 1982, Pete moved to the States.

He stayed a couple of years and met two producers and writers on his return to London in 1984. Mike Stock and Matt Aitken. Stock, Aitken and Waterman – that was their handle as producers – or SAW for short. Their first hit came after only four months of working together. No one will admit to owning Hazell Dean's 'Whatever I do (Wherever I Go)' now. It's no 'Yesterday' or 'Street Fighting Man', but Pete had spotted a niche in the marketplace. He had used all his knowledge of blues, disco and pop and blended it to create a new trend called Hi-NRG.

Within a year they had a No.1 record with Dead Or Alive's 'You Spin Me Round'. And by the end of the '80s Stock, Aitken Waterman were household names, or at least in most household's record collections. They were the most successful pop writers and producers in Britain and, before splitting, amassed more than 100 Top 40 hits, although the quality varied. Deep-voiced Rick Astley was of the '80s and will never be hip. Sexy Bananarama were Britain's all-time bestselling female group, pre-Spice Girls. And then there is Kylie. Pete put the Australian soap actress on her first steps to becoming the slick act she is now.

In 1989, Waterman also conceived a new TV show, *The Hitman And Her*, which featured him and Michaela Strachan introducing new groups and bands to the nation. Naturally, it became cult, then essential viewing. It exposed new music genres and gave exposure to unsigned acts.

Then along came Steps. Steps' debut single stayed in the Top 20 for 15 weeks and the debut album, *Step One*, sold in excess of two million copies. At the beginning of 1999, Steps reached No.1 with 'Heartbeat'/'Tragedy'. By October they were back at the top of the album charts with the release of *Steptacular*. The all-singing, all-dancing Steps was based on a simple, but supremely effective premise. Pete had thought if Oasis can get away with sounding like The Beatles, he could get away with Steps sounding like Abba. It worked.

No-stopping Pete. He had the first No.1 single of the new millennium and in the early years of the 21st century helped create a new branch of the manufactured pop phenomenon by becoming a judge on ITV's chief talent shows, *Pop Idol* and *Popstars – The Rivals*. The show's success stories were Will Young and Gareth Gates, who immediately stormed the charts.

Pete is about to start judging another series of *Pop Idol* when I tip up to hear his rant about students.

PWL, Pete Waterman Ltd, PWL Empire. 'Empire', that's what it says under the company's logo. Pete designed it himself.

It's like walking into an office in Marrakesh. This is Moroccan interior design – red leather, lots of brass studs, and the walls are lined with large wooden cupboards, floor to ceiling, in the same style with brass studs on each panel. I take a peek inside one – row upon row of manilla folders. Waterman stands in the middle of this, hands on hips. Something is bothering him for the minute. But it seems like he can't quite grasp what it is.

'Hello,' he says. He has a Midlands accent.

He now lives above the Empire – this office – or in Warrington. But he claims he hasn't had time to go home much this year. 'I've probably spent six nights there this year,' he adds. He's single now, for the last ten years. No bird. 'No time. I love my job too much,' is his explanation. And he does love his job. It's obvious. He wears his passion on his sleeve. He called his autobiography *I Wish I Was Me*.

He guides me into his office, which is just big enough for a big desk and a throne. I wasn't expecting anything less from England's most successful record producer – you can't beat a throne. Mock Moorish, I guess: heavy wood, red leather and those studs again. Pete takes the throne seat and, in front of him, on his desk, it's chaos.

It is strewn with CDs, paper, folders, sketches, architect's drawings, two identical retro chrome lamps. I notice two CDs – *Kick-Ass Polkas* and Meat Loaf's *Hits Out Of Hell*. One of his assistants brings in a piece of paper for Pete to check some figures. He approves some, rejects others. That seems to sort out his niggling problem. He relaxes, hands behind head, his white, subtle check shirt stretching across him.

When Pete doesn't produce, he models – railway engines and wagons. Anything to do with railways, really. I see a model on his desk and pick it up. It's a railway carriage, something that might transport cattle to market. It's very, very detailed – a beautiful scale reproduction. He's been interested in trains and railways all his life and the Waterman Railway Heritage Trust owns a vast 10mm (⅓in) scale collection of museum standard pieces like this.

'How many have you got?'

'Oh, thousands, thousands.'

'No, I mean real ones.' I know Waterman owns his own steam engines. He has a company called London & North Western Railway, which is the largest privately owned provider of rail maintenance services. He once also owned *The Flying Scotsman* steam locomotive.

'Oh, 17.'

He uses the modelling to relax.

'It keeps me sane. Railways have kept me sane.' I think about the Rick Astley records he produced. 'I use the modelling to concentrate on the songs. All songwriters will tell you that you need to be forced into doing it. Yep, I love my job, but you need to break the concentration, because there are only so many words in the well. I could write 20 songs in a day, but they wouldn't be any good so I need something that controls the balance.' Every time he finishes a song, he gets back to modelling, working on the 10mm (⅓in) scale models. That's when he's happiest.

And then I call Waterman Canute.

And he stands to curse and rant. 'I'm not King Canute. I say, "Bring it [the technology and downloading] on, but bring it on properly." I believe in technology. It would suit me if everything was off the Internet and we have been too slow to adapt to the new technology. The government should be doing something about it. [Music minister] Kim Howells should be doing a lot more about it,' shouts Pete. 'The government is condoning piracy. Let's not let them get away with it. Why are we tolerating this? Allowing it on their [government] premises. One thing Howells should do is shut down the universities' computing facilities that are allowing it. You could stop piracy tomorrow by putting a block on numbers. Is downloading giving students something they don't get?'

Uh-oh, I think. Waterman, the 15-year-old school-leaver, has a chip on his shoulder.

'Universities are seats of learning. Seats of learning paid for by the taxpayer, people like me and you,' says Pete, getting into his stride now. 'We can't allow one of our biggest industries to be put on the rocks by illegal downloading at universities.'

It's not Waterman who Waterman is fighting for. He is not being affected by the downloading phenomenon. Pete is fighting for the record industry because he cares passionately about that.

'They are not downloading Steps at university. If it's a pop act, they don't bother. The Russians don't bother with Steps.' The Russians? Waterman says many of the illegal downloading sites are based in Russia.

'That's not a coincidence,' according to Pete. 'That's a political motivation – to undermine capitalism.'

I'm shaking my head again.

'If you go to a market and can buy Eminem's greatest hits before Universal has officially released a record like that, it is not right.'

More seriously, Waterman thinks funds from the piracy are directed to terrorist networks like Al-Qaeda and the IRA. Actually, he claims he has proof. 'Credit card fraud and piracy, it is organised. Categorically Al-Qaeda and the IRA use copyright piracy.' He knows a bit about the IRA. He was in Warrington when an IRA bomb exploded in 1993 and killed Tim Parry.

But Waterman's thesis that the British government isn't doing enough for London record labels isn't his only gripe. He is also concerned about the power of the majors. As we talk, rumours in the mill suggest Warner's and BMG are in merger talks, serious negotiations. EMI has already explored the possibility of merging with both companies in the past, but was blocked by the European Union on the grounds of less competition.

But the political and economic landscape has changed and Waterman believes that by the end of the year there will only be four majors. This means less choice of record companies. Less choice is no good. Less choice means there won't be any independents churning out the edgy, left-field stuff. The music industry will be controlled by a handful of multinationals. He says, '25 years ago I had 20 mates who had 20 independent companies and if you bought something in to me and I didn't like it I could tell you three people you could take your record to. But I can't do that now. They're not around. I couldn't tell you three people.'

I suggest Waterman might have had the wrong 20 mates. Not bad lads, just ones who were not equipped to deal with the changing environment. You can't blame everything on the marketplace and economics. This is given short shrift.

And then there is the question of distribution. Waterman believes retail will soon be taken out of the equation. Everything will be pumped direct to people's homes and that will mean less choice, too. 'Once we take the retail out of the equation, then we will have no more than two portals. There won't be any HMVs any more, no traditional retailers. You will go to Apple to get EMI product because EMI don't retail to the public. I can make plain what will happen – the telecoms companies will own the product. Here is a revolution that needs to happen.'

So Pete wants a revolution?

'Yeah, but we don't want anarchy.'

A controlled revolution. I'm not certain that's possible, but let Pete continue. He's on a roll now, sitting back in his throne. He's not happy, though. The way the big corporations could end up in control of the source and supply of music is a big worry for Pete. 'Do we want majors dictating what we want? Our Top 50 has already really just become a Top 10. Soon retail will only stock what they are given by the majors,' he adds. Less choice again.

'I don't like Radiohead, but I support people's right to be able to listen to them. If I want to buy a Radiohead record, I should be able to. Like when I bought Tamla Motown when I was younger.' Waterman isn't convinced he will be able to do that shortly.

So Waterman is fighting back, in a way. He's setting up a recording studio complex to nurture new talent in London. On the banks of the

Thames, right next to the BPI. 'I am at least doing something positive. I've been here 40 years and in the past I would've said, "Look, I'll do it myself", but I am 56 now and can't do everything myself any more'.

After a booze-fuelled evening in a karaoke bar – Pete thinks he sang John Lennon's 'Imagine' ('I always sing Lennon') – with Mac Okamoto, the owner of County Hall, the pair hatched a plot to build a complex to train production skills and give something back to the London music scene. Pete also likes a challenge: 'If anything is a problem, I love that.'

Waterman wants to provide a breeding space for today's young producer talent to work and get a toehold in the London industry. 'Don't do it [produce] in your bedroom. Do it properly, because for everyone who is discovered in their bedrooms we miss 10,000 others. I am appalled at the facilities in this country for producers,' he says, adding that in Europe most towns and cities are full of studio space. 'Every little town in Sweden has a music school, teaching producers, but music shouldn't be funded by the government. It just seems like common sense to build studio facilities. This is all about encouraging young people to do what I did 30 years ago. There is no one else teaching young record producers and entrepreneurs in this country, and I think it needs someone like me who understands them.'

Open Studios is not a philanthropic venture, though. Rents will be around £15,000 ($25,000) per annum. But Waterman believes any producer worth his salt should be able to find the cash to pay that. 'People will be in charge of their own destiny. They will have to understand economics and they need to make enough money to make their next record. What we are saying is this is an easy way to start, to look professional when Sony or EMI come down, but you've got to pay the rent,' he says. 'They've got to want it.'

But will Pete be raising a trainload of producers in his mould? Simple answer – no.

'They can do whatever they want, as long as they have talent,' he adds, recalling a recent conversation with a producer who was pumping out what he thought his paymasters wanted, not what he wanted. 'I said, "Why are you producing such shit?"

'And he said, "This is what people want."

'There are some people in studios now, who are victims of their own treadmill. I want the arrogance of youth who believe in their own thing. I want people who can take their balls in their hand and produce what they want, and that is fucking hits.' Hits. That's what it's about.

I leave the PWL Empire and walk back up Borough High Street. Waterman's arguments and stratagems are still ringing in my ears. But, they soon fade, replaced by the constant drone of motorbikes and lorries clogging this drab thoroughfare running from the river to Elephant & Castle. As I near London Bridge, I wonder if Waterman sited his offices here because of the proximity to London Bridge railway station, the first large terminus in central London, though I know he isn't one of those anoraks who stands on chilly platforms clutching a pen, notepad and flash of sugary tea jotting down the numbers of Class 458 EMUs.

However, he must appreciate the history of Borough, one of London's most ancient areas, with a history stretching back centuries. Behind the unremarkable parade of pharmacies, bands and cafés right opposite the station is Borough Market, right in the shadow of Southwark Cathedral, which lies on the South Bank of the Thames on a site occupied by a church for over 1,000 years. The main structure of today's church was built between 1220 and 1420.

Southwark Fair Market flourished on the southern side of the river in pre-Roman Britain. The Borough market has shifted over the centuries, but has always remained near the southern bridgehead of London Bridge. It is now the oldest fruit and vegetable wholesale market still trading – since 1756 – in London.

Records traced back to 1014, when Canute built his bridge across the Thames, show that the market then sold fish, grain and cattle. By the Victorian era, most of the food arrived at the wharves by London Bridge and nearby Tooley Street, giving the area its nickname of the London Larder. Later, the produce arrived by train to London Bridge and was wheeled the few hundred metres to the market.

Today, a typical trader's day might start at 2am. Container trucks park up in Stoney Street, where pitching porters unload the fresh fruit and vegetables. In the early hours, greengrocers, hoteliers and restaurateurs from London's top eateries will turn up to select the best produce. Chef Jamie Oliver is a big fan of the market. By 9am, most of the trading is over and the debris is removed for another day.

More recently, the market has established stalls and shops selling fine food and wine to passing trade during the weekend. This kicked off with the arrival of Neal's Yard Dairies in the late 1990s, and now the gourmet market consists of around 50 stalls and stands showcasing English producers offering a wide range of top-quality fish, meats, ciders, wines, cheese, bread, coffee, cakes and patisseries.

I pick over a pile of cheeses – Stilton, Camembert. They remind me of a phone call I had with Dave Stewart the previous day. Stewart is into markets and communities. He would appreciate the community of Borough. 'Like in New York, there is a little local cheese shop. I'd rather go there than a big market. Communities are important. If I had billions of pounds, I would go and build communities. On three acres [1 hectare] you have a theatre, guitar repair shop, bread shop, cheese shop. Places where people work and live. An area where people go to buy something and then shop for something else, like records.'

Stewart had wanted to build a community with the Marquee Club. After the venue closed in Soho, Stewart and his Artist Network group built a new place in north London's Islington and called that the Marquee.

It came with an ambitious plan to build a multimedia company, with music as the common denominator. He wanted to use the club as an A&R source, a place to meet, make pop shows (one was for Channel Five, called *Pop*), watch bands, shoot videos, run a record store. Alongside that, Stewart started a new label.

He wanted to create a new community and be part of the community. Unfortunately, the dream ended and the Marquee closed. His vehicle, Artist Network, also went into administration because of lack of funds. However, Stewart is not pessimistic. Far from it. 'I'm not deflated and downhearted, it's been a lot of stress. It was all about building an artist-friendly environment. For me, it was about trying to work with new artists and create long-term careers. I don't want to go off trout fishing.'

Dave Stewart was one half of The Eurythmics with Annie Lennox. Stewart wore shades and played the guitar. The group sold millions of albums. He has directed a film, starring three of All Saints. A Renaissance man, he is currently writing a film, a musical. Stewart tells me his experiences – and problems – of trying to get a new club and label up and running are symptomatic of a record business in turmoil. 'It's a simple story. We never raised enough money. We were supposed to initially raise $10 million [£6 million], but got around $7–8 million [£4–5 million],' he says. People just aren't interested in investing in music. It's too risky at the moment.

Stewart learned that the hard way. He adds, 'The record business is spiralling, it's in a downfall. There are two reasons – one is the Internet and piracy, and the second is they have just not got product. Artists are just pushed into a pipe. What we want actually is to nurture talent and create ones with longevity.'

That was the idea behind Artist Network, to nurture and guide. And that is why Stewart is against the current model of record companies, which sign an artist and then keep hold over their copyrights for years. Under Stewart's ideal model, once an album is finished the artists should be free.

'You hear about some old Stax guys in a trailer park, who didn't get a penny and the record company made millions of dollars from him. In other businesses there are usually two businesspeople doing a deal, but in the record business the artist is not a businessman.

'It's like a mortgage for your house. With the mortgage, once you have paid it off, the house is yours, but with a record company they will give you an advance, and then when you've made the record they say they own it. People like myself don't think it is set up right. I'm very vocal. The record industry has slightly changed, with less deals where the rights are held time in perpetuity by the record companies. Those deals are ending.'

However, it is not just the restrictive deals he has a problem with. Stewart believes the A&R setup is wrong.

'It shouldn't be something that is just financial. I see labels that are signing up cabaret singers and they may turn away a real artist. I don't see the music industry as fast turnover, but they do. They'd rather sign up an act discovered through *Starsearch* or some other TV programme and sell half a million copies quickly. What I am saying is, "Sign someone with talent and you'll have them around for 25 years."

'There have been so many articles about the music industry in the last two years and lots of chief executives of record companies are saying the same thing – they have created an "analogue to monologue" fast turnover business. It's like the Ford car factory, where it is alright to have any music so long as it's the same.'

In spite of the initial failure of Artist Network, Stewart believes his ideas of community are still 'solid' and will eventually be adopted by the wider record industry. 'In the last three years, it has been catching up with what we were doing, inventing a new model.

'There is always a shift, but we ran out of time. We couldn't wait for the shift to happen,' he explains. Because of the Internet, the music business can't remain doing the same things and Stewart can also now detect a shift of power. 'In the future, because of the way the distribution is going on the Internet, anyone can become a record label. I think the telecoms and cable companies are going to be powerful. But I don't care what platform it is: the content has to be really real and really talented and creative.

'The Internet, all of these things together are making people paranoid. But you'll never stop a Damon Albarn. Singers and artists are all over the place, in garages, so it's really exciting when they come out and they are also getting more power, it is a slightly different ball game. And who knows what will happen in the next ten years or so?'

Stewart is now regrouping to come back again. He knows there is a finite limit to the number of 'pop bands pushed down the pipe'. He adds, 'Artist Network will continue in some shape. But when you try something radical, you put yourself in the front line and have to work out a lot of problems. Now what I think will happen is we will split into a lot of different "terrorist cells" and work stuff out and then come back together. Who knows what I will come back with.'

I leave the cheeses and the market, and pad back towards London Bridge, near where Canute built his Thames crossing.

I want to catch the bus down to Wandsworth to see an independent label in operation, to see if it is creating a community.

Behind Martin Mills's desk is a colour photograph of The Rolling Stones. Playing cricket, or pretending to, in a park. It's *Beggars Banquet*-era, when the Stones were street-fighting men. The album is one of Mills's favourites. It should be. After adopting the title as the name of his company, Mills has gone on to create one of the most successful British-owned record companies operating in London.

Through two decades, the label, through the association of its acts Bauhaus, The Cult, The Fall and Prodigy, has found a home in teenage record collections and has probably now eclipsed the 1968 album in many people's consciousness.

Mills probably wouldn't agree with that. He's a modest fellow. He keeps a low profile too, and hardly ever does interviews. He lets his bands do the talking for him and they've done a good job. Mills is now a millionaire. He sits atop a multimillion pound turnover group with several influential labels and has a hand in shaping some of the most innovative, world-beating acts, including The White Stripes.

Mills was at the Stripes's gig in Brixton. The Detroit duo are on XL Recordings, a label venture Beggars Banquet is in joint partnership with.

'Brilliant, very good,' he says of the duo when I catch up with him in the sprawling, higgledy-piggledy offices in south London. He grins a toothy smile. He smiles a lot, usually when he has just delivered a point or argued his case. Like a kindly doctor, telling you 'not to worry' while wondering if you have taken on board his prognosis.

I find Mills at Alma Road, just off Wandsworth Common. The open-plan offices are a long way from Sony's swish minimalism in Soho. There are no fierce young ladies in Prada manning the reception. At Beggars, everyone looks like overgrown students. This is more design by DIY, comfort and convenience.

Mills himself has white hair, a beard and glasses. He is sitting, bent up rather, in a faded black zip top and shapeless pants. He has found himself a quiet corner. It's not that quiet, though – TV sets are blaring from reception and someone is playing a song on their own stereo.

On Mills's black desk there's just enough room for a stereo and a Sony laptop, which Mills is 'pleased with'. He taps keys on it and looks for stuff during our conversation. The desk is the same cheap wood chip as the others in the building. It's the same size, too. It may even be smaller than some – and there are no shot-blasted glass panels to define Mills's office. If he wasn't twice the age of everyone else in the room, he would be difficult to place as the boss.

Mills occupies an unusual place in the London music industry. He's not just a hired gun like many executives working for multinational corporations. And he still mixes it in the mosh pit, getting out to watch bands two or three times each week.

'I think the world divides into those who like live music and those who listen to recorded music,' he reveals. Despite owning a record company, Mills is in the live camp. 'I get more of a kick out of that,' he adds, reaching for a large diary. He runs his finger down entries for the last week. 'Yes, last week I was at the Barfly, the Union Chapel and the Lyric Theatre in Hammersmith.'

He built Beggars on the back of 'Shadow', a single by The Lurkers in 1977. Where hundreds have failed, Beggars has flourished at the cutting edge, managing to adapt itself through different styles and tastes. He believes for any label to be successful they have to reinvent themselves. 'The independent labels, which have been great, but have not survived, are the ones that have not reinvented themselves. Creation was a great label, but it's one picture really [Oasis], not a succession of pictures. The same was true of Rough Trade and Factory, who put out music every bit as good as we did but didn't reinvent themselves,' adds Mills.

In the process, he has proved that an independent doesn't have to adopt the same values as a major to succeed. Mills has made his own rules. He knows it isn't possible to catch every musical wave, but he has been successful at catching 'successive waves'. He discovered that was the way to compete with the majors – not to compete head-on, but to find the niche and take things beyond that niche.

He explains: 'I think over the years our success has been the ability to catch those waves and also having a stable of labels with a lot of different identities all of which are compatible. Each bit adds up to a whole.'

But, the most important rule is releasing music he believes in. If commercial success follows, that's alright with Martin. And, largely it has. In addition to the Beggars group, Mills has also a hand in helping to shape the future of the London music business. He has sat on the boards of both the BPI and AIM, having a foot in the camp of the majors and independents. 'I'm always fighting as an independent label. When you stop fighting, then you start dying. But, you always have to strike a balance, to be part of the system and to be outside of the system.'

He's also helped drive the UKMO (UK Music Office) project in New York. Now he wants to create a London-based super-council, made up of bigwigs in the industry, to tackle a whole spectrum of issues and talk to outside agencies like the government. He's always doing things, Martin Mills. 'I'm busy,' he says and smiles. People seek out his advice. They want his views.

Mills has just got back from Brussels. He's been hobnobbing with officials at the EU and MEPs. He was talking to Macmillan's Earl of Stockton about copyright. That's Mills – he can talk about anything, and for the next couple of hours we do. From the anti-capitalism riots in Seattle from a few years back, through the effect of London property prices on the music business, to one of Mills's new spots, Scout Niblett. She plays drums for half the set and then switches to guitar.

Like a one-woman White Stripes?

'Yes, I suppose.' Mills smiles his toothy grin.

Mills didn't start off in the record business. He used to work for the Office of Population, Census and Surveys, writing reports on abortion law. But he liked music. So he started running a mobile discotheque in London in the '70s. They were popular then – play a tune and then tell the punters what it was: '...and this next record is "Sympathy For The Devil" by The Rolling Stones, off their album...*Beggars Banquet*...'. Mills's mobile disco was called Giant Elf – bad name. But he ditched that when he linked up with another DJ. They called this outfit Beggars Banquet – good name.

Then he started working for a secondhand record store in Shepherd's Bush, the Record and Tape Exchange. They have stores all over London. You either get cash for selling records, or double your money and exchange what you're selling. This experience gave the budding entrepreneur the idea to establish his own record store in Earl's Court in 1972, selling a mix of new and old records. By 1975, he had a few stores and was also branching into other areas of the business, such as promoting.

The first gig he put on was Tangerine Dream – at the Royal Albert Hall. In at the deep end, he concentrated on acts that weren't mainstream. Then The Sex Pistols and punk arrived, and with it Mills's first big break. Suddenly the world wasn't interested in albums any more; they were interested in singles. Suddenly the same people who had been listening to *Deodato* were buying the first single by The Sex Pistols.

It turned what the record industry did upside down. Mills became a promoter of punk gigs. He also launched a record label.

A basement beneath his record store in Fulham was being used by punk bands. Billy Idol and Tony James's group Generation X rehearsed there, as did The Lurkers. The Lurkers hadn't got a label deal and Mills, who was also helping to manage the band at this point, couldn't get one.

Mills decided to release the record himself. DIY records – something common today, but almost unheard of in the late '70s. There were no small independent record companies at that time, so Mills worked it out himself, pressed the record and hooked up with a distributor. Beggars became part of the first wave of independents with 'Shadow', funding the record label with the cash flowing through the tills of the record stores. Stiff, Small Wonder, Chiswick, Radar. They all started around the same time as Beggars, but have subsequently faded.

Mills says now that early success came easily because punks were starved of records and would buy anything that remotely sniffed of punk. Then along came Tubeway Army – Gary Numan's late '70s outfit with the man in black leather standing behind a synthesiser.

He earned Beggars Banquet its first No.1 single with 'Are Friends Electric?' It was over five minutes long and, according to Mills, had 'no tune'. It changed the fortunes of the company. As Mills points out, where it took A&M something like 15 years to have its first No.1 single, by 1979 Beggars was scoring at the top of the charts with Numan as a matter of course.

In 1982, Beggars established the first of what was to become a long line of sister labels: 4AD. Ivo Watts-Russell, one of the managers of one of the record shops, ran it. The idea was that it would be like Beggars in the early days – a place to nurture acts, which would move onto Beggars as they got bigger. Bauhaus started out on 4AD and moved to Beggars.

4AD began to develop its own identity, with acts such as Nick Cave's The Birthday Party and Cocteau Twins. Under Watts-Russell it grew parallel to Beggars. It, too, had hits, lots of them. And later, it reinvented itself as being a label for fey female vocalists and a home for alternative US rock groups such as The Pixies and Throwing Muses. Watts-Russell effectively suspended the label a few years back and is now semi-retired from the music business, building a house in Santa Fe.

Mills got the taste for new labels. A year later, in 1983, he launched Situation 2. The magic continued, with The Cult and The Associates starting out on Beggars Banquet's little brother imprint.

However, it was the Northampton goth band Bauhaus that was opening doors for Beggars. From the singles 'Dark Entries' and 'Terror Couple Kill Colonel', records played by the DJ in Camden's Devonshire Arms, and the band's debut album *In The Flat Field* on 4AD, Mills's record company became home to the '80s goth scene.

Bauhaus opened the doors and Beggars thrived with the dark gothic bands that followed. However, it wasn't all goth. In 1987, 4AD released the MARRS track 'Pump Up The Volume'. This was a seminal record, which delivered the first independently distributed dance No.1. For Mills it proved that his company and other independents could compete with the big players. Suddenly 4AD and Beggars weren't the poor relations in the record industry and, when the house music scene followed, Mills was ready.

A couple of years later, and another label, XL, was born on the back of the house sound. And so came The Prodigy. The way Mills sees it now was that, at the turn of the '90s, kids were either into dance music or alternative guitar bands. They were mutually exclusive. One thing or the other. But The Prodigy broke that barrier down, creating a dance/rock fusion that in itself helped create a new-look Beggars catering for both markets.

Suddenly kids who would only have had guitar records in their collections a few years before were now buying dance records too. Progression is the key for Mills. And, with The White Stripes on XL in 2003, there has been a huge progression. 'XL is like the ultimate alternative label,' he believes. 'What makes it exciting and also successful is this ability to adapt.'

And keep adapting. At present Mills believes the industry is going through one of its largest shifts. There are myriad external factors being brought into play. The Communications Bill is creating concerns about media consolidation and 'homogenous playlists'. There is the Licensing Bill and its effect on live music. And then the Internet. Another threat, perhaps.

Mills isn't scared of that, though. He sees opportunity. His group was one of the first to sell its back catalogue online. He's an indie and that gives him flexibility. Mills grins again. I then notice the packet of Pringle crisps and bottle of whisky on a filing cabinet behind him.

'People say the music industry is in trouble, but that's not true. The numbers of people going to concerts is booming. It is the traditional recording model, which is the sale of CDs. And then CD sales have only fallen to the levels they were at in the mid-'90s. But that is not counting the sale of DVDs, which are becoming more important to the music industry and are increasing.'

However, Mills concedes that 'there are a lot of battle grounds and there always will be'. The future of the singles market, for one. 'The promotional value only makes sense if it drives sales of physical product,' he argues. 'There is a huge culture shift going on with the whole record industry. It is so used to deriving 95 per cent of its income from sales on records.'

Mills believes that because independent groups like his own have been licensing music as a core part of their business for years, they are also 'extremely well placed' to take advantage of the potential gains offered by the Internet and digital distribution. 'The essence of a major is vertical integration. To manage the process from top to bottom. We [the independent record labels] exist in licensing. In the Internet age, that is more comfortable.'

However, he accepts that with recent Web-based developments such as the Apple initiative, the majors are 'abandoning their old attitudes... They are becoming willing licensees, but it is a difficult process for them,' he argues. Maybe they'll catch up, but it is a tough transformation for them, 'when record companies are faced with a new means of distribution where the products are free. That is difficult to confront.' He believes the Apple launch has 'transformed the landscape' and will encourage the availability of more subscription models.

Beggars has been a progressive Internet user because Mills believes it is a useful tool for people to find and discover music and tell their friends about it. The file sharing issue is, therefore, potentially a boon because Mills believes it could introduce new consumers to Beggars' artists. But, there has to be an economic element underpinning it. Mills is no fan of piracy. 'It's not a battle that will be completely won, but commercial piracy has to be fought.'

In the future he is certain the Internet will completely change the way music is consumed. He says music will be received in a variety of different ways: by buying the product in stores, buying a digital copy to store on a computer at home, or subscribing to a music provider. Future consumers may demand a few hours' worth of music from a provider that serves up particular genres such as rock or pop.

And what about the music that will be demanded? Mills, who was around during two music revolutions in London, punk and house, believes we are entering another new phase. He thinks the dominance of pop music that has sustained – and benefited from – TV talent shows such as *Pop Idol* and *Fame Academy* is on the wane. People are bored of it, and also record companies are realising that 'pop music is very transitory' and has no lasting value.

However, Mills is too laid-back to have let that worry him. 'It's just part of the world we live in. It would be pointless if it depressed me. It is what it is and there is demand for that music... It is very interesting at the moment. I think we are in one of those phases. It is a historical fact that pop music's dominance, the whole boy-band thing, we will get a reaction against it and we have one of those phases now,' he says.

That explains The White Stripes, Yeah Yeah Yeahs, The Strokes. 'Kids are reacting against the pop stuff we have been having for the last few years.' I point out that those bands are from America, not London. Is London booming? 'Yes, there's a lot of exciting stuff happening in this country, too. But it is fragmented, it is not coming out of one particular place. There is not much to connect them musically.' No movement, then, like punk rock. Mills has already done that.

16 E1

Shoreditch is a little self-conscious. But that's what you get when you're the hippest square mile in the world. They should have passports to gain entry to the place and to its little-brother neighbour, Hoxton.

This is where London's newest styles originate: new haircuts, new T-shirts, new slogans, new slang, new ways of wearing your trousers. The ideas, the fashions, they burst out of the pores of Shoreditch society and Hoxton humanity like a rocket. These ideas breed by word of mouth over Negroni cocktails in the chichi bars bordering Hoxton Square. These styles are adopted first by the tastemakers, aching with attitude, skulking out of the clubs lining Rivington Street. Then they are passed on to the rest of London, discarded, fed to the masses in Fulham or Chiswick. But by then the new way of wearing your trousers has become the old way on Shoreditch High Street, E1. The denizens of Hoxton will have moved on. It's so hip here, a haircut can go out of fashion before you've left the hairdresser.

I think about this as I amble past the White Cube Gallery on Hoxton Square. Yeah, that's right. The White Cube is hip. It shows the work of London's most happening artists. It's owned by Jay Jopling, married to Sam Taylor Wood, friend of Damien Hirst. I'm trying to find the Red Lion pub. Chris Taylor wants to meet there. Taylor is now. I only need to look in this month's copy of *Vogue* to find that out. The fashion, music, art issue. The world's grooviest smudger, Mario Testino, snaps the world's most gorgeous style-shakers and louche pop stars. Kate Moss models David Bowie's outfits, and Chris Taylor and his band Menlo Park strike a pose for Testino.

The Red Lion wants to present itself as a down-at-heel working men's boozer. It looks like one. It might even smell like one. But a working man hasn't been inside it for years. It's a second home for the area's artists – when they're not holed up in their enormous bare brick studios. In the Red Lion, regulars wear jeans made by obscure Belgian designers. But it's shut. I call Chris on his cellphone. He's late anyway. Fashionably late, of course.

'OK, OK.' He's got a velvet soft American accent. 'Er, er. OK, let's meet in the Hoxton Square Bar. It's next door to the old Blue Note.' I'll find it.

I set off back across Hoxton Square, worrying my jeans are a little bit last-season. The square is a tiny rectangle of grass bordered by Georgian houses, Victorian warehouses, 1970s offices and 21st-century bars. I pass a man, mid-20s, knife-sharp asymmetric haircut. He's sporting army surplus fused with Vivienne Westwood from a few seasons ago. The look is too self-conscious, even for these streets. He must be a tourist. In Shoreditch you don't try. You don't try too hard. A beautiful woman, early 20s, blunt bob. Sitting on a wall outside near the White Cube. She's drinking Coke, wearing Oxfam teamed with Matthew Williamson. She's not going anywhere she doesn't want to, probably doesn't need to. That's Hoxton.

Hoxton has history. It gets a mention in the Domesday Book in 1086. But then it was called Hogesdon, a possible reference to a farm called Hog in the area. Some evidence of medieval housing has been unearthed north of here, up Hoxton Road, near Nuttall Street. And in the 13th century the grounds of Robert de Wenloc's estate were laid out. That is now Wenlock Barn, a few streets west of here.

The Romans also made an imprint on the area, building Ermine Street to run north from London Bridge. Ermine Street survives to this day as Shoreditch High Street and, to the north, Kingsland Road. Now, instead of merchants travelling its length, postmodern urban commandos skate by.

Famed for its taverns and archery fields in the 18th century, the area later became a hotbed of non-conformist religion. Then, during the tail end of the 19th century, Shoreditch was one of the most hopeless slum areas in the whole of London, renowned for three things: poverty, crime and prostitution.

Poverty is now largely a thing of the past in these parts. Hard-up artists, attracted by industrial-sized studios began moving into the area in the late '70s. The area soon boasted a sizable artists' community. However, as the '80s turned into the '90s and developers heard about the area, the artists were forced further east, down Bethnal Green Road. The developers turned the run-down warehouses into designer apartments. Property prices went through the roof. However, the prostitution industry is still thriving. On Commercial Street, on any night of the week, 'Any business, Sir?'

As I negotiate Hoxton Square, I notice the architecture beyond the Victorian housing. It is basically shambolic. Urban planning took a holiday in Hoxton. Planted next to the beautiful old warehouses are concrete slabs – 1970s office blocks and low-rise council estates pepper Old Street and the streets a few blocks north. Derelict buildings are common.

In addition to the self-consciousness, I realise Hoxton also has an arrogance about it. It doesn't cater for anyone living in the real world. OK, it has the influential White Cube and a good art-house facility, the Lux Centre on Hoxton Square. However, the area boasts few other cultural attractions and even fewer amenities. Zero shops. What it does have is style bars. But that's almost all it has. It seems the area's chief function is a collection of bars and fancy restaurants. I count them.

TV chef Jamie Oliver opened his new restaurant 15 here. There's The Real Greek; Bluu on the corner of Coronet Street sits where the Blue Note used to (it's got obligatory concrete and brown leather sofas); Cantaloupe on Charlotte Road serves up Mediterranean food in a cavernous building; the Great Eastern Dining Room on Great Eastern Street is hipped up to the eyeballs; Lime on Curtain Road is clinical with LCD screens in the wall; Liquid Lab on City Road serves cocktails and cool. People sit in dentist chairs; Pool on Curtain Road has beanbags and pool tables; there's Soshomatch on Tabernacle Street for old-skool types; and Shoreditch Electricity Showrooms on Hoxton Square, the epitome of local cool.

I fetch up at the Hoxton Square Bar and Kitchen. Of course, there is no sign indicating that. That wouldn't be cool. Just a massive glass window overlooking the square. Inside I see concrete, a long bar, steel extractor ducts from a large kitchen, green office chairs, brown sofas. There's a girl in combats trying to make her skinny latte last all afternoon. I order a Jack and Coke, and wait.

Live, Menlo Park is an experience. There is no separation between music, theatre and cabaret. Taylor and his band, which includes Paul Simon's son Harper on guitar, have a couple of neat adjectives to describe their sound. Voodoo folk and hip-hop country. They're not being descriptive enough. It could be Cajun voodoo southern-fried country folk meets Edwardian music hall bedsit blues, informed by Captain Beefheart, Dr John and Elvis, and delivered with the aid of a viola and accordion.

The look is equally distinctive. Sporting modish moth-eaten trilbies andand threadbare Oxfam suits gives them an eccentric sartorial peg. A mix of 19th-century travelling circus and tramps. Harper Simon models the poacher look. Viola player John Gresswell's hat would be at home on a racing tipster. And there's a shock-headed drummer, Sebastian Roachford.

When I arrive at a seedy, east London concert hall, a cockroach race has already started. The hall has been transformed into a hillbilly fair. There's tequila apple-bobbing, flea circus, stuffed owls, string quartet and a cage full of chickens. At other Menlo Park gigs, the performance has included pigs on a spit, arm-wrestling transvestites and bare-knuckle boxing. Chris Taylor skids on stage in a garish pink suit, pink chiffon scarf and joke-shop Napoleon hat. 'The whole band's look... It's full on. Heavily theatrical – vaudevillian and cabaret meets Captain Beefheart, early Stones. Everything is weird,' explains Taylor.

After this theatre the music could seem incidental. However, the avant-garde clatter keeps the audience is transfixed. Menlo Park sing songs about colostomy cowboys and wayward whores. Taylor writhes through the set like an effete aristocrat. Sometimes he vibrates on the spot. He holds an arm high over his head, twitching. He could be wired into the mains. All this goes over big with the dressed-to-the-nines crowd.

Taylor tells me, 'What we're really good at is rocking a fucking crowd. We do a great live show with lots of energy – everyone plays like fuck. I sing on everything. I go crazy. I'm not a bad singer. The others are all older than me and committed themselves to being musicians. We're getting good. Shows are a spectacle. We've used horns and orchestras. We've had 25 extra players. It's a whole showoff thing, but everyone loves it because we can back it up with music that's fast and wild and with a lot of emotion. People go crazy when they see us. They don't want to go home.'

And the band can play. Dark and twisted, a hybrid of alternative country, folk rock, Cajun, swamp blues and gypsy jazz – all sawing violins, guitars and skittering drums. There's bluegrass and thumping polka band in between the country and western melodies telling stories about trailer-trash gals. There's a raggedy hoedown version of Madonna's 'Like A Virgin', complete with hot-pickin' banjo and fiddle and a song called 'Paraplegic Dancer', about a colostomy-bag-wearing cowgirl and a paraplegic who win a dance contest.

And then, when the mood takes him, it's time for the big party piece. Taylor swings out from the stage on a rope, like a mad trapeze artist, high over the heads of the audience.

Taylor appears at the Hoxton Square bar. He pulls up a chair. He drinks Hoegaarden beer. The Philadelphia-born ringmaster is dressed in a curious ensemble: Dr Who scarf, double-cuff shirt (no links), scrubby Levis and his hair is all over the place. He has arrived on a 500cc motorbike.

Why not?

'My lifestyle is pretty rock 'n' roll. London is great for that, unbelievable. I'm always in situations I can't believe. You never know who you're going to meet or where you'll end up,' he says by way of explanation. 'I like going out all the time, I like going out. I like film premieres. I'm still living way above my means, but it's fun when you know that the royal jeweller is having a party and it's in this fantastic place and the drinks are free. I love all that. When you put your mind to it, partying in London, you can do it to a really high level. It still feels new. I should be over it, but I still have a love of flash parties and free champagne.'

I toss a copy of *Vogue* on the table – the issue featuring Menlo Park. Taylor grins. The people who do production for Testino are fans of Menlo Park. 'They come to our gigs so when it came to do a music issue in *Vogue* they put us up for it. We did the shoot and Testino was up for it. We played a gig for them. Everyone else was getting their picture taken against walls. We brought our own instruments and played an acoustic gig. They started freaking out and took the pictures of us playing,' says Taylor.

Taylor has lived off Shoreditch High Street for about five years. But he was born in Philadelphia. He came to London when he was 17. 'In America I had done a TV show. I hadn't done very well at school. I grew up right in the middle of the city and I went a bit wild as a kid. Not wild in an awful way, just getting up to lots of mischief. I created a TV show on a public-access channel in Philadelphia. I started it with another kid. It was a comedy TV show. We would drive around Philadelphia. It was called *Freak Town*, about the freaks in Philadelphia,' he says. Sounds like Taylor's *métier*.

They'd chase The Beastie Boys around, interview them and intercut the footage with the same questions put to Bill Clinton or a homeless guy. He takes up the story. 'Then you'd have this montage with all these people answering the question, then you'd have live footage from the gig. Whatever was happening that week. It was all super-low budget paid for with illicit money. It was really fun.'

Next stop was MTV at 16. 'The kid I was doing my show with was brought in as a consultant so I was brought in to help. We were 16-year-old kids on the 52nd floor of the MTV building in Times Square – a whole floor was devoted to this show. That was "whoosh", my first experience of the entertainment business. I thought this is what I wanted to do.'

Taylor didn't go back to school after that. In fact, he hit Ireland and then Europe with a Eurorail ticket. Finally, he pitched up at Victoria

station, not knowing anyone, not having a place to stay, not having any money. 'I didn't know anyone. I started walking the streets, walking around pretending I was writing a magazine article for a New York hip-hop magazine, and I'd go into shops and people would invite me along to gigs and stuff.'
0

Somehow he found a job as assistant casting director on 40 quid ($65) a day, which was a big life change. 'I was living on £1 ($1.70) a day and my rent was £20 ($30) a week, so that was a massive amount of money, and within a few days of working there I realised I'd landed into this really crazy world.' Parties with Kate Moss, Calvin Klein ads, Nick Cave videos, work for Hugo Boss. Taylor did it and he loved it.

'Life was great. I was straight into the upper echelons of London society and people assume if you're at that level then you must be someone. It was like a movie, people would say, "He's so-and-so's friend", and I'd blag my way into parties. I still had no social life apart from this silver lifestyle at these fancy parties, where I'd eat canapés, drink champagne and get the night bus home. I was trying to find out how the London life connected up. How do these people connect to those people? What do they do? These mysterious posh people.'

Then he met guitarist Adam Holden. Taylor takes up the story again. Words spill out of his mouth. 'Me and another guy who I met at a casting party. He lived like a down-and-out rock star. His name is Adam. He had a rock-star vibe about him. Supermodels like Kate Moss were turning up. I met him and we became friends. He told me he was in a band. I'd never thought about music. He said, "Hey, man. Can I stay with you for a week?" He came to stay at my house and the first night he stayed there he was playing guitar and I started joking around and singing over the guitar. We recorded two songs that night and we'd never done music ever. The songs are on our first album. They're good little songs.'

It all started going really fast for Menlo Park from there. Within three months, the pair had signed to Cutty Shark.

'We'd never played live, there was only the two of us, no band as such writing songs about paedophilia, just really fucked-up dark country love ballads. But people liked it. We got a record deal and a bunch of money, and we were in a position that we had to put the whole project together but we didn't have anything, no band. We had to make it from scratch.'

Then Adam went off the rails. And now he's out of the picture.

'I didn't talk to him for a year, but we're friendly now. We wouldn't have him back. It would be too messy. Anyway, as soon as we had money he was straight back into the pool of nastiness. It was really bad. We'd built this studio and it was a hellish year and a half. This was about three or four years ago. An album that should have taken four months to do took a year and a half because of the messiness of the whole project. That was the hardest time of my life, but we made the record and it was amazing.'

Then things got faster.

Chris discovered drummer Seb playing during a lock-in.

'I wandered into this pub in my street,' Chris explains, 'and all these shifty people were going upstairs. They'd shut the pub and there was this full-on, open-mike jazz night going on upstairs and it was cool – a huge, fat black woman screaming away and this guy laying down drums. I'd never seen anyone like that before. He had real crazy hair. He was so shit-hot.' Equally impressed by his Afro as his jazz chops, Seb was on board.

The next guy was John Gresswell, the viola player. He is also Taylor's business foil.

'I was walking through Tottenham Court Road tube station. We'd already started making the record at this point and I heard some amazing gypsy Spanish guitar player and a guy playing what I thought was a violin. I stood and watched and it sounded great. I liked the vibe coming from the violin guy. I wasn't interested in the guitarist. I said I was making a record and I took his number. Then we were thinking of what to put on the record and I said to the band, "I know this shit-hot viola player." So I called John and he was really nice and we all got on like a house on fire, and now three years on he completely runs the band. We're all really committed'.

Finally New York-born Harper Simon was persuaded to join.

'I met him in London. He's a great guitarist. Country stuff. This was in a dark time after we'd kicked Adam out. All of a sudden I met his weird American guy in a bar. Really weird short guy with a funny voice. He looked cool, but in a kooky way – he was wearing a suit.'

Taylor slugs back his first bottle of Hoegaarden and I order another. The girl in combats making a latte last all afternoon is still making it last.

'The music just came out that way. I'm from Philadelphia. I like hip-hop, that's what I grew up with and I started singing really dark lyrics over country music. I thought I'd try hip-hop, but I thought country was really funny. I'd never really listened to country before – I never really listened to music that much. I'm one of these people that are a bit behind. I wasn't the kind of kid who had loads of records. I liked to watch TV. We had about ten records. We call it alternative country, but that's not really what we do. I don't know what we do. I'm still trying to figure what to call ourselves. Country is in there. It's not really blues. We're all country people, but not Nashville. It's Johnny Cash meets Elvis meets punk meets Dr John. It's all mandolins, violas and weird sounds. There is an eastern European sound, too.'

The alternative country scene in London is growing. The Barbican has a festival called Beyond Nashville. Menlo Park have played it twice.

'It's very American, what we do. There is an alternative country scene, but we don't fit in with scenes. We're not part of the rock scene. We don't play Camden. We never play normal venues. We kind of created our own scene, because a lot of people come to see us. You kind of never know who you're going to see. Sometimes I look out and it's a massive celebrity audience. We get Jarvis Cocker and Jade Jagger turning up. Some people think we're prissy because we get articles written about us in the *Independent* and *The Times*.'

And there's the rub. Taylor has little time for his contemporaries. In fact, he thinks 'new bands are so shit'. The A&Rs are after them. He can't understand it. 'The rock thing is boring me. Straight-up standard rock bores the shit out of me. People who aren't fucked up enough shouldn't be doing rock. I don't have any problem with The Strokes and The White Stripes, but there are so many other bands trying to be like them. Normal rock is a bit boring. Throw another musical genre in. Rock isn't new, it's a rehash of old stuff.'

But what really riles him is they are getting the deals and Menlo Park is unsigned at the moment. They lost their label deal a year or so back, and the band are now having to put out their own records. And being unsigned is 'a pain in the ass'. Menlo Park would like a bit of support. To get the push a big label can give a band. To have some weight behind them. 'The shows are brilliant, but in the UK the record industry has no interest in us. It's a mystery to me. I've sent press packs out to every major label and got no calls back. We're not new, but they sign shit bands every day,' he argues. 'We're OK, we get releases out on time, but we've got no real distribution. Our ad budget is zero. We get lots of press. We have our own label, which has a distribution deal. We have a press agent and a plugger, so we get stuff out.'

Fortunately, Taylor has a second job to fall back on. With John he has a company called MPM (Menlo Park Music). This helps source music for ads and films. Taylor listens to thousands of tracks, which he marries to products. 'My music knowledge is increasing exponentially every day. Producers call me up and say, "I need a track." We do all the edgy ads. It's very particular, because only a few tracks will really work. We do things against the grain, because you can add so much to the picture with music.'

He might listen to 5,000 songs for one ad before narrowing it down to ten. He's worked for Saatchi & Saatchi, put music to T.Mobile ads, spots for Nurofen and contributed a Menlo Park track for a high-profile Guinness campaign.

'We look in millions of places for the agency,' he explains. 'It's quite boring, but it's OK money and allows you to be in a band. We've got a good show reel.'

His real ambition though may lie somewhere else. His stage show is the clue. Taylor has the acting bug. 'I'm a fucking showoff. That's my problem. I'd like to give it a shot, though.' He's knocked around the movie festivals in Berlin and Cannes and is getting a feel for film.

'It's interesting seeing the film business from inside. It feels like the early days when I first got into music. Mmmm. I can feel that bug and my band can feel it, too. I'd like to play around with that.'

It's about ten at night when the taxi passes the Bethnal Green Working Men's Club. This is it, I shout to the cabbie.

'What?'

'Here.'

He slams his foot on the cab's brakes and looks around.

'You sure, mate? It doesn't look like much to me.'

It isn't much – an old turn-of-the-last-century building, probably Edwardian just off the Mile End Road. This is the old East End of London, Kray country. The two '60s gangsters lived just down the road in a two-up, two-down on Vallance Road.

Then the area was predominantly white working class. Now it is predominantly Asian. Nearby Brick Lane, in the heart of the East End, is world-famous for its curry houses. It's also home to a thriving Bangladeshi community. Bangla Town, that's what they call it now.

There's a mad mix of styles. A stew of Bollywood meets drum 'n' bass. The dress is Asian street: market jean jackets, sometimes distressed over Indian pyjamas and a pair of cool kicking trainers, new skool – Nike, preferably.

This part of London has long provided a community and refuge for immigrants fleeing persecution. In the 18th century, nearby Spitalfields was occupied by silk weavers descended from the Huguenot refugees (French Protestants escaping Catholic persecution in France). Many of their houses on Fournier Street – built in the 1720s, with large attic windows to provide light for the looms – have been restored. A hundred years later, Jews fleeing the pogroms in eastern Europe settled here and founded a community.

Brick Lane mosque, on the corner of Brick Lane and Fournier Street, is a good barometer for the area, serving a range of religious needs for successive immigrants. Originally built as a Huguenot chapel in 1743, it briefly served the Jewish community. Then it became a

Methodist chapel and in 1898 it became a synagogue. By 1976, the building was converted again, into a mosque to serve the Bangladeshi community, who moved into the area in the early '70s.

The Brick Lane market first developed during the 18th century so that farmers could sell livestock and produce outside the city boundary. Today the market opens every Sunday and offers a wide variety of fruit and vegetables, saris, jeans, silk and music – lots of it. And at the Whitechapel Bell Foundry, at 34 Whitechapel Road, there is a music room housing the only permanent collection of music published for handbells.

Food, though, is the currency here. There are curry houses everywhere, cheek by jowl. In the late 1920s, Sylheti sailors from northeast Bangladesh started to open cafés in the Brick Lane area. One of the earliest was The Gulshan Restaurant at 13 Sandys Row. Now Indians and Pakistanis also run the restaurants up and down the narrow street. The success of these curry houses was down to the willingness of restaurateurs to adapt Indian food to British tastes. Creating dishes like chicken Madras, Chicken tikka masala and lamb vindaloo. Madras is hot. Vindaloo is very hot.

I wish I hadn't had the vindaloo when the cabbie hits his brakes. Hard. 'Yeah, this is it. We're here.'

Outside the window, there isn't much sign of the Huguenot invasion in this part of town – I'm outside 42 Pollard Row, Bethnal Green, E2. It was bombed in the Blitz and is scarred with big tenement projects dating from the war.

At the steps leading up to the Working Men's Club, there is a knot of party animals. They're waiting for the bouncer to nod them in. This is Workers Playtime. Dress tonight is not optional. The dress code is workwear. I'm dressed like a writer. I don't know what writers wear, but, I guess this rig will do it. I was thinking Hunter S Thompson – jeans, T-shirt and French army jacket.

I know I'm underdressed when I see Bruce. Bruce runs Workers Playtime. Bruce the promoter, Bruce Marcus aka the Count, Count Indigo. Count Indigo is wearing a yellow hard hat, ripped road builders' jerkin, blue overalls, rolleddown, and steel toecapped boots.

Indigo goes to work.

The first thing I notice about Bruce is his moustache. Salvador Dali has nothing on this guy. Waxed and spun, two prongs spin out from under his nose.

'Hey, how are you doing?' Bruce has a deep, mellow voice. He's from Northamptonshire. He plays rugby in Blackheath and, back in the day, went to Bauhaus gigs dressed in spats and jodhpurs.

Tonight, though, it's a blend of easy listening, sleazy rock and electroclash. The crowd, in polyester shirts and bright slacks, sway to Bacharach and John Barry compositions. I catch a drink at the bar and look at my watch. I want to be across town before 11. There's a tribute to Joe Strummer at the Tabernacle in Notting Hill. I want to be there. I might catch up with a few faces from the funeral.

I leave the Count, dressed as a chef, booming out his lounge set from the stage and slip out the front door to catch a cab. Fifteen minutes later, I hail one. I call Paul from the Percy. No answer. I guess he is already there.

'Is there any reason why it's taking place today?' the cabbie asks.

'What?'

'Any reason it's on tonight?'

'No, I don't know. Why?

'Well, it's the resurrection, isn't it?,' he says. We both laugh at that.

'You know, I saw The Clash at the Rainbow...' Yeah, yeah, yeah.

The omens look bad. The Tabernacle, a marvellous old church-turned-community centre on Powis Square, looks quiet. The lobby is almost deserted – a couple of bouncers and some staff chatting idly. It's all over, I think.

I check out upstairs. And, as soon as I open a fire door, I can hear it. Like a battle cry: 'White riot – I wanna riot/White riot – a riot of my own'. I spin around a corner, and the door to an upstairs theatre is open. Inside the place is slamming. Middle-aged men, who should know better, are pogoing. The rest are jumping, lungeing, pushing, pulling, slapping, clapping, crying, wailing, waving, shouting, screaming, singing. Making a racket – enough to wake the dead. They wanna riot. And it looks like they're making one.

After babies, divorce and redundancy, they probably haven't had this much fun since the '77 Anarchy tour. Behind the stage are flags – one red, green and gold with a picture of Strummer in the middle, 1952–2002. And in front of the flags, in the thick of it, Strummer's old bandmates from The 101ers and The Clash's Mick Jones, attacking his guitar like it was year zero.

Now everyone is screaming: 'Are you taking over/Or are you taking orders?/Are you going backwards/Or are you going forwards?' Then it's over – 1 minute, 58 seconds on my vinyl single, including the police sirens. This seemed quicker. The lights go up.

There was only one man missing tonight. Joe Strummer... He was 'only looking for fun'... He would have found it tonight.

Appendix 1

TWENTY OF LONDON'S HOTTEST MUSIC VENUES

100 CLUB (See Map 1)
From jazz to punk, this world-famous basement venue has seen them all and is still a coveted venue for 'secret' gigs.
100 Oxford Street
London
W1
Tel: 020 7636 0933

ASTORIA (See Map 1)
The old Crosse & Blackwell factory is a no-nonsense venue capable of staging Kylie-style pop to hard rock.
157 Charing Cross Road
London
WC2
Tel: 020 7434 9592

BRIXTON ACADEMY
Brixton Academy attracts up-and-coming acts and big-name stars looking for a warm-up venue.
211 Stockwell Road
London
SW9
Tel: 020 7771 3000

BULL & GATE (See Map 2)
A rough and ready venue, which is a good supporter of local live music scene in its back room.
389 Kentish Town Road
London
NW5
Tel: 020 7485 5358

DINGWALLS (See Map 2)
One of Camden's first live music venues and still one of the best in the area, with a diverse range of bands.
Middle Yard
Camden Lock
Camden High Street
London
NW1
Tel 020 7267 1577

DUBLIN CASTLE (See Map 2)
Standing room only in this famous Camden venue, which has seen everyone from Madness to Blur play in its back room.
94 Parkway
London
NW1
Tel: 020 7485 1773

ELECTRIC BALLROOM (See Map 2)
A superb straight-ahead rock venue, which every band worth its salt has on its CV.
184 Camden High Street
London
NW1
Tel: 020 7485 9006

FORUM (See Map 2)
The Forum is a regular stop-off point for touring acts from all over the US and Europe.
9–17 Highgate Road
London
NW5
Tel: 020 7284 1001

THE GARAGE
A lively little indie venue, which has attracted its fair crop of well-known US acts.
20–22 Highbury Corner
London
N5
Tel: 020 7607 1818

HAMMERSMITH APOLLO (CARLING APOLLO)
All-seater theatre-style venue, which provides good views and has good tube connections.
Queen Caroline Street
London
W6
Tel: 020 8563 3800

JAZZ CAFÉ
A large, well-equipped venue hosting everything from world music to free-form jazz.
5 Parkway
London
NW1
Tel: 020 7916 6060

THE MONARCH (See Map 2)
Hugely popular room above a Camden pub, which attracts well-known bands and also upstarts who are looking for the first rung on the live ladder.
49 Chalk Farm Road
London
NW1
Tel: 020 7916 1049

NOTTING HILL ARTS CLUB
A small basement club often showcasing up-and-coming bands.
21 Notting Hill Gate
London
W11
Tel: 020 7460 4459

OCEAN
Recent addition to London's live experience, this purpose-built venue is popular with R&B and dance acts.
270 Mare Street
London
E8
Tel: 020 8533 0111

RONNIE SCOTT'S (See Map 1)
This smoky, atmospheric jazz joint draws the best-name acts from around the world.
47 Frith Street
London
W1
Tel: 020 7439 0747

SCALA (See Map 3)
Night club and venue complex in King's Cross, which is often used by record companies to showcase their new acts.
275 Pentonville Road
London
WC1
Tel: 020 7833 2022

SHEPHERD'S BUSH EMPIRE
A decent-sized, comfortable venue, which has seen a range of acts tread its boards from Lou Reed to The Sex Pistols.
Shepherd's Bush Green
London
W12
Tel: 020 8354 3300

UNDERWORLD (See Map 2)
A good live venue below the World's End pub, which has attracted bands on the way up, such as The Datsuns and Queens Of The Stone Age.
174 Camden High Street
London
NW1
Tel: 020 7492 1932

UNION CHAPEL
A small north London church that comfortably handles acts mixing in world music, indie, rock or folk.
Compton Terrace
London
N1
Tel: 020 7226 1686

WATER RATS (See Map 3)
Small pub and theatre, which is a good starting point for up-and-coming unsigned bands.
328 Gray's Inn Road
London
WC1
Tel: 020 7436 7211

TWENTY LONDON RESTAURANTS

ANDREW EDMUNDS
Lots of candles in wine bottles, but if you overlook the decor the modern European food more than makes up for it.
46 Lexington Street
London
W1
Tel: 020 7437 5708

BRASSERIE DU MARCHE
Based in trendy Portobello Road, this relaxed brasserie offers topnotch dishes – their eggy brunches with the obligatory Bloody Mary is perfect for a hangover.
349 Portobello Road
London
W10
Tel: 020 8968 5828

CAFÉ ALGARVE
A real authentic Portuguese restaurant, unbelievably basic and unbelievably cheap.
129a Ladbroke Grove
London
W11
Tel: 020 7727 4604

CAFÉ NAZ
Indian restaurants abound in this area of London and Café Naz is one of the best – it's often busy and the music's loud, but the food is good and authentic. And if you don't like it, slope off to another further down the street.
46–48 Brick Lane
London
E1
Tel: 020 7247 0234

CARLUCCIO'S CAFÉ
Hearty Italian food is served throughout this chain of stylish cafés, and they do great coffee, too.
8 Market Place
London
W1
Tel: 020 7636 2228

THE COW DINING ROOM
The Cow is in a cramped space and can get overrun with Notting Hillbilly types, but the food – particularly the seafood – is great and there's always the Guinness if you prefer a liquid lunch.
89 Westbourne Park Road
London
W2
Tel: 020 7221 0021

E&O
If you fancy watching Kylie Minogue and Nicole Kidman grapple with their tempura prawns, this glitzy, sleek hot spot with a Pacific Rim menu is for you.
14 Blenheim Crescent
London
W11
Tel: 020 7229 5454

THE EAGLE
One of London's earliest gastropubs, all bare boards and unfussy decor, serving tasty Mediterranean grub.
159 Farringdon Road
London
EC1
Tel: 020 7837 1353

THE ENGINEER
Popular with combat-wearing bright young things, it's loud and hip, and dishes up staples such as steak and chips and rack of lamb.
65 Gloucester Avenue
London
NW1
Tel: 020 7722 0950

THE FINCA
Excellent Spanish tapas, a spacious bar area where you can sip Sangria until you keel over, as well as a salsa club upstairs for when the rhythm really starts kicking.
96–98 Pentonville Road
London
N1
Tel: 020 7837 5387

THE FISH SHOP
Good old fish and chips feature, of course, but seafood platters, pots of winkles and bouillabaisse get a look in, too.
360–362 St John Street
London
EC1
Tel: 020 7837 1199

FOX DINING ROOM

A gem of a pub in one of London's fashionable quarters, which serves good-value dishes from a daily set menu and doesn't skimp on the portions.
28 Paul Street
London
EC2
Tel: 020 7729 5708

GARLIC & SHOTS

It's shabby and a haven for heavy metallers, but the food – mainly Swedish – is surprisingly delicious.
14 Frith Street
London
W1
Tel: 020 7734 9505

IZNIK

Typical Turkish dishes and the backdrop of Ottoman lamps and incense burners add to its charm.
19 Highbury Park
London
N5
Tel: 020 7354 5697

MANGO ROOM

Serving traditional and modern Caribbean cuisine in edgy Camden Town – not surprisingly, the rice and peas is a triumph.
10 Kentish Town Road
London
NW1
Tel: 020 7482 5065

MESON DON FELIPE
Noisy and hectic, but the tapas are delicious and you're but a spit away
from the South Bank, home of the National Theatre.
53 The Cut
London
SE1
Tel: 020 7928 3237

MILDRED'S
For tofu lovers everywhere, this vegetarian restaurant could turn even
die-hard carnivores onto beans and sprouts.
45 Lexington Street
London
W1
Tel: 020 7494 1634

MR KONG
Based on three levels, although the two lowest are cramped, Mr Kong
serves topnotch authentic Chinese food without compromising itself
toward delicate Western tastes.
21 Lisle Street
London
WC2
Tel: 020 7437 7341

THE RIVINGTON GRILL
Based in super-trendy Hoxton, this restaurant offers white walls, wooden
floors, celebrity diners – artist Tracey Emin and designer Vivienne
Westwood have been known to pop in – and comfort food, including
home-made fish fingers and mushy peas.
28–30 Rivington Street
London
EC2
Tel: 020 7729 7053

THE SOCIAL
A happening bar where DJs spin the grooves and you can chomp away
on comfort food such as home-made fish fingers and beans on toast.
5 Little Portland Street
London
W1
Tel: 020 7636 4992

TWENTY PLACES FOR THE LONDON EXPERIENCE

BOROUGH MARKET
Excellent food market open on most days of the week and selling the
freshest produce shipped in from all over the country.
Borough High Street
London
SE1

BRICK LANE MARKET
Cheap, busy and friendly East End market, which is worth the visit alone
for the bagels or a curry.
Brick Lane
Cygnet Street
London
E1

CAMDEN MARKET
Whatever obscure rock T-shirt or body piercing you're after, you'll find
it at one of the many fashion-crazy markets around Camden High Street
and Chalk Farm Road. But arrive early – it gets very crowded.
Camden High Street
London
NW1

COVENT GARDEN
Right in the centre of London, the Apple and Jubilee markets in Covent Garden sell T-shirts, antiques and crafts, and is open most days of the week. Also, a good spot to watch street performers.
The Piazza
London
WC2

GABRIEL'S WHARF
Designer craft workshops, bars and restaurants based in a small courtyard on the South Bank.
56 Upper Ground
London
SE1
Tel: 020 7401 2255

HOUSES OF PARLIAMENT
London's best-known building, where visitors can watch the government in action from the public galleries.
Parliament Square
London
SW1
Tel: 020 7219 4272

INSTITUTE OF CONTEMPORARY ARTS (ICA)
Centre for contemporary arts and also performances by bands and artists.
Nash House
The Mall
London
SW1
Tel: 020 7930 3647

KENWOOD HOUSE
Neoclassical villa in north London, with classical concerts in the summer.
Hampstead Lane
London
NW3
Tel: 020 8348 1286

LONDON EYE
Next to County Hall, the Millennium Wheel takes people for a 30-minute
ride, offering the best views of central London.
South Bank
London
SE1
Tel: 0870 500 0600

LONDON ZOO
Animals aplenty, of course, but also some stunning architecture.
Regent's Park
London
NW1
Tel: 020 7722 3333

PORTOBELLO ROAD MARKET
The world-famous west London market selling everything from antique
military wear to the latest hip-hop records. Visit at the weekend.
Portobello Road
London
W11

PRIMROSE HILL
Spectacular views can be had of London from this open stretch of land
in north London.
Primrose Hill
London
NW3

ROYAL BOTANICAL GARDENS (KEW GARDENS)
Over 40,000 plant species plotted out over some 120 hectares (300 acres) of land.
Kew
Richmond
Surrey
Tel: 020 8940 1171

ROYAL FESTIVAL HALL
One of London's major concert venues, and a good starting point to explore the rest of what the South Bank has to offer – from the Hayward Gallery to County Hall.
South Bank
London
SE1
Tel: 020 7960 4242

ROYAL OPERA HOUSE
First built in 1732, it is London's main opera house and recently underwent a multi-million-pound redevelopment.
Covent Garden, between Floral Street and King Street
London
WC2
Tel: 020 7304 4000

SHAKESPEARE'S GLOBE THEATRE
The original Globe recreated on the South Bank utilising the same materials and building techniques from the Elizabethan era.
21 New Globe Walk
Bankside
London
SE1
Tel: 020 7902 1400

SPITALFIELDS MARKET
Once the capital's leading fruit and veg market, now the listed building is home to clothing stalls, organic goods and hip cafés and restaurants.
Commercial Street
E1

ST PAUL'S CATHEDRAL
Sir Christopher Wren's masterpiece, and the site of many royal weddings.
St Paul's Churchyard
London
EC4
Tel: 020 7246 8348

TATE MODERN
The world's largest modern art gallery, with works by all the major artists of the 20th century, including Dali, Duchamp, Matisse, Rothko, Warhol and Picasso.
Bankside
London
SE1
Tel: 020 7887 8000

VINOPOLIS, CITY OF WINE
A 1 hectare (2½ acre) site devoted to the world of wine, including an exhibition and tastings – you learn a lot and get nicely inebriated at the same time.
1 Bank End
London
SE1
Tel: 0870 241 4040

Appendix 2

SOME HOTELS IN LONDON

THE COLUMBIA
A favourite for touring rock stars, with everyone from Oasis to Ocean Colour Scene booking in at this Bayswater stayover.
95–99 Lancaster Gate
London
W2
Tel: 020 7402 0021

GARDEN COURT HOTEL
Family-run B&B close to the Portobello market.
30–31 Kensington Gardens Square
London
W2
Tel: 020 7229 2553

GREAT EASTERN HOTEL
Recently reburbished railway hotel with a Conran restaurant attached.
Liverpool Street
London
EC2
Tel: 020 7618 5000

HOLIDAY INN EXPRESS
This hotel is a short stroll from the Tate Modern as well as a jolly good bargain.
103–109 Southwark Street
London
SE1
Tel: 020 7401 2525

THE HOUSE HOTEL
Large Victorian mansion conversion, which has easy access to the Hampstead's attractions.
2 Rosslyn Hill
London
NW3
Tel: 020 7431 8000

JURY'S INN
Modern, stylish north London hotel just around the corner from Islington's bars, clubs and venues on Upper Street.
60 Pentonville Road
London
N1
Tel: 020 7282 5500

LE MERIDIEN RUSSELL
Victorian landmark in the heart of Bloomsbury featuring an elegant and well-stocked bar.
Russell Square
London
WC1
Tel: 020 7837 6470

MYHOTEL BLOOMSBURY
Modern chichi design in a good, central location near Tottenham
Court Road.
11–13 Bayley Street
Bedford Square
London
W1
Tel: 020 7667 6000

THE PAVILION FASHION ROCK 'N' ROLL HOTEL
Hot crash pad for the fashion and music set in Bayswater.
34–36 Sussex Gardens
London
W2
Tel: 020 7262 0905

THE PORTOBELLO HOTEL
This is where Kate Moss and Johnny Depp bathed in a bath full of
champagne. Pricey but elegant rooms, and just round the corner from
the Portobello Road.
22 Stanley Gardens
London
W11
Tel: 020 7727 2777

GETTING THERE

HEATHROW AIRPORT
The world's busiest international airport is home to over 90 airlines, handles 63 million passengers a year and serves 170 destinations.
Tel: 0870 000 0123 or www.baa.co.uk
Getting into London:
Heathrow is 19km (12 miles) west of the city.

For speed, catch the Heathrow Express, which takes between 15 and 20 minutes to reach Paddington Station – Tel: 0845 600 1515 or www.heathrowexpress.co.uk

The Piccadilly Underground line is cheaper and connects the airport to numerous stations, but takes about 50 minutes to reach the centre – Tel: 020 7222 1234.

National Express coaches run from Heathrow to Victoria Coach Station – Traveline 0870 608 2608 or www.nationalexpress.com

An Airbus service picks up at all four terminals and drops off at various destinations in the city – Tel: 020 8990 6300 or www.airlinks.co.uk

Taxis are expensive (around £40/$70), but usually available.

GATWICK AIRPORT
The second largest UK airport, with 30 million passengers a year, home to 70 airlines serving 200 destinations.
Tel: 0870 000 2468 or www.baa.co.uk
Getting into London:
Gatwick is 45km (28 miles) south of London.

The Gatwick Express is a nonstop 30-minute service from the South Terminal to Victoria station – National Rail Enquiries 0845 748 4950.

South Central Services run from the airport to Clapham Junction and Victoria, taking about 40 minutes – Customer Services 0870 603 0405.

The Thameslink rail service departs every 15 minutes and stops at various places including King's Cross – Customer Services 020 7620 6333.

The National Express Shuttle, no.25 runs to Victoria station – Traveline 0870 608 2608 or www.nationalexpress.com

Taxis are about £50 ($80) into central London.

LONDON STANSTED AIRPORT

The fourth busiest airport in the UK and the fastest-growing major airport in Europe, Stansted is the main home of the leading low-cost scheduled airlines flying to short-haul destinations.

Tel: 0870 000 0303 or www.baa.co.uk

Getting into London:

Stansted Airport lies 54km (34 miles) northeast of the capital.

The Stansted Express runs every 15 minutes and takes about 40 minutes to reach Liverpool Street station. This also serves Tottenham Hale, which links with London's Underground for the West End – Tel: 0845 850 0150.

An hourly local service calls at all principal stations between the airport and Liverpool Street station, including Tottenham Hale and Hackney Downs – National Rail Enquiries 0845 748 4950.

The National Express A6 coach service runs to Victoria Station, stopping at St John's Wood and Marble Arch (among others) en route – Traveline 0870 608 2608 or www.nationalexpress.com

The Terravision Shuttle Express is a nonstop service between the airport and Victoria station – Tel: 01279 662931 or www.terravision.it

LUTON AIRPORT

Handling mainly charter flights to UK and European destinations (Britannia Airways and Monarch Airlines are based at the airport) and home to budget airline EasyJet, Luton serves over 6 million passengers a year.

Tel: 01582 405100 or www.london-luton.com

Getting into London:

Luton airport is roughly 55km (35 miles) north of the city centre.

The Thameslink rail service runs from Luton Airport Parkway station to King's Cross and other stations in central London – National Rail Enquiries 0845 748 4950.

The Greenline no.757 bus takes about 90 minutes to reach central London, stopping at Baker Street, Marble Arch and Victoria, among others – www.greenline.co.uk

Taxis are very expensive, in the region of £70 ($110), and take about an hour to get into town.

GETTING AROUND

THE UNDERGROUND

The Underground (or tube as Londoners call it) is the quickest way to get around town. The system comprises 11 different tube lines and six zones – Zone 1 is central London and increasing the further out from the city centre you travel. Fares increase according to the number of zones travelled.

Each line has its own colour and name – tickets must be bought in advance from automatic machines or from a booth at the station. If you don't have a valid ticket for your journey, you could get an on-the-spot fine of £10 ($17). A single journey in the Central Zone costs £1.60 ($2.70). If you're making several trips, it's cheaper to buy a Travelcard, which are available on an annual, monthly, weekly or daily basis (after 9:30am for day-passes) and can be used on buses and local trains as well as the tube.

The first trains start running at about 5:30am, Monday to Saturday, and 7am on Sunday. The last trains are at about midnight Monday to Saturday, or 11pm on Sunday.

BUSES

The capital's red buses are fun to ride on and offer good opportunities for sightseeing, but can get stuck in traffic. There are two types of buses. Routemaster buses have an open platform at the back of the bus with a conductor who you can buy your ticket from or show your pass to. If the bus is a driver-only bus, the doors are located at the front and you are expected to pay the driver as you board.

Tickets for all bus journeys within the Central Zone cost a flat fare of £1 ($1.70). To find out what you need to pay, state your destination.

Check what type of bus stop you are waiting at. If the bus stop states 'request stop', you must indicate to the bus driver that you want it to stop by holding out your arm as you see the bus approaching. Ring the bell once to indicate that you want to get off at the next bus stop.

You can buy a Travelcard for the entire London transport network, and also a one-day bus pass is available.

Regular buses run between about 6am and midnight, and a network of night buses (prefixed with the letter N) operate outside this period.

OVERGROUND TRAINS

For those destinations not covered by the Underground, use the suburban train network (Travelcards valid), which you can catch from the main city stations. If you're planning to use the train frequently, you can buy a Network Railcard, which costs £20 ($33) and is valid for a year and offers 33 per cent discount on fares to destinations in and around the southeast. Useful train lines that cross the capital include the Silverlink or North London line, and the Thameslink service. For further information, call National Rail Enquiries on 0845 748 4950.

TAXIS

London's metered black taxis can be hailed in the street or found at designated ranks. If you're hailing a taxi in the street, look for the orange light on the roof, which indicates that the taxi is for hire.

The cost of a cab journey is regulated through a metering system, which is displayed inside the cab. Extra charges, such as evening and weekend journeys, are also shown here. A 10 per cent tip is customary, although not compulsory.

London cabbies complete an intensive series of examinations, known as 'The Knowledge', before receiving their licence, which means they know the shortest routes. Minicabs are less reliable than black cabs, as their drivers are private individuals, but they are considerably cheaper. They can't be hailed, and touting is illegal, so the best way is to get a number from the phone book.

CONGESTION CHARGE

Central London congestion charges came into force in February 2003 in an effort to reduce the number of cars in the capital. The charge is £5 ($8) per day and only applies on weekdays, between 7am and 6:30pm. You have up to midnight on the day of travel to pay the charge and you can pay at a range newsagents, off-licences and petrol stations across the capital.

FURTHER INFORMATION

For further information regarding all methods of London Transport, go to www.londontransport.co.uk

The main LT travel information office, providing free maps and details of bus and tube services, is at Piccadilly Circus Tube Station with other desks at Heathrow, Euston, King's Cross, Liverpool Street, Paddington and Victoria stations.

The 24-hour information phone line has details of all bus and tube services – 020 7222 1234.

Index

Maps

SOHO, CAMDEN AND KING'S CROSS

London's live music venues are located, in the main, around three distinct areas: Soho, Camden and King's Cross. The following pages pinpoint the whereabouts of a selection of the hottest venues discussed in this book.

MAP 1 - SOHO

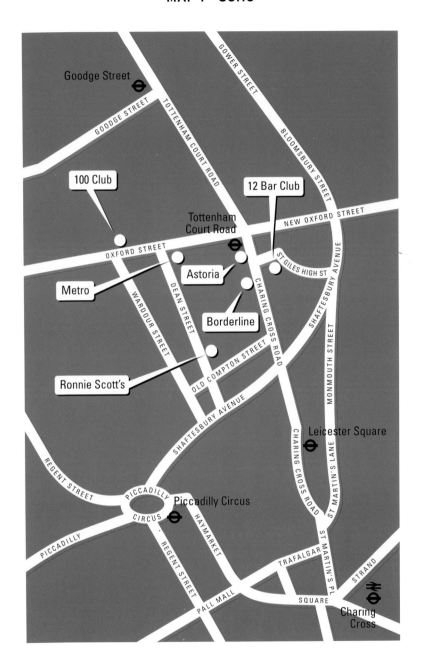

MAP 2 - CAMDEN

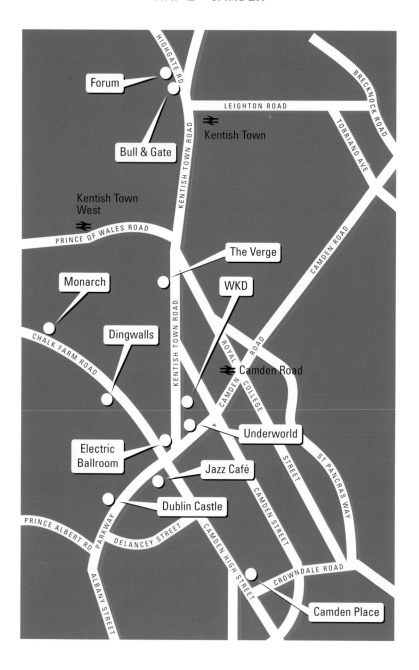